DAGNY

DAGNY JUEL PRZYBYSZEWSKA,
THE WOMAN AND THE MYTH

DAGNY

DAGNY JUEL PRZYBYSZEWSKA,

THE WOMAN AND THE MYTH

MARY KAY NORSENG

A SAMUEL AND ALTHEA STROUM BOOK

University of Washington Press   *Seattle & London*

For S. D. S.

This book is published with the assistance of a grant from the Stroum Book Fund, established through the generosity of Samuel and Althea Stroum.

Copyright © 1991 by the University of Washington Press
Printed in the United States of America
Design by Richard Hendel

Library of Congress Cataloging-in-Publication Data
Norseng, Mary Kay.
Dagny : Dagny Juel Przybyszewska, the woman and
the myth / Mary Kay Norseng.
p.   cm.
Includes bibliographical references.
ISBN 0-295-96999-7 (alk. paper)
1. Juell, Dagny, 1867–1901—Biography.   2. Authors,
Norwegian—19th century—Biography.   I. Title.
PT8903.J84Z79   1990
839.8'28609—dc20
[B]   90-30147
CIP

The paper used in this publication meets the minimum
requirements of American National Standard for Information
Sciences—Permanence of Paper for Printed Library Materials,
ANSI Z39.48-1984. ⊗

I want to tell my life's strange story. Perhaps not
everyone will find it so strange. Perhaps the same
thing has happened to others.—But I have never heard
of it, and therefore I think I am the only one who
looks this terribly tragic, mysterious fate in the eye.

Dagny Juel Przybyszewska, "Rediviva"

CONTENTS

ACKNOWLEDGMENTS

Writing this book has brought me into contact with people of very generous spirit. First of all, I wish to thank Dagny's descendents. Her daughter, Iwa Dahlin, gave me her precious time, her wise insights, and her trust, and she asked her family to be open to me. Dr. Lennart Hellström, Dagny's sister's grandson, gave me access to Ragnhild Juell Bäckström's invaluable correspondence, which in turn gave me access to the private lives of the Juell family. Some of those with whom I met and talked have since died. Dagny's son, Zenon P. Westrup, at the age of ninety, received me and charmed me. Jadwiga P. Westrup, Dagny's granddaughter, welcomed me into her home as a colleague and a friend. Astrid Holmqvist and Eva Hellström, Dagny's nieces, shared letters, photographs, and their memories with me. More than anything else, the members of Dagny's family, individually and collectively, helped me to understand the notion of the spiritual aristocrat that so informed the personality of Dagny herself.

The scholars whom I met, most importantly Ewa Kossak in Poland and Ole Michael Selberg in Norway, could not have been more generous with either their time or their materials. Ewa said that writing her own book about Dagny had changed her life. She predicted that writing this one would change mine. She was right, and I thank her for seeing herself in me.

The curators and librarians in the museums and libraries of Scandinavia and Poland were extraordinarily helpful and expert, in particular Jaga

Kvadsheim at Universitetsbiblioteket and Sissel Biørnstad at the Munch Museum in Oslo, and Anna Polakowska at the University of Poznań.

My Polish translator, Roma King, has been thorough and knowledgeable, and there whenever I needed her. With the exception of the Polish, unless otherwise indicated the translations of the texts are my own.

I am especially grateful to Chris Juzwiak for his splendid collaboration on the index.

A series of annual grants from the Academic Senate of the University of California, Los Angeles, made my research possible in Denmark, England, Norway, Poland, and Sweden. The Norwegian Government, represented by Ekspedisjonssjef Bjørn Jensen, awarded me funds for a longer stay in Norway.

Finally, I would like to thank everyone who has read my manuscript at one stage or another. In particular, I thank my friend Pamela Ball, who has read it in all its stages and given me her perceptive criticism and her warm, humor-filled, and vital support.

INTRODUCTION

Hot winds sweep through the valley of the night,
A thousand wild eyes quickly tremble,
The sleeping earth moans anxiously in its dreams.
Feels the kiss on its will-less mouth.

All the golden leaves in a whirl!
The last dance . . .
My golden hair: a wreath of fire!
And soon so pale . . .

The earth opens its wide womb
And seething floods flow forth:
Glowing flowers
Grand as rainbows,
Blood and fire!
With terror's might
Raise their arms toward the shining stars.

Gentle winds sweep through the valley of the night,
A thousand golden stars quickly tremble,
The sleeping earth smiles calmly in its dreams,
Feels the kiss on its closed mouth.

("Vinden stryger hedt igjennem nattens dybe afgrund")

Dagny outside Kongsvinger Fortress, summer 1893.

Dagny Juel Przybyszewska seemed to leap like a flame from an unearthly womb. Mysterious, provocative, and inexplicably beautiful, she was the central woman in two of the major European cultural bohemias of the 1890s, first in Berlin, then later in Kraków. She had lived the first twenty-five years of her life in the decorous anonymity of the Norwegian upper class, when suddenly, in 1893, she stepped into the role of the elegant, erotic queen of the bohemians. She fulfilled people's fears and expectations of the role so well that they came to dissociate her completely from her past. A woman from Kraków wrote that "here nobody believed that she came from any home at all, people didn't even believe she had any parents. They thought she came out of thin air, who knows from where. Maybe she was a sorceress."[1]

By the time Dagny died at the age of thirty-three, her reputation as the angel/demon of the *fin de siècle* was so widespread that the thought that she had been anything else took people aback. A Norwegian feminist who had met her a year earlier at the home of her uncle, the Norwegian prime minister to the king of Sweden-Norway, wrote upon her death: "Last year I was with her in Stockholm at a reception at Prime Minister Blehr's, where her [piano] playing inspired great admiration, and I got to know her as a fine, talented woman."[2] The remembrance was actually shocking by virtue of the nonprovocative picture it painted of the celebrated Dagny Juel Przybyszewska.

The truth is that Dagny belonged to both the world of the bourgeois and the world of the avant-garde. As opposed as they were, she seemed to be able to traverse both worlds with grace. She refused to be limited by the conventions of either and was not compelled to condemn the one to the other. She married Polish writer Stanisław Przybyszewski in 1893, and with him presided over the *Schwarze Ferkel* bohemia in Berlin—among its members were the Scandinavians Edvard Munch and August Strindberg—and later over the *Paon* bohemia of the Young Poland movement in Kraków. She wrote, she acted as a cultural agent for Scandinavian artists, including Munch, and she lived the life of the *bohême par excellence*. She had two children, she kept in close contact with her parents and her three sisters, and she often returned home to Norway.

The truth also is that Dagny grew increasingly alienated from both her worlds, falling victim to the burdens of the conflicting roles she assumed. In the process of breaking down the limiting notions of what a woman might become, she became a woman dispossessed. She was a love goddess who was imprisoned and betrayed by love, a wife who returned again and again to her childhood home, a mother who left her children, a writer who preferred silence. She died estranged from everyone and everything she had known, shot by a neurotic young man in a hotel room in Tiflis (now Tbilisi) near the Black Sea. He wrote, "She was not of this world, she was far too ethereal for anyone to understand her true nature."

The young man was right in a way he could not know, for Dagny Juel Przybyszewska, at once extraordinary and ordinary, personified far ahead of her time both the rise and the fall of the myth of the modern woman, a being intellectually, sexually, and spiritually free.

Nina Auerbach, in her book *Woman and the Demon* (1982), took as her subject the myth of womanhood engendered by the Victorian cultural imagination. Though her material is derived from late nineteenth-century England, it has much broader application, certainly to the continental European culture of which Dagny was a part. Auerbach wrote:

This imagination is essentially mythic, though it tries to be scientific, moral, and "real"; its most powerful, if least acknowledged, creation is an explosively mobile, magic woman, who breaks the boundaries of family within which her society restricts her. The triumph of this overweening creature is a celebration of the corporate imagination that believed in her.[3]

Dagny's life proves Auerbach both right and wrong. People were indeed anxious to believe in her, but they were equally anxious to wish her away. The reality of the "modern woman," both for Dagny and for others, was as painful as it was inspiring.

Dagny was a woman of extremes—extreme desires, extreme conflicts, extreme contradictions. She lived more intensely than others, giving those around her a heightened sense of their own potential. Yet at times she seemed plagued with the passivity of a sleepwalker. She was a bohemian and a bourgeois, in love with life and obsessed by death, a rebel and a handmaiden. Still, of the brilliance, bravery, struggle, failure, and pain of her short life, only the scandal was remembered.

Word of her death spread like wildfire in dry heat. Articles about her appeared in the newspapers of France, Germany, Poland, and Scandinavia, one account more sensational than the last. She had been murdered by a jealous lover. He had dared her to laugh, and when she did he shot her. A friend, Maya Vogt, wrote to Dagny's sister Ragnhild from Paris:

> Good God—so many lies have seldom been printed at one time. I have to tell you about something that appeared in a French newspaper. You just have to laugh. That the poet Strindberg had loved her, and when she didn't return his love, in desperation he had traveled with Andrée to the North Pole and there met his death! It's unbelievable what they print.[4]

In the face of the scandal, Dagny's family kept silent. Her mother ordered all correspondence relating to her destroyed.[5] She was seldom spoken of. Dagny's granddaughter remembered that her great grandmother and aunts "only wanted to relate idyllic details" from that earlier time.[6] The "idyllic details" were piled up like stones on Dagny's name, the memories of the real woman buried under a rubble of silences and scandalous stories, until her own grandchildren scarcely knew who she was.

Yet it must be said that Dagny's own silence contributed equally to the entombment of her past. Her few surviving letters tell little, for she revealed so little, out of a need to protect herself or others. She tended to keep her anxieties well concealed. A friend and associate of the Kraków theater, Lucyna Kotarbińska, wrote: "And did any word of complaint ever come from her mouth? Sometimes, unwillingly, with a half-smile, she let slip, 'Oh yes, it is difficult.' But then she'd immediately come with different facts that were meant to change the difficult to something easier." Neither did Dagny defend herself in the face of accusations, whether they were made privately or publicly. She was who she was, and she seemed never to justify or apologize. In Kotarbińska's words: "She knew how to bear everything, and live through everything without accusing anybody, without a word of complaint. Never any hurt, never feeling the injustice. Always full of dignity."[7]

Dagny's only real personal legacy is her writing, four plays, a short story, a collection of prose poems, and a cycle of lyric poems. Whether she wrote more is not known. But these few works reveal an emerging voice that was strong, lyrical, dark, and erotic, at one and the same time defiant and despairing.

Even as she lived, Dagny was perceived to exist in a borderland between myth and reality, sensationalism and silence. Compounded by the distortions effected by time, she has slipped almost irretrievably from view. Since her death, many people have written about her, though few have striven to bring her life, much less her art, into focus. The tendency to fictionalize, both because of the provocative subject and the scarcity of historical facts, has been too tempting.

This fictionalizing process is changing with the growing respect for the accomplishments of women of the past and the accompanying legitimacy awarded them by the intellectual establishment. In the early 1960s, the Swedish scholar Erik Vendelfelt included a chapter on Dagny in his biography of Bengt Lidforss, suggesting that she should be viewed as a modern woman rather than a femme fatale. At approximately the same time, the Norwegian literary critic Sonja Hagemann wrote a compelling article entitled "Genienes inspiratrise" (Inspirer of the geniuses), attempting to raise Dagny's image from the realm of the seductress to the realm of the muse.[8] Hagemann also made the point, for the first time, that Dagny had written poetry, concluding the article with one of her prose poems. Still, it was the image of the passive muse, "the prism that threw back the reflections" of the "geniuses," that took hold in people's minds, most likely because the notion of the muse is so closely wedded to its demonic counterpart, the femme fatale.

In the 1970s, two Norwegian scholars, Ole Michael Selberg and Martin Nag, discovered and published unknown literary works by Dagny: a short story, a number of plays, and a cycle of poetry.[9] Selberg and Nag wrote seriously about her impact as a cultural figure and as a writer. Ewa Kossak, Polish author and journalist, wrote the only book about Dagny, *Dagny Przybyszewska: Zbłąkana gwiazda* (Dagny Przybyszewska: Wandering star), in 1973. It is a lengthy, sympathetic biography which was translated from Polish into Swedish in abridged form in 1978.[10] A remarkable work in many ways, it traces in detail the course of Dagny's life and amasses a voluminous number of her contemporaries' reactions to her. Kossak had access to all that has been written about Dagny in Poland, where she has long been an adored cult figure.[11] My own book would not have been possible without Kossak's, upon which I have depended for much source material. But Kossak's book can also be problematical. Kossak could not resist romanticizing Dagny, freely mixing biographical and literary portraits, sometimes confusing facts or substituting imaginative supposition. She also virtually ignored Dagny's writing, thus failing to make use of Dagny's authorial voice in telling her own story.[12]

The process of reassessing Dagny's intellectual contribution to her time is most recently reflected in two new Norwegian literary histories: *Kvinners spor i skrift* (Women's tracks in writing) (1986) and *Norsk kvinnelitteraturhistorie: Bind 1, 1600–1900* (The history of Norwegian women's literature, vol. 1) (1988).[13] Whereas Scandinavian literary histories of the past, without exception, treated Dagny as the provocative companion of Munch and Strindberg, these studies from the 1980s treat her straightforwardly as a writer.[14]

Yet Dagny's prevailing femme fatale image is so firmly fixed that it must first be dismantled if it is to be lastingly rebuilt. I have, therefore, tried at once to deconstruct and reconstruct our ways of "seeing" her. I have broken the image up into the different faces of the woman—celebrity, myth, girl, artist, mother, daughter, sister, wife—in an attempt to illuminate each in a starker light. This approach is the most intrinsically effective. On the one hand, it both breaks down the stereotype and opens up new angles of interpretation. On the other hand, it issues inevitably from Dagny's personality, which was one of many conflicting images, not a harmonious whole. My hope is that I can restore her varied images and recover the woman and her work from the melodrama of her life: from the sensationalism that surrounded it, the silence that fell upon it, and the clichés that have issued from it.

I have employed a nontraditional, essentially musical structure borrowed from the *fin de siècle* prose poem, which sought to elicit the deeper truths locked beneath the surface of traditional poetic language. Like the authors of the poem, I introduce a major theme and then return to it in its various manifestations, in an effort to elicit the deeper truths of Dagny's life locked beneath the melodrama. I rejected the more traditional, linear biographical structure because it automatically imposed on her life a fictional development that is historically unfounded, if not false.

One of the most serious problems in writing about Dagny is one she experienced in life: an overabundance of unreliable material about her, on the one hand, and the lack of reliable material about her, on the other. The extant literature, primarily on her as a public personality, is characterized by conflicting accounts, by a shockingly shoddy tradition of scholarship, rampant with falsehoods and sexist biases, and ultimately by the complex personalities of the artists and men who have been largely responsible for telling her story. In the opposite extreme, the memoirs and correspondence of Dagny and her family that could come closer to revealing the private woman have for the most part been destroyed or lost.

To correct the imbalance I have relied heavily on the personal correspondence that *has* survived, in particular the private family collections.[15] I use the everyday voices of Dagny and her relatives and friends to reconstruct a portrait of her that is at once immediate and authentic. As much as possible I have used Dagny's own literary voice to tell of her internal life. My synchronic approach to the material has enabled me as well to suggest what the Juell family dynamic might have been like as Dagny was growing up, based on letters from the later years. Virtually nothing exists from her girlhood. Yet understanding her family is a key to understanding how she came to be simultaneously so well and so poorly prepared for her role as one of the most modern women of the European *fin de siècle*.

I have sifted through the more sensational secondary material in an attempt to separate fact from fiction, though as I demonstrate in chapter 1,

"The Lady and the Literary Establishment," divining the "truth" is often an impossible task. I do not whittle down every account in the literature in an effort to expose the grains of truth each may contain. Rather, I use the sources to show how the emotional and ideological yearnings of the times both willed into being and finally destroyed a fantastic woman like Dagny. Whenever it is possible and constructive, I indicate the discrepancy between fiction and fact, though I usually relegate such information to endnotes so as not to interrupt the surface of the text. I consider the endnote apparatus to be an integral, corrective part of the reconstructive process. It can suggest not only how "fictions" became historical "facts" but how the "fictions" were used to trivialize or distort Dagny's persona.

The "truth" about Dagny Juel Przybyszewska does not lie in the mere forward flow of events, but rather in the myth of the modern woman she inspired and the attending ambivalence she provoked (chapters 1 and 2); in the shattering discrepancies between the myth and the realities of her life, be they her relationships to those she loved, her own conflicted personality, or her attempt to be an artist (chapters 3, 4, 7, and 8); in her writing (chapters 5 and 6); and in her fatal confrontation with the very ideology that made of her a modern goddess (chapter 9).

Dagny was a woman in historical and personal transition. Everything about her reflects this fact, even her name, even her face. Of her name: she was born Dagny Juell. In the early 1890s she experimented with the spelling of her maiden name, writing Juell, then Juel interchangeably in her books. Finally she dropped the last "l." After she married Przybyszewski, she signed her name Dagny Juel Przybyszewska[16] or simply Dagny Przybyszewska, the name she used as a writer. It is perhaps a reflection of the difficulty she experienced in breaking down tradition that people still insistently refer to her as Dagny Juell. I have chosen to call her Dagny, since it was her common signature through all the phases of her life.[17]

Of her face: she was irresistible to painters, sculptors, and photographers because of her elusory countenance. After her death, her friend Maya Vogt wrote to her sister Ragnhild, thanking her for Dagny's photograph: "My, how beautiful it is, as good as a photograph could possibly be, I think; the interesting thing in Dagny's face can't be reproduced well except in a painting. . . . I have longed so for her and suddenly I can see her so clearly with her fine head and her charming, graceful smile."[18] Yet the most interesting thing of all is how varied and contrasting the individual portraits are.

Dagny Juel Przybyszewska represents transition and change, both as a woman in her own right and as the paradigmatic modern woman. In any transition the changes are wrenching, often threatening and seldom elegantly executed. No exception was made for Dagny. Yet she brought to her life, in all its stages, a seemingly inevitable dignity. Her powerful attraction, for her contemporaries and for us, seems to me to derive not only from her remarkable life but from the intensity with which she embraced it.

DAGNY

DAGNY JUEL PRZYBYSZEWSKA, THE WOMAN AND THE MYTH

1 : THE LADY AND THE LITERARY ESTABLISHMENT

It is worthwhile having a picture of her. I do not know whether there was anything more rewarding [than her] in the entire Berlin circle. The others had talent, and were beset by talent; visionaries, filled to bursting with their obsessions and barely able to move; maniacs, possessed, poor devils. Fine, we have their work. If you take the time, you will get to know them, for they have transmitted every inch of themselves, down to their fingertips, through their art and literature. But Ducha was the Lady. There they stood with their stories and there she stood with her flickering eyes.

[*Julius Meier-Graefe, Berlin publisher and member of the Schwarze Ferkel circle*] [1]

The "Lady" was Dagny. "They" were some of Europe's most avant-garde, late-nineteenth-century artists and thinkers. In the winter of 1892–93, before Dagny came upon the scene, "they" came together, daily and nightly, in a Berlin tavern they called *Zum schwarzen Ferkel* (The Black Piglet).[2] They were the revolutionaries of the art world, most notorious among them the Norwegian painter Edvard Munch, who would befriend Dagny; the Swedish playwright August Strindberg, who would malign her; and the Polish cultural revolutionary Stanisław Przybyszewski, who would marry her within months of their first meeting. Munch and Strindberg went on to change the state of their art forms. Przybyszewski would not leave such a mark, but at the time and in this group he was the most inspirational of them all, a kind of dionysian devil who wanted every old law broken in the name of art and life.

The year Dagny came to Berlin Munch was twenty-nine and riding high on scandal and success. That fall in Christiania (or Kristiania, now Oslo) he had held a private exhibition, his "secession" exhibition, signaling his break with the Norwegian art establishment. Almost immediately the German Art Guild invited him to show his works in Berlin. The exhibition sent shock waves through the city, and the Guild voted to close it down on only the second day, ensuring its success as even the most enthusiastic review could not have done. Munch immediately signed a contract to exhibit his paintings in Düsseldorf and Köln, and by December he had brought them back to Berlin. He had suddenly become "a big name . . . , and he could delight in hearing unknown people talk about him on the street."[3] That spring he would paint his beautiful portrait of *Fru Przybyszewska* (p. 00).

Strindberg was forty-four when he first met Dagny. He had already written *Fadren/The Father* and *Fröken Julie/Miss Julie*, two of the plays that would alter the face of the modern theater. His works were not being performed in Sweden, but these two revolutionary dramas, both staged briefly in Berlin, then shut down—*The Father* by the censorship office, *Miss Julie* mainly by outraged women in the audience—had gained him a following in the city. Poor and depressed in his own country in the fall of 1892, Strindberg was brought by friends and admirers to Berlin, where *Fordringsägare/Creditors* was performed in January, at the same time as *Miss Julie* opened in Paris. His reputation as a European playwright was on the rise, and he himself was lionized by his fellow artists and intellectuals, in particular the mostly younger men of the *Ferkel* group. Four, five, and six years later, when the group had long since dispersed, he would explore his fears of the disturbing Dagny in works like *Inferno, Klostret/The Cloister*, and *Brott och brott/Crimes and Crimes*.

Przybyszewski was twenty-four, one year younger than Dagny, who would soon change the course of his life. He had come to Berlin in 1889 to study architecture but was ultimately more interested in the structures of the psyche than of the city. Literally hell-bent on exploring the unconscious, he read Nietzsche, studied neurology, steeped himself in mysticism, occultism, witchcraft and satanism, and made sex a near religion. In 1892 he published three psycho/physiological essays on Nietzsche, Chopin, and the Swedish poet Ola Hansson. In 1893 he published his first novel, the satanic *Totenmesse* (The mass of the dead). He would go on to write novels, plays, and long poems, all of them inspired by Dagny, to whom he gave the name Ducha, "duch" being Polish for soul. He was heralded as brilliant in contemporary circles in Germany and Poland, and though as an artist he did not transcend his time, he was the life force of the *Ferkel* circle by virtue of his intensity, his passion, and his diabolical will to revolutionize art. As Dagny would become the queen, he was the king of the bohemians, a "meteor" in their midst.[4]

Strindberg had found the tavern, originally called *Das Kloster* (The Cloister), on the corner of Neue Wilhelmstrasse and Unter den Linden. He renamed it for the three, blackened Armenian wine sacks hanging outside its door, looking, at least to him, like a little black pig. He made the tavern his home-away-from-home, and then the others came too: Munch, Przybyszewski, and a host of writers, painters, and patrons of the arts, some integral, some peripheral to the group, most of them Northern Europeans, almost all of them men. There were the Norwegians: Tryggve Andersen, Thomas Krag, Gunnar Heiberg, Christian and Oda Krohg, Sigbjørn Obstfelder, Fritz Thaulow, Gustav Vigeland; the Swedes: Ola Hansson, Bengt Lidforss; the Finns: Karl Gustav and Gabrielle Tavastjerna, John Sibelius, Adolf Paul, Axeli Gallen-Kallela; the Dane: Holger Drachmann; the Germans: Max Dauthendey, Richard Dehmel, Fidus (Hugo Höppener), Max Klinger, Julius Meier-Graefe, Franz Servaes, Johannes Schlaf, Carl Schleich; the Poles: Stanisław Sawicki, Alfred Wysocki.

The owner of the *Schwarze Ferkel*, Julius Türke, welcomed them and catered to them. He was said to have nine hundred different kinds of liquors, one for their every conceivable mood. The multicolored bottles lined the walls and gothic windows of his tavern so the bohemians "literally saw the sun come up through the alcohol!"[5] There they sat, day and night, close together, drinking, smoking, talking about art, love, and, of course, themselves, sometimes in hushed tones, sometimes raised. When an outsider came in they stopped talking until he left. Then they resumed their intimate conversations.

The regulars of the circle would later make a legend of it. They exaggerated, distorted, and fictionalized it in their nostalgic attempts to recreate the atmosphere of creativity and dissipation, camaraderie and rivalry, calm and chaos they experienced there and would never know in quite the same way again. There are favorite bits of *Ferkel* lore that suggest the way it was. Przybyszewski, famous for his impassioned, improvised piano play-ing, would suddenly race to the piano and fill the room with the sounds of Chopin, filtered through his wild fingers. Strindberg would sing ballads on his guitar, which he kept forever out of tune. Late one night Richard Dehmel, the German poet whom Strindberg called "the madman," was said to have jumped up on the table, brandishing his cape like a sword, sending many of the nine hundred liquor bottles crashing to the floor, all a drunken backdrop for his recitation of a poem he had written in honor of Strindberg, "a giant, mist-filled grotto/in which an age-old badger dreamed of new worlds."[6]

Before Dagny, a few women came and went,[7] but the atmosphere was almost exclusively male. They were enjoying themselves, these bad boys of the art world, setting themselves apart, delighting in how shocking and how interesting they could be, revelling in their own elite company.

Then early in March 1893, Dagny Juel, twenty-five, came to the *Schwarze Ferkel*. She made her presence felt the moment she walked in the door. The men, absorbed in their own brazen uniqueness, suddenly found themselves confronted with someone possibly more unique than they. Dagny seemed to understand. She wrote in one of her prose poems: "She was young, and her beauty was of the multifarious and changing kind that caught your imagination and held it captive. Her smiles were full of riddles and those who wished to solve them were many" ("Sing mir das Lied vom Leben und vom Tode").

Berlin publisher Julius Meier-Graefe would contend that Dagny was the most interesting member of the entire *Ferkel* group, of all of them the most enigmatic, the most all-seeing, at once the most deeply spiritual and pro-foundly sensual. In his attempt to describe her, he referred to her as "the Lady," *die Dame*, the name Munch originally gave her; but he suggested that Munch and the others did not understand the full implication of the name. "None of those *litterateurs*, trained in the psychological, sensed the phenomenal degree to which Ducha was a Lady." Meier-Graefe did not mean to suggest that she was ladylike. On the contrary, he meant to convey that she had an undefined, powerful, feminine presence. "In retrospect," he wrote, "I can think of no comparable, authentic female aristocrat."[8]

Dagny Juel caught the imagination of the *Schwarze Ferkel* group and, indeed, "held it captive." Tradition has it that she instantaneously became their muse, turned their heads and broke their hearts. They all were said to have fallen in love with her, vying with each other for her favors. Rumors persisted of her many romances. Supposedly Munch brought her to the tavern and loved her first; and then came Strindberg, and others, and then Przybyszewski, whom she finally chose. Some saw her as a modern love goddess of the literati, akin to Lou Salomé, sensual, intelligent, provocative, and free. For others, such as Strindberg, she was a femme fatale without equal, a destructive, erotic queen in the midst of these hungry bohemians.

It is difficult to divine the degree of truth in all the stories that grew out of the *Ferkel* air of spirits and smoke, and lived on in exotic variants for years to come. Dagny's relationships to Munch and Strindberg, in particular, have been primary subjects for titillating fantasy. They are good examples of the distorted *Ferkel* lore that has been perpetuated as historical fact, and that in great part has determined how Dagny has been viewed. Though I delay her entry upon the scene, I would like to use the Munch and Strindberg "stories" to expose the hysteria and falsification that riddled them, even at their inception, as well as to demonstrate the difficulty of determining what was "real" and what was "imagined," whether by the *Ferkel* participants or by the scholars who later became so fascinated with them.

One thing is clear. As Dagny was a victim of sexist attitudes while she lived, so she became a victim of sexist scholarship after her death. The male artists with whom she associated appropriated her for their personal and creative fantasies. Most researchers have subsequently been interested in her only in so far as she has lent excitement and sexual stature to their more famous subjects. Others, though perhaps better intentioned, have simply accepted the stories as they have been passed down by the authorities. A few have been interested in the truth, as relative a concept as that may be.

Before turning directly to Dagny, it is worthwhile to reveal, if only in isolated ways, how the stories might have come about, and how they have been used to reduce her to the sexual companion of the great men. Only when we understand how her image has been trivialized, can we genuinely appreciate the powerful impact she actually had *on her own* as the incomparable, "authentic female aristocrat" of Meier-Graefe's memory: "What they made of her defines them, and were she not the femme fatale, or had they made of her the Maid of Orleans or an Iphigenie, then that too would have identified them. Of course, there was something of her in the stories, but even three hundred of those would not yet give outline to her."

The tale about Dagny and Munch, generally accepted, even in the main by Kossak, is that they were childhood friends who became lovers in the infamous Christiania bohemia of the 1880s. In the winter of 1893 she supposedly went to Berlin for Munch's sake. During her first weeks there Munch kept her to himself, fearing his fellow bohemians would take her from him. In early March he finally brought her to the *Schwarze Ferkel*, where he lost her first to Strindberg, then to the Swede, Bengt Lidforss, then the German, Carl Schleich, and finally the Pole, Przybyszewski. Munch, sick with jealousy, nevertheless clung to the intimate circle around Dagny, remaining best friends with both her and Stach, and using her as the model for his most celebrated paintings of the 1890s, those of *Livsfrisen* or the Frieze of Life series, among others, *Madonna*, *Vampyr* (Vampire), *Jalusi* (Jealousy), *Kysset* (The kiss), *Aske* (Ashes).

Through the years some or all of the elements of this tale, with attending flourishes, have appeared in a variety of studies of varying quality, for example: in Adolf Paul's *Min Strindbergsbok* (My Strindberg book) (1933), the first, very biased account of the *Schwarze Ferkel* by one of its intimate members; in Strindberg's second wife Frida Uhl's colorful but colored remembrances in *Strindberg och hans andra hustru* (Strindberg and his second wife) (1933), like Paul's written years later, and also like Paul's very influenced by Strindberg's highly emotional interpretation of events; in art historian Polo Gauguin's study, *Edvard Munch* (1933); in Ewa Kossak's respected biography, *Dagny Przybyszewska* (1973); in Olof Lagercrantz's fine, highly esteemed biography, *August Strindberg* (1979); in Reidar Dittman's unscholarly study, *Eros and Psyche: Strindberg and Munch in the 1890s* (1976); in Swedish writer P.O. Enquist's *Strindberg: Ett liv* (Strindberg: A life) (1984), the screenplay written for Swedish Television's Strindberg series in 1985; in *Northern Light: Nordic Art at the Turn of the Century* (1988), an introduction to *fin de siècle* Scandinavian art edited by art historian Kirk Varnedoe.[9] Scholarly credentials have by no means ensured the exclusion of fictions in these studies.

In 1978, Norwegian art historian Arne Brenna, frustrated by a flagrantly inaccurate article proposing Dagny as Munch's erotic liberator in art and in life, wrote his own article in defense of the facts.[10] He showed that Dagny and Munch could have been neither childhood friends nor acquaintances much earlier than 1892,[11] and that their relationship, which lasted until Dagny's death, was not one of passion but of friendship. He reminded us that Munch had documented in detail his erotic obsessions in the early 1890s,[12] never once mentioning Dagny. And, he reasoned, had Munch been having an affair with her, he would hardly have responded with chivalry to losing her, nor would he have remained on intimate terms with the Przybyszewskis. "Anyone who has read Munch's own descriptions of his love relationships, with their intense strain of jealousy, must find it unbelievable that he in 1893 could play the purveyor's doubtful role and give up to another a loved woman, continue to be best friends with them both and be a constant guest in their house." Brenna also argued very convincingly that Dagny was not the actual model for the *Madonna* and the other paintings of the Frieze of Life.[13]

My research tends to support Brenna's conclusions. Dagny and Munch probably met in Christiania in the early 1890s, but not before that. Dagny and her sister Ragnhild did know some of the young artists in the city at that time, but they were not members of the Christiania bohemia and neither was Dagny. Certainly she may have met Munch during these years, but there is no direct evidence that she did. Supposedly Munch painted Dagny and Ragnhild at his artist retreat at Åsgårdstrand in the summer of 1892. The painting, entitled *To musiserende søstre* (Two music-making sisters), does indeed exist, having formerly belonged to Ragnhild's family and now owned by a private collector in Japan. Brenna questioned the dating of the painting, however, and suggested that Munch might have painted it several years later in Berlin. That is possible, since Ragnhild Juell and her new husband, Helge Bäckström, spent their honeymoon with Dagny and Stach in Berlin in January 1894. Munch painted his portrait of Ragnhild, *Fru Bäckström*, at that time, and he may have painted the two sisters as well.

It seems apparent that Dagny did not go to Berlin for Munch's sake, but for her music's sake. She originally intended to go to Paris in the winter of 1892–93 to study piano. At the last minute she changed her plans and went to Berlin to study specifically at Holländer's Conservatory. She may not have known Munch at all until she arrived there, but rather met him through Sigrid Lund, a young, upper-class Norwegian woman like Dagny who was already studying piano in the city.[14] Whether Sigrid and Dagny knew each other from Norway is not known. But they, along with another young Norwegian pianist whom Dagny *had* known in Christiania, Arne Sem, were very close during the Berlin years. Before Dagny came upon the scene, Sigrid was well acquainted with the artists of the *Schwarze Ferkel* group, in particular Munch and Strindberg. It is equally possible that Sigrid introduced Dagny to Munch.

Dagny's personal relationship to Munch, as evidenced by their surviving correspondence, was direct, supportive, very calm and constant, if not always frequent through the years.[15] Their letters showed no sign of passion, past or present. Stach himself, however, probably contributed to the gossip that he had taken Dagny from Munch. In his novel, *Ueber Bord/ Overboard* (1896), the first in the *Homo Sapiens* trilogy, the writer, Falk, steals the beautiful Ysa from the painter Mikata. Word of the novel apparently reached Munch who in turn apparently wrote to Dagny and Stach. Munch's letter is lost, but Dagny's reply has survived:

> What you write, that a book of Stachu's should be uncomfortable for you, is absolutely inconceivable.
>
> Maybe it's because in a book called "Overboard" there is a man who is a painter. The artist in question is, indeed, as different from you as two people—all of whom are created in God's image—could possibly be—but the evil here in this world is immeasurable.
>
> If it should be this painter in "Overboard" who is the object of gossip, then it is of interest, since the book has still only come out in Danish and you can only have heard about it from your beloved, little countrymen. Probably Obstfelder or Thiis or some such.
>
> I simply do not understand how you could think for a moment that Stachu would write something that was uncomfortable for you. I hardly know of a person who is so fond of you. [Undated, but written sometime in the late summer, fall of 1896]

In spite of Dagny's comforting words, *Overboard* was about a tavern possibly resembling *Schwarze Ferkel*, a trio of artists with some characteristics possibly resembling those of Przybyszewski, Munch, and Strindberg, and a central woman possibly resembling Dagny. Strindberg later added fuel to the gossiping fires with his novel based on the same period, *The Cloister* (originally written in 1898 though not published until after Strindberg's death),[16] in which he employed a similar surface plot. Both Przybyszewski and Strindberg, it must be remembered, were authors and men who were known to take great liberties with the truth. Both were also obsessed with their sexual identities. An interesting discrepancy in their fictional accounts is that in *Overboard* the woman is desperate to meet the Przybyszewski-like character, in *The Cloister* the Strindberg-like character. Finally, however, both were artists who were experimenting with a new kind of fiction that was from life but not the same as life. They wrote fiction, not reportage, and both knew the difference, even if they played games with their public. Dagny rejected the idea out of hand that Przybyszewski's "painter" had anything to do with Munch. But the rumors persisted.

I could not conclude with Arne Brenna's certainty that Dagny and Munch were never lovers. But if they were, it was to Munch's credit, and even more so to Dagny's, given Munch's well-documented, pathological anxiety over women, that their friendship flourished and that he became her great admirer and champion.[17] For that is the role he chose to play vis-à-vis this woman he called "the Lady." After her death he gave the only positive account of her life to appear in any Scandinavian newspaper, portraying her as an intellectual, cultured, and kind woman who actively participated in the creative endeavors of the *Ferkel* circle.[18]

I do agree with Brenna that Dagny was not the actual model for the paintings of the Frieze of Life series. It has been taken for granted by many that she *was* the Madonna. Munch himself seemingly intended to put that idea to rest. A fragment of a letter from Munch to a certain lawyer, copied in Munch's sister's hand, is in the archives of the Munch Museum:

> With regard to the picture the wave (the lithograph) which D. has bought I can inform you that the model or the inspiration for this picture is a model I had in Berlin in the 90s. It is the same model I used for the big lithograph Madonna—Prszybyschevski [sic] was allowed to use one of the drafts for a poetry collection. It had a certain resemblance to fru Dagny.
>
> It is the same type that you find in the tiger in Alpha and Omega— When we spoke about whether it was supposed to be fru Dagny or

whether she was the model, then that's all wrong. There is, however, a certain likeness. . . .[19]

Since Munch's original letter has not been found, the copied fragment cannot serve as absolute proof of the role Dagny did *not* play in the creation of the Madonna painting. Yet Munch's meaning seems clear. At the same time it is unthinkable that Dagny, as Munch's close friend and the central woman of the *Schwarze Ferkel*, did not play a crucial, if indirect, role in the creation of the paintings.[20]

In interviewing Munch about Dagny after her death, the reporter for the Christiania newspaper asked him:

"What if you drew a picture of her for *Kristiania Dagsavis*? You have been so close to her."—Munch shakes his head. "It's precisely because I've been so close to her that the whole story has affected me so deeply . . . I cannot draw her right now."

Munch concluded the interview:

"Upright and free she walked among us, encouraging and at times comforting, as only a woman can be, and her whole apparition had a very special calming and at the same time inspiring effect. It was as if her mere closeness gave new impulses, new ideas, and the urge to create, which had gone to sleep, awakened anew."[21]

The tale of Dagny's relationship to Strindberg emanates almost exclusively from Strindberg and is highly unreliable. Nevertheless, it has had a far more determining influence on Dagny's image than any other. As Olof Lagercrantz wrote in his respected Strindberg biography from 1979:

. . . in terms of a bad reputation [Dagny] could match just about anybody. This was primarily due to Strindberg who reviled her with incomparable malice and never relented in his hatred of her. . . .

Dagny Juel incarnated [for Strindberg] a phase of woman as sexual being. She was the opposite of the virginal, motherly creature Strindberg usually projected onto those women he loved. The ruthlessness with which Strindberg treated her during the following months arose from the fear of something in himself that she threatened. Therefore one cannot take his infamies really seriously.[22]

Strindberg claimed that Dagny was his lover for three weeks in March when Frida Uhl, to whom he was secretly and soon to be publicly engaged, was out of town. He tired of Dagny (just as Frida returned) and, in his own words, "bequeathed" her to the young Swedish scientist and Strindberg admirer, Bengt Lidforss[23] (who was homosexual, as well as syphillitic at the time). Strindberg's version has gone down in history as fact, repeated not only by authors like Adolf Paul and Frida Uhl in their fanciful accounts, but also by reputable scholars such as Evert Sprinchorn in his introduction to the English translation of *Inferno, Alone and Other Writings* (1968) and Nils Beyer in his biography of Bengt Lidforss (1968).[24]

Another variant, supposedly told by Stach Przybyszewski, is that Strindberg asked Dagny to marry him, at which point she laughed and said he was old enough to be her father. This is the version preferred by Kossak,[25] though she accepted the story of their affair.

Without question, Strindberg reacted intensely to Dagny. If she reacted equally intensely to him, it is not known. But whether Dagny spurned Strindberg, ignored him, loved him, or simply infuriated him by virtue of who she was, he interpreted her as his persecuting demon, and he waged a vicious war of words against her, as only a writer could, attacking her first in his letters and later in his literary works.

The discrepancy between Strindberg's "reality" and others' "reality" is demonstrated by two letters he wrote in the spring-summer of 1893. Having learned that Bengt Lidforss was about to be evicted from his Berlin hotel because he could not pay his bill, Strindberg wrote to Birger Mörner, an acquaintance from Lund, urging him to mobilize friends to bring Lidforss home. Blaming Dagny for Lidforss's plight, he urged that she be "taken" home too.

> I'm newly married, on Helgoland, and things are fine.
>
> But our poor Bengt is sitting in a hotel in Berlin, ruined by that miserable devil of a woman, Dagny Juel (who was also my lover for three weeks!). In a letter from Paul today I learned that the hotel manager is threatening him with the police, you know that in Germany the police are called in, if one can't immediately parry a hotel bill. . . .
>
> If you can recall Dagny it would be good, for her parents' sake.
>
> She has rented a room in a prostitute street and is so struck with moral insanity that she too will soon be taken by the police.

Oh, there is a novel! She destroys families, and men, distressed but with talent, squander money, leave house and home, duties and professions!

It shouldn't concern me, because I gave her away as a lover, and morality doesn't matter to me. But for Bengt's, others', her own, and her relatives' sake . . . let her be taken home! [May 9, 1893] [26]

Mörner contacted Dagny's oldest sister, Gudrun Juell Westrup, who was living in Lund. Gudrun went to Berlin and found all to be well. (Dagny, incidentally, was already intimately involved with Przybyszewski and considered herself engaged.) Gudrun returned to Lund, furious with Mörner and Strindberg. On June 22, Strindberg wrote to Adolf Paul that "Mörner, who is at the district court sessions in Skara, has finally written me a cool summer letter. Says he has gotten hell in Lund from Aspasia's sister. She had namely (listen!) found 'everything in order' in Berlin and left happily in the given belief that the whole thing was 'a villainy of Strindberg.'" [27] Gudrun was a very intelligent, very conservative, correct, and perceptive woman who was not easily fooled by anyone, certainly not her younger sister.

Strindberg's personal situation must be taken into account. At the time he met Dagny, he was becoming more deeply involved with Frida Uhl. As Lagercrantz wrote, "At the same time passion is awakened, hostility is as well, and Strindberg is gripped by the fear of being despised as the weaker one and of seeing his protective walls crumble." [28] It seems possible that in order to allow himself to enter into a relationship with Frida, he desperately needed a female scapegoat onto whom to project his debilitating fears. The time of his most violent persecutions of Dagny began when he married Frida, and they continued throughout the first year of his marriage. [29]

There could also be another, not conflicting interpretation. In his study, Lagercrantz suggested that Strindberg used his letters and journals as preparation for his literary works. This was particularly true, he believed, for the letters connected with the so-called "inferno" period. Lagercrantz put forward the interesting idea that Strindberg did not really undergo his famous breakdown, supposedly documented in his letters from the time. Rather, Lagercrantz proposed, Strindberg used the letters to prepare the psychological groundwork—nurturing his creativity in precisely the way he needed—in order to write *Inferno*, his book about a modern's descent into hell. In other words, the letters were actually early drafts of the final fiction. The same theory could apply to the letters of 1893–94.

Strindberg went on to use "his" Dagny as the model for the destructive woman of many of his works, including Aspasia in *Inferno* and *Svarta fanor* (Black banners), Laïs in *The Cloister* and *Karantänmästarns andra berättelse* (The quarantine officer's second story), and Henriette in *Crimes and Crimes*. But these are *literary* creations. As Lagercrantz brilliantly argued, even Strindberg's so-called autobiographical works, including *Tjänstekvinnans son/The Son of a Servant*, *En dåres försvarstal/A Madman's Defense*, *Inferno*, and *The Cloister* must be understood as fictions. "Strindberg the confessor and self-revealer is a myth. When he feels like confessing, he always disguises himself, while the purported self-portraits are designed to lead us on to false tracks." [30]

Increasingly throughout the 1890s Strindberg was experimenting with a new kind of fiction in which, as Lagercrantz expressed it, Strindberg the author and Strindberg the subject coexisted but were not one and the same. The "author" was attempting to create a universal out of the "subject." Strindberg wrote *The Cloister*, the supposed autobiographical novel about the *Schwarze Ferkel* [31] and his marriage to Frida Uhl, in 1898. Lagercrantz pointed out in connection with the Frida-character: "Strindberg was developing a symbolist mode of creation, in which there was no room for individuals. There had, of course, always been little room for such people, except himself, in his works." [32] The same certainly applies to his Dagny-character, which has, unfortunately, come to stand for the real woman.

In all of my research I have found nothing specific that illuminates the relationship between Dagny and Strindberg. She did have in her possession in Poland a copy of *Kamraterna/Comrades* (1888) originally belonging to Ola Hansson. [33] That is all. Strindberg created a female monster in her image. She kept silent.

Dagny may have had affairs with both Munch and Strindberg, or she may have had affairs with neither. A friend of hers from the time, Polish writer Alfred Wysocki, wrote in his memoirs from Berlin:

> To me, Dagny Przybyszewska and Sigrid L[und] stood for representatives of a highly interesting and earlier unknown type of woman. They had gone to school with boys and thought of the men as friends.

They leaned familiarly on their arms, they told them down-right out-spoken stories, they changed their wet stockings in their presence and drank bonhomie-toasts with them, but all of this meant nothing more than that.[34]

The significant point is that Dagny felt free to form relationships with men. This may have been threatening to some, but it neither was nor is the truly interesting thing about her.

It is time to destroy the individual Strindberg/Munch fictions and to resurrect the woman her contemporaries *as a whole* actually thought they saw. Dagny inspired strong reactions not just in the famous men but in many people. Initially I propose to use their reactions to her, not for their historical "detail," right or wrong, but for their composite truth. The first real "truth" about Dagny, I believe, is to be found in the symbiotic relationship between her and her time. In collaboration with her contemporaries she generated a myth of feminine dynamism and transcendence. Whether people were responding to "real" or "imagined" situations is initially unimportant. They longed for and feared a woman of mythic proportion, and Dagny fulfilled their fantasies. In the course of time, however, the myth has been adulterated and trivialized. Dagny has continued to pique the interest of scholars, writers, and film makers, but in personae splintered and isolated from her original mythos, in particular in diluted versions of Munch's muse and Strindberg's femme fatale.[35] Both personae contain their half-truths, but as isolated aspects of the myth Dagny came to embody, they lie. The femme fatale is far too destructive, the muse far too passive. Both rob the myth and the woman of the real energy and integrity they had.

I intend the subsequent chapter on the "myth" to be read as if one were listening to a chorus of voices from the turn of the century. It seemed to me to be the most creatively authentic way to rediscover Dagny, "the female aristocrat"; Dagny, the "worshiped modern woman." Only when we separate ourselves from the subjectivity of individual responses and listen to the chorus, are we able to appreciate Dagny's powerful impact on her time.

2 : THE MYTH

You had to experience her to be able to describe her," Munch was to have said of Dagny,[1] Munch who "described" a woman of unique beauty and complexity in his painting of her from 1893. She seems to rise out of a translucent blue mist, slender, clothed in a black dress that barely exists, a hint of bat's wings in its puffed shoulders. A nearly invisible halo of increasingly larger rings emanates from her white face, the focal point of Munch's vision. Her expression is open, inviting, seemingly benign, somehow sad. Her eyes are veiled. She may be holding her hands provokingly behind her back or protectively in front of her. She is at once spirit and flesh, angel and demon, in ecstasy and in mourning, of life and of death.

Munch could not resist making a mystery out of Dagny Juel Przyby-szewska. Neither could most who met her. Within weeks of her arrival in Berlin, she had become the undisputed if controversial "muse" of the artists of the *Schwarze Ferkel* circle. An anonymous author wrote just after her death:

> . . . spirit shone in her smile, in every movement of her supple limbs, that were wrapped in a loose hanging gown, and everyone she spoke to became spiritual. She only had to look at you, to lay her hand on your arm, and suddenly you found expression and form for one thing or another that you had long gone and wrestled with. She was the intellectual mid-wife for these poets born in pain.[2]

Adolf Paul remembered her as Strindberg did:

One day she walked into 'Ferkeln' with Munch—blond, slender, elegant and dressed with a refinement that well knew how to accentuate the body's suppleness but avoided revealing too definite contours. . . . she wound around between the narcissistic genius-snobs, captured them one by one and masterfully played the role of the ideal for each, until she had him in her net and could see behind the scenes of his life's mystery! Then she laughed at him and threw him out of the boat! [3]

Stach Przybyszewski wrote to Paul in the first months of his relationship with Dagny:

Yes—I knew no love, knew not myself. And all that was unknown to me—the unconscious mainsprings of my behavior and actions, that which was my soul's great secret, she elicited; in her the mysteriousness of my soul was embodied, yes, you see, she is my highest intellectual and aesthetic pleasure. [4]

Strindberg named her Aspasia, [5] mistress of Pericles, friend of Socrates, a woman known for her great intellect, sensuality, and influence with men of power. Dagny's ability to inspire myth-making reached beyond the intimate inner circle of the *Schwarze Ferkel,* and the myth she inspired grew beyond the muse, whether dangerous or benign. She was an "angel," a "wood-nymph," a "vestal" striding toward the temple, "Eurydice" gliding into the night, "Judith" sneaking to Holofernes's tent. She was the New Woman.

. . . the singular, phenomenal and fascinating creature . . . Ducha—who was then twenty and some years, was an amazing woman with whom all men fell in love, and whom all women admired. She had slightly wavy hair that fell seductively about her temples and cheeks. In a word: she was in a certain sense the prototype for the worshiped modern woman. . . . She acclimatized herself completely to her new role and in return enjoyed the admiration, if not to say worship, Przybyszewski in his literary ecstacy paid her. A similar legendary radiance encircled her in the bohemian circles in Berlin. [Franz Servaes, literary critic and member of the *Schwarze Ferkel* circle] [6]

Wherever they [Stachu and Ducha] went they were followed by a group of young people. [Ida Auerbach Dehmel][7]

The same aura that surrounded Dagny's presence in Berlin followed her to Poland, where she once again was made the queen of the avant-garde bohemians, the artists of the Young Poland circle, who held court in the Kraków tavern known as *Paon* (The Peacock). One of Przybyszewski's admirers wrote:

We only knew that she was Beautiful and that she was always with him, she had to become our Astarte, goddess, queen, sovereign, the Prophet's companion, consequently the Prophetess. . . . In Dagny we saw the Prophet's mistress and friend, Androgyny, the Absolute, his happiness, his origin, the original source of ecstacy, madness and inspiration.[8]

And once again she drew a following of the young, the romantic, the rebellious, and the artistically inclined, so much so that they were said to have come to *Paon* after the theater just to get a glimpse of her.[9]

The myth took on meanings far beyond her person. She became akin to a living work of art. "All the billowing, the elusiveness, the moving that we later met in excess in painting, we had seen born in her," said Ida Dehmel. People literally saw her as if she had been cut out of a masterpiece. One described her as a Botticelli:

I noticed her curly, silken hair, that surrounded her narrow, oval face, hid her ears and formed something of a golden frame, broken by fine coils in convolutions around her head, like airy, golden yellow down. Under her regularly shaped eyebrows gazed light blue, peaceful, cool eyes, with dark rings under them. [Alfred Wysocki][10]

Another described her in terms suggestive of Rosetti's overwhelming, Pre-Raphaelite women:

Not at all beautiful and still seductive like no other. Tall, lean, supple with dark bangs and light eyes under the half-shut, tired eyelids. Completely dry, stiff, curly, brown-red hair, that bristled with every touch like ripe rye before a storm. A mouth that was way too big, as it shone so brightly purple-red over the sharp, snow-white, genuine Norwegian . . . teeth. [Anonymous][11]

A third saw her bathed in Rembrandt twilight:

> The salon was large and dark. Two empty bottles served as candle-sticks. The whole interior was atmospheric, like a Rembrandt twilight painting. Dagny was carried away playing music at the piano. [Johannes Schlaf] [12]

Many were reminded of Leonardo's *Mona Lisa*:

> [This] distinguished and silent woman seems secretive and distant— as distant as her smile, distant as the look in those oval, veiled eyes, half covered by her heavy, shimmering, gold eye lashes. [Someone from Kraków] [13]

Dagny Juel Przybyszewska, as she lived even, became part of the romantic iconography of the *fin de siècle*. Where the woman ended and the myth began is in a very real sense impossible to determine. Dagny, in collaboration with her contemporaries, generated the myth, and though she was separate from it, she was inextricably and actively at its core. She was a sophisticated, intellectual woman in love with the art of the avant-garde. She lived at the center of a group of artists caught up in the excitement of breaking new ground. These were the early moderns, distrusting of all authorities save the unconscious, anxious to turn their own lives into art. Dagny was just as anxious.

It would be a mistake to see her simply as a victim of the fantasies she inspired, a woman undone by the overwrought, misogynous male imagination of the late nineteenth century. This would be to deny the woman and the myth their very *real* power. Though she could not control the exaggerated forms it took or its ultimate impact on herself or others, she was obviously aware of the myth she generated. As a writer she self-consciously chose it as the subject of her texts, exploring its seductive allure and its tragic underside.

The myth was fed both by truths and by lies. Whether people encountered Dagny first or second hand, they found her persona so provoking that they easily distorted fact in an attempt to recreate the woman they thought they had experienced. They found her as unique as they felt they themselves were. Depending on predisposition, some responded to the beauty in the vision, some to its sensuality, or spirituality, many to the duality of body and soul. Everyone seemed to be, though, when all was said and done, a little mystified. They were prepared to see something, but they were not sure what they saw. They responded with both marvel and anxiety to a woman so indeterminate. Intense subjectivity gave rise to a web of often conflicting fictions.

> Her entire person and being had a strangely calming, at the same time inspirational effect, like fresh forest air. [Munch] [14]

> . . . comfortable in her presence, no one was, not even those who desired her the most. [Anonymous] [15]

And again,

> Dagny was unresistant, lacking strong will. The wave of life had been carrying her—without any resistance. [Lucyna Kotarbińska] [16]

> She had a provocative word for everyone, raised him up to her and thrust him away again. She was a very elegant queen, full of arrogance, bold impudence and boyish superiority. [Julius Meier-Graefe] [17]

> With unaffected obviousness she surveys our room, completely calm, and gives herself a lot of time, as when one looks at one's own room in which the furniture present is well-known and is in its place. It's only on me the curious eyes loiter, surveying and testing, as if on a new piece of furniture. It is a test, almost to my advantage, there is something benevolent and still painful, surprising in this approbation between two women. Absolutely nothing malicious or hateful, but openly curious and strictly matter of fact. Purely an accountant's look, weighing an affair and contrary to expectation finding the object serviceable. [Frida Uhl] [18]

> That's the way she always is! That's just it. The snake remains cold. That doesn't make it less deadly. Now she's going to take aim at your heel. [Strindberg, as filtered through Uhl] [19]

> And how she could set to work and help. It was Dagny almost more than myself who took hold of my exhibitions in Berlin. [Munch] [20]

> . . . she sat upright and silent on the rug in the simple gallery, where her friend, the Norwegian painter Edvard Munch, ran back and forth hanging his paintings. [Franz Servaes] [21]

There was not even any agreement on the color and texture of her hair: "gilded hair, fine like silk"; "completely dry, stiff, curly, brown-red hair, that bristled with every touch like ripe rye before a storm"; "curly blond hair"; "hair that formed a gilded halo around her face"; "frizzy, dark blond hair"; "golden red hair."

In addition to being tainted by subjectivity, many of the memories were recorded after Dagny's violent death at a very young age, which made her an even more provoking subject. Time dulled the facts. And her many acquaintances, who became mini-artists in their unusually emotional attempts to recreate her, were given an even freer hand with the truth.

Yet, within the very confusion of history lies a key to understanding the powerful myth Dagny embodied. A myth by very definition grows out of a combination of falsehoods and truths. As Nina Auerbach has written, myth is "an uncomfortable word, poised uneasily between rejection and embrace, apocrypha and dogma, arousing our trust and dispelling it simultaneously, remaining with us longer, perhaps, than do those things we know to be lies and truth."[22] At the same time, if it is firmly rooted in the age from which it springs, a myth becomes its own truth, a distillation of the essence of a culture, a projection of its dreams and fears.

Auerbach convincingly argued that in the last half of the nineteenth century a myth was born of a female hero, "a single vivid creature of seemingly endless mutations and personae." She was "queen," "victim," "angel," "demon," "fallen woman," able to change shapes at will, "alone and in command." In the composite of her manifestations, she became a shaping principle for new forms of life. "Victorian culture," said Auerbach, "had no firmly rooted imagination of adult womanhood and so envisioned a creature of almost infinite mobility."[23]

In the northern European circles in which she lived, Dagny Juel Przybyszewska generated precisely such a myth of feminine transcendence. She seemed to break down temporal and material limitations, giving rise to fantasies of new, ever-changing forms of life. No single persona captured the essence of all the others as did the "solo dancer," who seemed to defy the laws of matter.

She was also something that was for that time very unusual, a kind of solo dancer, the only one in our closest circle. There was something of the wood-nymph, the mirage in her dance, something fantastic and magical, that completely bewitched the spectators. [Franz Servaes] [24]

. . . her body found limitless possibilities for expression in the measured, nearly commonplace rhythm. . . .

With the first glance her arms seemed to fasten themselves immovably around your body. With a movement full of promise she stretched them out, let them flutter in the air and lift over her head. In her hands she held wreaths of flowers. Like a vestal she strode toward the temple, like a Eurydice she glided into the night, like a Judith she snuck to Holofernes's tent. Her well-formed head bobbed like a little boat and disappeared into the cloudy mist. In this cloud her face shone with a phosphorescent light. [Julius Meier-Graefe] [25]

. . . Ducha's party, Ducha's evening. Never before in my life had I seen anything like her dancing. She was as shapely as a rush and just as supple. She rested in men's arms as lightly as a veil, a flock of clouds. You thought undeniably of the movements of a flower, when you saw how proud she carried her beautiful, little head on her straight, well-formed neck. [Ida Dehmel] [26]

Alone, constantly in motion, and endlessly mutable, Dagny awakened dreams of undiscovered possibilities. And they were ripe for it, these artists of the *fin de siècle* with whom she associated, the famous and the not-so-famous, desperately seeking forms through which to move beyond the barriers of their own consciousness. Dagny seemed to her contemporaries to speak a mute language pregnant with mysteries from beyond the grave. She gave them the electrifying feeling that she had something to reveal to them, if they could only understand her. A Pole who, as a boy, had met her in the mountain resort town of Zakopane, wrote:

Today it seems to me—though it may be just my imagination—that she had a remarkable intuition that reached far beyond the boundaries of the present. She was surprised herself by these mysterious premonitions, which gave her material for new dreams and fantasies of unknown combinations. [27]

If we are really to understand the power of the Dagny myth, we must first isolate its parts in order finally to suggest the essence of the whole, i.e., a myth of feminine redefinition. All the elements are contained in the persona of the "solo dancer," but it is illuminating as well as restorative to view the individual faces of this fascinating, modern "Woman."

SHE WAS UNIQUE...

> Dagny not only appreciated eccentric people, she was herself eccentric, very talented. [Munch] [28]

> She was talked about with admiration and interest, as if she were the only woman of her kind. [Julius Bab] [29]

Dagny was perceived to be different in intellect, looks, and allure. Though people identified her "difference" in varying ways, all seemed to agree that they had never seen anything like her before. She fades in and out of the persona of a tall, slender, dark blond woman with a Greek profile and aristocratic hands, to become something else entirely, like a statue coming to life in unexpected ways. Frida Uhl experienced her to be less, then more than she had imagined.

> All at once we [Uhl and Strindberg] hear steps, light steps nearing. And suddenly the door, shoved by a hard hand, flies wide open and gapes blackly at us. Two women. The first one walks past so fast that her flame red blouse still flashes like fire. But the other one stands there demonstratively and looks in without setting her foot in the door or greeting us. Strange. It seems to me I've seen her before, or rather her beautiful sister. She herself is actually not half as pretty as my dim memory. A beautiful figure; tall and smart. Dressed in distinguished, colorless gray. Curly blond hair over her eyebrows. Underneath rises up a fine, Greek nose. Her lips are narrow and nervous, her teeth white.
>
> The most beautiful thing about her are her aristocratic hands, the well-dressed feet and her lack of weight. "Une belle femme" she is hardly. The traditional "femme fatale" she is not either. She makes her impression through her expression. [30]

For some, like Uhl, beautiful did not seem to be the right word to describe her.

Not at all beautiful and still seductive like no other. [Anonymous] [31]

She was perhaps more charming than beautiful, distinguished, dressed with studied simplicity. [Polish friend from Paris] [32]

For others, beautiful was precisely the right word.

Physically she was extraordinarily beautiful. Not even the time's terrible fashions could distort her figure. She wore with regal dignity the old clothes she inherited from her rich sister in Stockholm. [Tadeusz Boy-Żeleński] [33]

Many responded with a kind of totemistic reverence to a curious energy in her body. [34]

—The face is singular, aristocratic, winningly full of life. There is something searching in it, something testing the air; there's a trembling around the nostrils, she holds her eyelids lowered, but the eyes still stare out audaciously. [Strindberg, as filtered through Uhl] [35]

There was something regal about her, something enchanting in the very way she moved. She was very beautiful, and she had the most perfect hands I have ever seen, unbelievably white and restless. [Jappe Nilssen] [36]

Her eyes still look at me. I cannot forget them, not because they bewitched me, but because they had something to tell me. It was not a hypnotic look, rather the opposite, passive but at the same time curious, a kind of mute language I could not understand. [The Pole who, as a young boy, met Dagny in Zakopane] [37]

It is impossible to determine from where Dagny's enticing energy came. It does seem certain that it was due in great part to her being perceived to be a woman of remarkable spirit, sensuality, and, significantly, intellect.

Mme Dagny was characterized by her unusual intelligence and her extraordinary breeding. [Polish necrology] [38]

She was . . . the best educated. [Munch] [39]

Without any doubt I see it such that the center, the original source of the fantastic ideas which they embraced and played with in this circle was Mme Dagny. Her opinions and formulations, her grasp of the questions seemed almost like revelations, even old foxes thought so. [Polish friend from Paris] [40]

At that time Stach was really a poet—I didn't doubt for a minute that it was thanks to Mme Dagny that he had reached the heights. She had a penetrating and quick intellect, she was so straightforward and had such a sensitive and warm heart, as one only sees in such people who have come into the world to experience and understand all human feelings. [Polish zoologist from Paris] [41]

Her intellectual niveau was also in every sense "modern." [Frans Servaes] [42]

A woman who was highly intelligent, physically alluring, and kind was a most uncommon phenomenon, particularly in a time when women were divided into those of the upper classes, who were taught to cultivate their heads and hearts, and those of the lower classes, who were forced to cultivate their bodies. Even some of the most progressive women adhered to the "rightness" in this dichotomy. For example, critics and writers such as the Swedes, Ellen Key and Laura Marholm, and the Norwegian, Amalie Skram, saw the sexual woman both as a victim of male abuse and a threat to women of substance. Scandinavian women writers of the 1890s in general revealed a crippling ambivalence to the sexual woman, preferring to fashion heroines who could rely on their intrinsic innocence as the most profound truth of their identity.

Dagny, as a woman and as a writer, rejected innocence in favor of the more complex woman who incorporated the sexual as a significant determining aspect of her "self." In Dagny the unnatural divisions disappeared, making the sensual seem spiritual, the intellectual seductive, the spiritual so astonishingly physical. Munch saw it:

Her unbelievable beauty and electrifying nature and intelligence— and so Norwegianly feminine and personal, and kind and cheerfully attentive to everyone! exotically aristocratic—all of this did not give the scandal mongers peace in their dark corners. [43]

Adolf Paul saw it in his more conflicted way:

A classically pure profile, her forehead shaded with a confusion of curls, so that one could at one's pleasure estimate its height and thus even the possibilities of intelligence. A smile that awakened the longing for kisses but at the same time fear of the two rows of pearl-white, sharp teeth, which behind the thin lips waited for the chance to bite![44]

She was awe-inspiring, this complex woman who was redefining what women could be. Not surprisingly she gave rise to wonder and contempt.

ALONE...

Her primary magic power consists in the fact that she is the only unmarried woman in the camp and she knows how to make use of the situation. [Strindberg, as filtered through Uhl][45]

Now, after her death, when I try to recall what she looked like, I always see her dressed in black, disheartened and with bowed head. She didn't seem to notice her surroundings at all. Actually I never saw her like that while she still lived. She was always surrounded by people, she was always loved. [Gabriella Zapolska][46]

Dagny was remembered not only as being unique, but as being alone, in spite of the fact that she gained her reputation primarily in the crowded haunts of the bohemians in Germany and Poland, and that her fame presumably derived from her associations with famous men. In the descriptions of her from the *Ferkel* group, whether as Munch's nurturing angel or Paul's serpentine temptress, she rises out of the mass of others, as the men become her blurred backdrop. The sheer numbers of men with whom she was rumored to be associated, both in Berlin and Poland, ensured that they would recede into the shadows, interchangeable somehow with one another, as she gained her reputation for being interchangeable with no one at all. She was the one, they were the many.

Julius Meier-Graefe, for example, describing the atmosphere in Dagny's and Stach's Berlin apartment in Louisenstrasse, remembered Stach playing the piano, Dagny dancing with one friend, while two others watched. "One danced with Ducha, and the two at the table looked on, the one was Munch, the other as a rule Strindberg. The four men were all in love with

Ducha, each in his way, and didn't let it show." As Norwegian critic Sonja Hagemann pointed out many years ago, Strindberg could not have been a member of the foursome,[47] though people continue to be tantalized by the notion that he was. In terms of the myth about Dagny, it does not really matter who was there. The one abiding truth was that she was sovereign.

The man with whom Dagny was magically wedded in people's minds was, of course, Stach. They were thought of as inseparable. Ida Dehmel wrote about:

The harmony in their voices, when they spoke to each other. Stach spoke a gentle, broken German, Ducha just as little German as Polish, but their conversation rang like the most beautiful chord, as if a maestro played the viola and was accompanied by a finely tuned violin. I will always be able to hear their hushed voices.

Yet even as the two seemed to be as one, it is Dagny who is seen as the shimmering soul of the pair. Again Dehmel:

Stach without Ducha was a person who lived at loose ends, a homeless eccentric, a typical bohemian. When Ducha was at his side a center was suddenly created, a focus from which a magical and enchanted sheen was cast over those people who knew enough to appreciate art.[48]

The Norwegian sculptor, Gustav Vigeland, said later in his life:

And the only woman was Fru Przybyszewski [sic]. She had green eyes, [a] red dress and danced for us, and we all desired her.

Vigeland's sculpture *Vals II* (Waltz II), possibly inspired by Dagny and Stach, gives the woman the same exaggerated status that Dagny was perceived to have. It is she who determines the parameters and the sweep of the piece.[49]

Traditionally a woman alone was a dreaded metaphor for inferiority of soul and failure in life. Dagny's "aloneness," however, was a fantasy of unlimited possibilities and thus a well-spring of strength. Spiritual, animal, ordinary, and magical, she seemed to dissolve into sheer energy.

Her long, tight-fitting gown became a burning streak when she danced. [Julius Meier-Graefe][50]

Gustav Vigeland's Vals II, *1896.*

At the same time, there was something ominous in such omnipotent singularity, a hint of tragedy that played in the shadows of the myth, as if such a woman was doomed. As the Polish writer and critic, Gabriella Zapolska, wrote:

An aura of bewitchment hung about her, one sensed that she belonged to a race of women who are destined by fate for destruction.[51]

...AND MAGICAL

She was compared to a wood-nymph, this magical creature that constantly appears in new shapes. She exuded an indescribable enchantment in her manner of talking and being, but above all in her dancing. Her inventiveness was inexhaustible. She entertained no apprehensions when it came to getting herself out of the material difficulties that constantly arose. She was born to be queen in this group of artists. [Julius Bab][52]

Ducha is enchanting. If she carried white lilies in her hands she would be seen as a symbol of forever changing life. I always envision her as a singing angel—an angel with a cigarette in her mouth. She even smokes in a nearly ethereal way, and small, heavenly rings float like a halo around her lips. [A woman friend from Norway][53]

Dagny gave the impression of being of several worlds at once. As the "smoking angel" she was both angelic and demonic, as the "solo dancer," of matter and air, as the "muse," creative and destructive. She was of the poetic and the prosaic, the sublime and the mundane.

It is said that she is frail, she looks like an ethereal dream. When her husband speaks Polish when they're alone at home or out in a restaurant, and she doesn't understand anything or is tired of listening, she lies down and sleeps on the sofa where the men have thrown their coats. She, who makes such a poetic impression, must look funny there, in those surroundings, sleeping on the coats. [Helena Pawlikowska][54]

The woman seemed to slip invisibly into other forms of life, flowers, birds, and animals, even as she remained woman. Johannes Schlaf remembered her one summer day in Berlin as the huge sunflower she wore.

> She was tall and well-built, dressed in a thin dress. Her blond hair was shiny but not very well-combed. She had gotten the original idea to fasten a large sunflower on her breast. Because of her unbelievable figure she gave the impression herself of being a sunflower.[55]

Others remembered her as a bird or a butterfly, sometimes with life under her wings, sometimes death. An acquaintance from Paris saw her as a bright bird on a winter morning.

> One sunny winter morning I stood outside the entrance to the Jacob Hotel. My attention was caught by a young woman who just walked out through the gate. She hesitated a bit and walked slowly down rue des Saints-Pères straight toward boulevard Saint-Germain. Her gaudy clothes caused a sensation. Her dress was brown, her jacket and cap red, around her neck she wore a very yellow fox, on her feet, green shoes. She looked like a goldfinch. She had a beautiful figure and her movements were soft, her face tired, her eyes bright.[56]

Another in Poland saw her as fey creatures of the air.

> Tall and serious, wrapped in black tulle covered with black spangles —she looks like a butterfly in mourning, like a stormy petrel—A kind of deep seriousness in her barely visible little smile, in her amiable, hushed conversation of few words in a foreign language.[57]

A young girl from Lund had seen her as a wild creature of the forest.

> . . . in the middle of a ray of sun Dagny and her young son danced and played. With his dark green velvet frock and his leather belt, with his blond, tangled curls and his amusing, expression-filled face, the boy looked like a little, high-spirited, gracious Puck in Midsummer Night's Dream. The mother's frizzy, dark blond hair, parted in the middle, had fallen into disorder when, light as a bird, she jumped up on the big library table. The bun at the back of her neck had come loose, the color had risen in her otherwise ivory cheeks—she actually looked at that moment like some kind of Titania or wood nymph. I

stood in the doorway, not wanting to disturb the beautiful sight. It was like accidentally surprising a deer with her young in the deepest thicket of the forest—far from humans' narrow domains.[58]

One of the most astonishing descriptions of her was inspired by her eyes. To the boy who met her in Zakopane she took on the persona of a sacred goat.

> . . . a unique, very beautiful woman. Her golden red hair was parted in the middle and fell down over her ears. She squinted a little with her fascinating and curious eyes when she looked at me. I was just a boy then and shorter than she. These light, cold eyes under equally light eyelashes reminded me of the lighthearted and enigmatic eyes of a goat. . . . If you have never seen a goat's eyes, a white goat—then look at them next time. An eternal, mild smile rests over such eyes, a smile that can mean everything and nothing. . . . These wise goat eyes, this cold intellect, that picked up something beyond time and space![59]

Perhaps the most powerful polar-personae Dagny inspired, the one in which all the others are somehow subsumed, is the angel/demon, the saint concealing the serpent, Venus the vampire. Some, in particular Strindberg and his sycophants, responded to the demon.

> I've only seen her in passing. She didn't make any special impression on me. I'm not taken with that kind. I go more for the solid, substantial ones. . . . —in all senses of the word—there seems to be something a little lean about her person. She is more snake than Eve. But however it is, she can bring about the fall. [Strindberg, as filtered through Uhl][60]

Others, like the Polish painter Stanisław Wyspiański, responded to the angel, but an angel with the curiously powerful eye of a goddess, and the sensual woman, defenseless, and under siege.[61]

Munch responded to both the angel and the demon, the ethereal and the sensual woman, in a prophetic way, allowing the one to inspire the other, giving might and grace to both. And indeed Munch may have understood

Stanisław Wyspiański's Dagny.

best the powerful myth that his friend Dagny inspired. For both the angel and the demon are fantasies of transcendence, the angel to innocence, the demon to omnipotence. And there can be no greater fantasy in life than to be both innocent and all-powerful.[62]

Munch's vision of Dagny remained attached to the human artist who created it. We understand that he viewed her with reasonable wonder and reasonable fear. But there were those who lost sight of the human longing in the vision. For them she became, literally, the Supreme Being, and they had to destroy her. There was something of this in the Strindbergian hysteria that could not see the woman for Satan. But it culminated tragically in the crippled imagination of the young man who could not see the woman for God.

Wyspiański's cartoon on the Paon *canvas.*

Edvard Munch's Dagny Juel Przybyszewska, *1893.*

That she appeared to be an incarnation of the absolute, that she was God, you will learn from others. I just want to tell you, to express it in an earthly way, she was a saint. She was goodness itself, the kind of goodness that is called regal, and that arises from contempt. [Władysław Emeryk—the man who shot Dagny, then himself—in a letter he had earlier written to her five-year-old son, Zenon][63]

3 : DAGNY JUEL PRZYBYSZEWSKA

The discrepancies between myth and reality were many, if initially they may not have seemed so profound. There was little in the first twenty-five years of Dagny's life to suggest the fame and final tragedy of the last six; though it is apparent, even from the few known facts, that she had the upbringing, the cultural background, and the personality necessary to play the mythic woman people imagined her to be.

JUELL/JUEL

Dagny was born in Kongsvinger, Norway, on June 8, 1867. Her father, Hans Lemmich Juell, then twenty-seven, had begun his medical practice in 1863 and would become one of the most prominent doctors and political leaders in the district. He traced his aristocratic lineage back through more than a century of Juells who had served the Danish kings in the district of Hedmark, and much further back than that through generations of high-born Juells in Denmark. Her mother, Minda (neé Blehr), twenty-two, was also from an old Hedmark family. Minda's brother, Otto Blehr, would become the Norwegian prime minister to the king of Sweden-Norway in 1891, two years before Dagny went to Berlin.

Dagny was the second of four sisters, closely knit as they grew up and strongly, if at times ambivalently, supportive in their later lives. The sisters

Dagny at Rolighed, summer 1893. This photograph, probably taken upon Dagny's return from Berlin, seems to me to resemble closely Munch's portrait. The bonnet suggests the faint halo, the neckline and the puffed arms of the dress are similar, the head is cocked in a like manner, the arms are held close to the body.

Rolighed.

were reputed to have been among the most beautiful and talented young women of Kongsvinger. Since Dr. Juell was the attendant physician to the Swedish king, when he visited the queen at her summer residence at nearby Ridabøl, the Juell daughters were invited to the royal parties. When the oldest of the sisters was first presented to the king, he is said to have asked if there were many pretty girls in Kongsvinger. She is said to have replied, "There are four of us."[1]

The Juells lived at Rolighed (Serenity), an estate on the edge of the city limits, with grounds that led down to the river Glomma. They had a large, white, thirteen-room house, twenty-five acres of cultivated land, large vegetable and fruit gardens, and forest land on which Dr. Juell built a shooting range and the area's first ski jump. The sisters tended to identify themselves as coming from Rolighed, not Kongsvinger. Their social life seemed to revolve around Minda Juell's sisters and brothers who lived on farms and estates in the surrounding area.

Dagny's years as a girl and young woman are like a darkened landscape, the illuminating facts are so few. She had scarlet fever when she was ten.

She was confirmed at the age of fifteen and then traveled to Germany, apparently on a pleasure trip.[2] The public records reveal that she completed the traditional six grades of school. It would have been possible for her to continue her studies, as did her oldest sister, Gudrun, but she did not. Perhaps she had already formed her contempt for "the academic." The Swedish writer Amelie Posse remembered Dagny's advice to her when they met in Lund in 1900. Posse was then a girl of only twelve, aspiring to become a painter. "She warned me against continuing to study with the nice, old professor with whom I had just begun. She maintained that I would just grow moldy and petrify. She pronounced 'academic' with such obvious drudgery, indeed disgust, that in her beautiful mouth it became a dirty word."[3]

In her twenty-first year Dagny emerges briefly from the darkness of the past. She acted as governess to the children of her Uncle Otto and Aunt Randi Blehr from the fall of 1888 to the fall of 1889. Otto was then serving as district minister in the small, west coast town of Førde, northeast of Bergen. The weather was harsh that winter, the nights were, of course, long, and Førde was a very small town. Dagny and her relatives were like "foreign birds in an odd menagerie," as one of her aunts said.[4] Yet Dagny seemed to take to her changed world. She wrote of meeting new people, of a certain young man named Bull, of putting on plays, of staying up late with her uncle and his chess-playing friends.[5] She also wrote to her Aunt Randi, who was away for a longer stay, "Actually [I am] at home every day. I really think it's most fun to be with the children and the piano, at home in peace." Her nieces and nephews remembered, in particular, her sense of humor and the stories she read them.[6] Dagny herself was very fond of the children. When her year as governess was over she wrote to her aunt, "Say hello to those sweet, good children of mine and tell them I think about them terribly often, and tell them they don't have permission to forget me."[7]

Dagny seemed most excited, though, when she went to Bergen to visit her Aunt Birgit Blehr and Randi Blehr's mother, whom she called "Grandma Nilsen." They were equally excited to have her. After a visit from Dagny and Randi Blehr in the fall, Birgit wrote: "Thank you to both you and Dagny for the breath of fresh air from Bruland, it penetrated deep into my bones. Oh yes, it was a lovely time, and surely and absolutely I'll live on it for a long time. One definitely needs to shake off all the cooking drudgery nonsense and that kind of thing."[8] She invited them for Christmas. There were "many beauties" in town, she added. "Dagny should be here."

Dagny did, indeed, go to Bergen for Christmas. She wrote to Randi Blehr upon her arrival:

> Yesterday afternoon—that is, 3:00, I arrived safe and sound; uff! What weather; terrible sea; though I managed well namely by being sensible enough to stay in my cabin most of the time. Bull was, of course, kindness itself, and I blessed my good fortune that sent me off in such good company. It was enormously fun to see Aunt [Birgit] again and Bergen and all of it. . . .

She was immediately swept up into the social and cultural whirl of the city, and she delighted in it.

> Imagine, right away last evening I was invited by your uncle R. Nilsen to a grand ball; very enjoyable to see all the city's young ladies on one platter; Honoraria Gram was charming in an elegant, gray-blue dress and Gina's friend, Miss Våge, absolutely beautiful. . . .
>
> Bull paid a visit this morning; he is supposed to have dinner with your parents today; but tomorrow he is eating here and then he invited Aunt [Birgit] and me to see "Zaar og tømmermand" with him tomorrow evening; the opera is supposed to be both beautiful and fun and, of course, we're looking forward to it.[9]

Dagny was having a wonderful time in Bergen that Christmas, and she did not want to leave any sooner than necessary. She wrote again to Randi on December 30: "I'm having a fantastic time, as you can well imagine. . . . Dear Aunt, would you please send me a few words and tell me which day you want school to begin and therefore me to come home? I would really, of course, rather stay here as long as possible."[10]

Dagny returned to Bergen a number of times during her year on the west coast. During one such visit, with her nieces along, she wrote: "Last Saturday there was a party and a dance; a lot of young people and fantastically fun. I've been with Hjalmar Jonsson several times; one day he came here to dinner with August, and since then we've continued the acquaintance; Marit [her niece] and I are both quite taken with him."[11]

But dances and operas and people were not her only joys. She also loved playing the piano. "Aunt [Birgit] and I were [at your mother's] yesterday, unceremoniously; no one was home except your parents and Andreas and Harald—I played my whole repertoire; it was so fun to play for your mother again."[12] Fru Nilsen enjoyed Dagny's playing just as much. She wrote to her in January 1893, as Dagny was on her way to the Continent to study piano: "Thank you for every time you have delighted me with your music, dear Dagny. . . . Farewell, my dear, kind Dagny. God protect you and bless you. When you play Rubinstein [sic], and Peer Lasson, my favorite pieces, then think of your devoted old Grandma Nilsen."[13]

Dagny's letters from her time in Førde and Bergen reveal a young woman excited by people, parties, and the arts. Yet there was an innocence about them. They were written by a charming, loved, and protected niece, not a femme fatale. Meier-Graefe's description of her years later as a member of the *Schwarze Ferkel* comes to mind. "She was intelligent and witty and ready for everything, but not for this circle's most beloved preoccupation [i.e., sex]."[14]

The letters also indicate that as a teenager Dagny had seriously studied the piano and that she derived great pleasure in playing both for herself and for relatives and friends. Then as later she seemed to be drawn at once to both the excitement of the crowd and the calm of the intimate circle.

After her year as a governess Dagny was met by her father in Bergen, and together they sailed back to Christiania. She returned to Rolighed, where she set up in what she called her "antique" room with old pieces of furniture she had acquired in Førde. But from a letter she wrote to Randi Blehr upon her return, she was also spending time in Christiania.

Dearest Aunt!

You think I'm a terribly ungrateful, impolite creature, who still hasn't written to you. Dear, don't despise me too deeply. I've been so on the go; and you know that letter writing is the weakest of all my weak sides. . . .

There was life and gaiety in Christiania—a lot of people on the street and very fun. . . .

Are you and Uncle going to Berlin? If only you'd all come to Christiania instead. . . .

I have heard de Gruf twice in Christiania. You can imagine how wonderful that was! Absolutely exceptional. *He* played Grieg![15]

Dagny in Christiania, early 1890s.

Dagny was twenty-two, in love with life, and apparently intent on pursuing her piano studies.

> I'm going to play with the pianist Westy Waalev, he is supposed to be fantastically good and talented and most of all he loves Grieg more than anything, and that of course clinched it for me. I've begun to practice with fantastic diligence—4 hours a day, quite a bit, don't you think?

Whether Dagny lived in Christiania in the early 1890s, or whether she traveled back and forth between the city and Kongsvinger, is not known. The latter is the likelier possibility; family letters to Randi Blehr indicate that Dagny paid extended visits to her uncles and aunts in Hedmark during that time, and when she wanted, she certainly had places to stay in Christiania. Her mother's sister, Maria Blehr, ran a school for young girls in the fashionable Victoria Terrasse,[16] and Randi and Otto Blehr themselves lived in the equally fashionable Oscarsgate from 1889 to 1891. Invitations from her aunt did not seem to be unusual. One December in 1889 or 1890 Dagny wrote to Randi Blehr on her way to Christiania from Hamar, where her father's relatives lived:

> You were so kind to invite Ragnhild and me to stay with you on our way home from Hamar; dear, if it is the least bit inconvenient for you, then you must definitely write and say. We're coming to the city on Thursday, the 2nd, and if you can put us up in any way possible, you would be terribly kind. So if we don't hear from you, then we're coming!
>
> You can believe we have had a lovely, fun Christmas; have danced and had fun non-stop.[17]

People have speculated that Dagny met some of the Christiania artists at the Blehr home. That was certainly a possibility. Otto was a liberal politician, Randi a leading feminist, and they apparently made the artists welcome. It seems unlikely, though, that the members of the infamous Christiania bohemia, dominated by free-thinker and writer Hans Jæger, and painters Oda and Christian Krohg, were actually guests of the Blehrs. In any case, there is little to link them to Dagny.[18] She and her youngest sister Ragnhild were friends with a less socially aggressive group of young, aspiring artists.

Ragnhild was studying voice with concert pianist Erika Nissen, who was also originally from Kongsvinger. Dagny may have been studying with Waalev. Whatever their professional status, the sisters, who were extremely close, seem often to have been in the city together. They became friends with the lyric poets Vilhelm and Thomas Krag[19] and Nils Collett Vogt; the pianist Arne Sem, whom Dagny would meet again in Berlin; Maya Vogt, Nils's sister, whom Dagny would also meet again in Berlin; and the writer and journalist Hjalmar Christiansen.

Dagny and Christiansen were possibly tied romantically. He was from Førde and then studied in Bergen, graduating in 1887. Dagny may have met him either place, or she may have met him in Christiania. The only evidence of their acquaintance from the early 1890s is a photograph of the sisters with Krag and Christiansen (p. 46). But Dagny had two of Christiansen's books with her in Poland, *En frisindet* (A liberal) (1889) and *Mat blod* (Tired blood) (1891), both personally dedicated to "Frøken Dagny Juell."[20] There is no further mention of Dagny and Hjalmar Christiansen until after her death in a letter from Maya Vogt to Ragnhild. "Do you take *Verdens Gang*? Hj. Chr. is very productive writing articles right now. You can believe Dagny was fond of *him*! I met him again *for the first time* in Paris, and we talked a lot about Dagny."[21]

In early February 1892, Dagny went to Berlin, probably to study music. Her sister, Gudrun, wrote to Otto Blehr in March, giving him Dagny's new address and asserting that "Dagny is extremely happy in Berlin."[22] Nothing was heard of her there, though. No one from the later *Ferkel* group suggested he had met her earlier. What she did or how long she stayed is not known. If the dating of Munch's painting of Dagny and Ragnhild, *Two Music-Making Sisters,* is correct, she and her sister were very likely in Åsgårdstrand, where Munch lived and had his studio, that summer of 1892. By the fall, and probably earlier, Dagny was back at Rolighed. By the end of the year she was restless and anxious to leave again.

Dagny spent the month before Christmas, 1892, with Gudrun in Lund and caused her first "public stir." She went to visit the younger members of the Professor Lidforss family who belonged to her sister's snobbishly respectable circle. Eleven-year-old Hedvig Lidforss thought Dagny was "sin personified." She later remembered the visit: "a little party was put together in the upstairs apartment. Gerda was there, Bengt and Erik. . . . Dagny Juel had on a long black dress that was smeared around her body like a shield.

Vilhelm Krag, Hjalmar Christiansen, Dagny, and Ragnhild in Christiania, early 1890s.

Around her waist she had a wide, green crocodile sash, something we had never seen in the city before. She had makeup on, drank and smoked like the others."[23]

Hedvig may have been shocked by Dagny, but her older brother, Bengt Lidforss, was said to have fallen in love with her. They met again a few months later in the *Schwarze Ferkel* circle, where Lidforss came as an intimate of Strindberg. If real, Lidforss's love for Dagny was doomed from the beginning, given that he was homosexual and was suffering from syphilis. His biographers contend, regardless, that he never got over her.[24] She seems to have treated him as a good friend, welcoming him to her and Stach's apartment in Berlin and confiding to him her efforts to write. He, on the other hand, in party with Strindberg, generated some of the most malicious gossip ever spread about her.[25] Resentment of her seems to have taken root even before she left for Berlin.

Whether Hedvig Lidforss was really so shocked by Dagny in December of 1892, or whether in retrospect she enjoyed being so, is impossible to say. Her reaction to Dagny as "sin personified," however, typified the reactions of those who saw in her something to fear. But many more would see in her something to inspire. Another young girl from Lund, Gudrun's friend Amelie Posse, remembered later that "she was a messenger from the great world out there that lay waiting for me with all its enticing promises and unlimited possibilities. In my heart I immediately called her 'Europa' —it was as if that was what she represented to me most of all."[26]

Dagny's Grandmother Nilsen wrote to her just before she left for Berlin: "A warm thank you for the picture of your sweet face. The pose is original. No one but you could have thought of turning your back to the camera. Still, nothing is lost of the face's profile. The picture is *remarkable,* and beautiful, and remarkably like you. We all agree that it is a remarkable picture of our dear Dagny."[27]

Dagny did have a flair for the dramatic, as her photographs from the time suggest. Sometimes she would wear a high-brimmed hat, sometimes an oversized bunch of dried flowers at her breast, or a big, metal salamander at her throat. She would stand in side profile, and she would not smile.

Perhaps the dramatic poses, like her experimenting with the spelling of her name, were symptoms of the fact that she was casting about in life, looking for her direction. She was twenty-five, unmarried, and without a "cause." She was not at all political, though both Randi and Otto Blehr provided potentially powerful models for her. Music was her one, abiding passion, but she pursued her studies with intermittent fervor. She was anxious for artistic and social stimulation and, judging from the way she responded to the *Schwarze Ferkel* group, existential resolution.

Dagny was used to a large and loving family network. The bohemians must have seemed her perfect forum, for they themselves were a kind of extended family into which she was welcomed. Albeit some of the most revolutionary artists of the time, they were not necessarily the most inwardly secure. Dagny—aristocratic, artistic, playful, and distinctive—lent them psychological stature, or exposed the lack thereof. They in turn confirmed her originality and desirability with an excitement she could not have imagined.

JUEL / PRZYBYSZEWSKA

Europa

At Christmastime, 1892, Dagny had written Fru Nilsen that she was about to fulfill her "life's dream." She was going to Paris to study piano, where her sister Ragnhild was studying voice.[28] For whatever reason, she changed her mind in the course of three weeks and decided to go to Berlin. On January 26, she wrote to her uncle, the prime minister, for a consular passport, which would allow her access to cultural events in the city. "I would be so appreciative. . . . You see, I'm going to Berlin on Thursday of next week and stay down there for three months in order to study at Holländer's Conservatory. You can believe I'm ecstatically happy."[29]

The first week in February 1893, Dagny left Norway for Germany. The *Ferkel* artists propelled her into the limelight within a month of her setting foot on the European stage. Thus began the dramatic, public years of her life which ended as abruptly as they had begun when, seven and a half years later, she was shot, at the age of only thirty-three, in Tiflis near the Black Sea.

If the myth was only an impossible dream, then Dagny's sensational death was its fitting end.[30] But there was also possibility in the myth. The tragedy for Dagny lay in the discrepancy between the worshiped modern woman of the myth and the modern woman of real life. She tried to be everything: artist, free woman, wife, mother, daughter, sister, friend, literally "breaking the boundaries of family within which society restrict[ed] her."[31] Yet it was she who was broken in the process.

Her geographical journey from Norway to Russian Georgia can be traced with considerable accuracy, with long stays in Berlin, then Paris, Spain, Kraków, Warsaw, and always returning home to Rolighed.[32] Her interior journey during those few short years remains for the most part uncharted. Dagny seldom revealed her feelings, even in the few surviving letters to her family and friends. Whether out of pride, helplessness, or ennui, she remained eerily silent about the ever more ill-fated turns her life was taking. An overview of the events suggests her decreasing ability to control them.

Her life had all the makings of a melodrama, and indeed, it was one on the surface. She and Stach Przybyszewski fell in love in the spring and were married in Berlin in the late summer of 1893.[33] Amidst constant rumors of other liaisons on both sides, they were at the same time perceived to be inseparable, their souls perfectly in tune, their strong wills as one. Ducha and Stachu were exceptional. As Ida Auerbach Dehmel later wrote: "If you took [those] two into your heart you felt yourself enriched by something you are vouchsafed to encounter only once in a lifetime."[34]

They became the king and queen of the bohemians, their one room apartment in Louisenstrasse 6 their *fin de siècle* court. Meier-Graefe described it: "In the middle of the room chairs and a table. Over it, hanging from a wire, a kerosene lamp with a red paper shade. Two beds partly hidden by a kind of standing screen. . . . They had rented a piano that could be muted, so you could play all night without disturbing the house. She played Grieg; he played Chopin."[35]

Strindberg claimed that the *Schwarze Ferkel* group soon split apart because of the rivalries Dagny engendered. Save for his own departure, however, the opposite was true, as Dagny and Stach held the group together for a time. They were its spiritual and emotional center. They agitated for the recognition of the Scandinavian artists among them. Dagny translated Sigbjørn Obstfelder, Stach wrote about Edvard Munch and the sculptor Gustav Vigeland. They were the motivating force behind *Pan* (1895), the most progressive European art journal of the decade and the group's brainchild, which Dagny had named.[36]

If they were an inspiration to their friends, they were even more so to

Stachu and Ducha, Kongsvinger, 1895. The Przybyszewskis used this photograph as a postcard.

each other. Stach wrote prolifically in his years with Dagny. He attributed his inspiration to her, used her as his model, and dedicated his works to her. He wrote that because of her "a whole new life began for me; I grew deeper, more intensive, while my consciousness was enriched with all the slumbering abilities and powers I earlier knew nothing about. Much in my soul was written with invisible ink. It only needed heat to be visible." Critics and biographers alike contend that Stach did his finest work when he was with Dagny and that he went into decline as a writer when his life with her ended.[37]

Dagny herself began to write, mysterious, rebellious pieces of poetry, fiction, and plays. She wrote a short story, "Rediviva," in December 1893, and sometime later a play, *Den sterkere* (The stronger), that was published in Norway in 1896. By the end of the summer of 1897, she had written at least three more plays. She started to write lyric poems and a prose-poem cycle.

They had two children, Zenon in September 1895, and Iwa in October 1897. When Zenon was nine months old Dagny wrote to Munch, "My son now says 'Mama' and that is without comparison the most interesting thing I've experienced in Norway. And he pulls out all the hair I have."[38]

Their difficulties, however, had long since begun. Stach was a serious alcoholic. His obsessions with satanism, sex, and drink darkened their environment. He was also a pathological liar and never to be depended upon. Dagny and Stach were *always* without money, due both to their mutual unconcern and to Stach's drinking. Some initially saw a charm in their poverty. Dagny herself was to have said that they got married because one day they just happened to have a mark, the very cost of a marriage license.[39] Ida Dehmel remembered:

> Both of them, Stachu and Dagny, entertained a bottomless contempt for all kinds of order. They found the thought of tomorrow ridiculous and unnecessary. In the spring Dagny pawned her winter clothes and redeemed them in the fall, when she left her summer clothes instead. When we were together, pawn tickets were always falling out of her purse. This happened of course not completely by accident, and with childish charm she cried: "Right, Mme Isi, you'll give me two marks before I leave."[40]

But their poverty was real. They did not always have enough to eat. Eventually they were forced to sell their personal belongings, including their furniture, their art, and their old family things, which were so important to Dagny. Both financially and emotionally they put themselves forever at the mercy of their family and friends.

They often came to Rolighed for long periods, because they simply did not have the means to survive on their own. Sometimes Dagny would come alone. Between the time they were married in 1893 and the fall of 1898 when they moved to Kraków, she spent thirty-three months, or a little less than three of those five years, with her parents at Rolighed. Stach spent just over a year there, the rest of his time, for the main, in Berlin.

Dagny gave birth to both her children at Rolighed, and she entrusted them to the care of her mother when she went off to join Stach, whether in Berlin, Copenhagen, Paris, or Spain. She left both children for the first time when they were about three months old. She was apart from Zenon for almost half of his first three years of life, and from Iwa for almost half of her first year. Dagny never took the children with her when she went to be with Stach. He did not see his daughter until she was over one year old.

It was, however, not only her poverty that brought Dagny back to Rolighed again and again. She was very close to all the members of her family. Inevitably, from her restless, uncertain life, she was drawn back to their peace and stability. She seemed to feel that her own children were safer with them. When she was about to leave Zenon within months of his birth, she wrote to her Aunt Randi:

> You can imagine how happy I am over my boy. I find him miraculously beautiful and sweet and handsome, and healthy he is too, which is of course the best thing of all. It is going to be terribly painful to leave him, but he's way too little for a long trip in the middle of winter. He's going to stay here at Rolighed this winter and as good a home as he has here he can truthfully not have with me.[41]

As Rolighed drew her home, Stach drew her away, both like invisible ropes pulling at her from opposite directions. The children became the victims of her inner tug-of-war.

In June 1896, three years after Dagny and Stach were married, their lives were shaken by real tragedy. When Stach had met Dagny in 1893, he was involved with a young Polish woman named Marta Foerder, who had already had two children with him. Stach continued to see Marta after his marriage to Dagny, returning to her when Dagny stayed behind at Rolighed. Marta gave birth to Stach's third child in February 1895, the same year Zenon was born, and may have been pregnant with a fourth child when she took poison on June 9, 1896.

It is not known how Dagny responded to Stach's relationship with Marta, or even what she knew of it.[42] But when news of the suicide came Dagny had only recently joined him in Copenhagen, reunited after three months apart. Stach had written to several friends that they were joyous to be together again, but they did not know what they were going to do. Marta's suicide decided for them. Together they went to Berlin, where Stach was implicated in the suicide, arrested, and jailed for two weeks. He was released, but the scandal was great and would take its toll. Most of their friends, including Richard Dehmel, abandoned them. They had no money, and Stach was initially so depressed that he could not function.

The picture that emerges of Dagny is a complicated one. She stood steadfastly by Stach. They remained alone in Berlin, where she not only kept him company and cooked for him, but rewrote his manuscripts, dealt with his publishers, gave piano lessons, begged for money from their friends, and played the lottery.[43] To the outside world she insisted they could manage. And she always found a way to put Stach in a sympathetic light. In a letter to Munch, written sometime in the summer of 1896, she wrote:

> Dear Munch,
>
> Stachu is sick and still cannot write to you. I'm writing just a few words to answer your questions.
>
> Dear, ask no one about money for Stachu. In the first place, it wouldn't do any good and besides, Pan has accepted something, so we're all right for the time being.[44]

It is in this letter that she also assured Munch that Stach had not used him as the model for his painter in *Overboard*. He was, as she said, too fond of him ever to misuse him.

Meier-Graefe wrote to Munch that Dagny and Stach were not "all right." "I have spoken to Stachu and Ducha, things are not going well for them, terrible."[45] What little money they managed to scrape together, Stach spent on drink. Their rent unpaid, they were forced to vacate their Berlin apartment. Just before Christmas they moved to Nieder Schönhausen outside the city, and though each in letters said they were enjoying being together in the greater quiet of the suburbs, they were obviously struggling day to day. Dagny wrote to Ragnhild on the birth of Ragnhild's second son around the New Year, 1896–97: "Think that I didn't have money to send you a telegram and it was absolutely impossible to get any."[46]

The Polish writer Alfred Wysocki was one of the few friends who did not abandon the Przybyszewskis. In his memoirs he remembered that they had so little money that Dagny often had to sleep away hunger and cold. The atmosphere was decadent, with Stach indulging his interest in satanism and drinking excessively. Yet Wysocki said Dagny denied Stach nothing. She made no protest when he spent in the taverns what little money they had. "Stachu needs such happy moments of relaxation," Wysocki remembered her saying.[47]

Dagny at this time showed not only great loyalty to Stach but ingenuity and courage in a desperate situation for them both. Wysocki saw her as the saving grace: "[She] was the one who always seemed unmoved, almost cold. In spite of her unreserved, comradely way and her outspokenness, Dagny created such respect that none of us in her presence would choose to use an improper word or an indiscreet gesture."[48] But as there is a suggestion of depression in Wysocki's description, there is, in the general description of events from this time, an even greater suggestion of something help-lessly obsessive about Dagny's dedication to Stach. Was it a defiant or a self-destructive woman who saw her husband through this crisis? I suggest both. She captured the ambivalence herself in one of a number of lyric poems she probably wrote at this time.

> I drank from your deep well
> One night when the moon big and bloody
> Burned between the pine trees' crooked branches.
>
> I saw the eagle fly away,
> Frightened by the moon in that gloomy gallows,
> And muddy the water in your clear spring.
>
> And the power I drank from your waters
> Became poison in my healthy veins,
> While I waited, sitting on the runestone.
>
> ("Jeg har drukket af din dybe brønd")

Marta Foerder represented Stach's greatest betrayal of Dagny during these years, but there were others, including Dagny's friend Maya Vogt, and there would be more.[49]

Dagny had become pregnant for the second time in January 1897. She was tired and sick and had not seen her son, who was at Rolighed with her mother, for over half a year. In March she went home, Stach came and went again in the summer, and in October, one month late, she gave birth to her daughter, Iwa. The last stages of the pregnancy had been dif-ficult, and Dagny almost died in childbirth. That summer she had written several short plays, including one titled Når solen går ned (When the sun goes down), about a young girl who dies from fear. She had called her protagonist Ivi, the name she also originally gave to her daughter.[50] Stach professed to be distraught over Dagny's critical condition, but he remained in Berlin. In December Dagny went to him, leaving both children with her mother. The Przybyszewskis first traveled to Paris, then to Spain in February–March, then back to Paris.

In early summer Dagny's father developed what was determined to be a cancerous tumor on his eye. All the sisters returned to Rolighed. Stach followed several weeks later. Dr. Juell was operated on and seemed to recover, but his condition worsened in the course of the fall.

In September 1898 Stach went to Kraków to take over the editorship of Życie (Life), the journal of the avant-garde Young Poland. Dagny and the children followed him there in the late fall. The move was bitter-sweet. Stach was received like a returning war lord by the adoring artists of the Kraków bohemia, and Dagny once again was the Lady, singular, enigmatic, Stach's queen, everyone's dream. Their friends rented them a house, kept them in food and liquor, and thronged around them day and night. But Dagny's father was growing weaker.

Dagny wrote to a friend shortly after her arrival that Kraków was a charming and beautiful little city, but that she was very depressed, for she could not think of anything but her father.[51] When it became clear that he was dying, she longed to go back to Rolighed, but decided she could not do so for the sake of her children. Her sister Astrid wrote to Randi Blehr on December 11: "It is so terrible for Dagny, since it is of course impossible for her to come home, she has two small children she cannot leave and neither does she dare to take them with her at this time of year." Dagny's mother wrote to her on December 27:

> Thank you for your telegram, which came so early in the afternoon and gave me a feeling that you were not so far away after all. I do know that your thoughts are here, especially during this *difficult* time . . . but to hear directly from you is always a great joy. Papa's condition has, "God be praised," not gotten particularly worse these past days, especially the last week before Christmas was exceptionally good. . . . I dread so terribly the moment that will take him from us forever, and though I know so well that it grows near and perhaps is not as distant as I hope, I cannot possibly accept that it really is so. You cannot imagine, Dagny mine, how beautiful he is, as he lies here, a picture of peace and devotion to God's will . . . , only gratitude and tenderness toward Astrid and me, who are with him.[52]

Dagny was in a foreign land in more ways than simply geographically. A friend from Kraków described the house in which she and Stach were then living at 53 Karmelicka Street.[53] It seemed to be a different planet, he said, where nothing existed except art. The walls were covered by works of Munch, Goya, and Wyspiański and on the table lay beautiful art books, unknown until then in Poland. It was an exotic land, full of visitors from early afternoon until late at night. The drinking was continual. Stach would play Chopin, and when he tired, Dagny would sit at the piano playing Grieg and other sad melodies from Norway. One day Zenon supposedly went up to his mother and asked her what kind of tears were rolling down her face.[54]

The Przybyszewskis' situation soon began to deteriorate. Stach drank even more than before. Dagny never really learned Polish, and though she had her following of worshiping men, she was isolated from Stach and the group as she had not been in Berlin. Her father died in January. The journal *Życie* went under. Dagny and Stach were literally kept by their friends, their relationship worsened and there were betrayals on both sides.

In June 1899, Stach became involved with two other women simultaneously. One, Aniela Pająkówna, would bear him a daughter the next year.[55] The other, Jadwiga Kasprowicz, the wife of one of Stach's best friends and Poland's major poets, would marry him after Dagny's death. That summer Dagny spent much of her time in the resort town of Zakopane in the mountains south of Kraków. She was said to have been seeing Tadeusz Boy-Żeleński, her and Stach's good friend from the *Paon* circle.

In January 1900, Dagny left Stach. Though the circumstances are unclear, the final phase of their relationship had obviously begun. They almost seemed to be engaged in some sort of terrible duet, unable to be together, unable to part. Dagny supposedly moved into a hotel with a young Polish/French poet by the name of Wincent Brzozowski. For a short time they stayed in Kraków. Then she either took or sent Zenon to her family in Scandinavia, and Stach sent Iwa to Aniela Pająkówna, his lover in Lemberg (now Lwów). Dagny, too, visited Lemberg, where Brzozowski was living. Then she seemed to flee from one city to the next, first to Berlin with Brzozowski, then back to Kraków alone, then to Prague alone, then to Paris again to be with Brzozowski. All the while Stach was still in the background, though the nature of the role he played is difficult to determine. He went to Berlin when he feared Dagny had gone there. He claimed that he gave money to her and Brzozowski because they were starving, that he sent her to Prague to be with friends, and that he brought her back to Kraków because she threatened to kill herself if she did not see Iwa again.

Were they acting out a kind of revenge imitation play, with their children and other lovers as pawns in their action? It is difficult to sort out the

Dagny, Zakopane, 1899.

Stach, Zakopane, 1899.

truth because all the information came from Stach, in letters he wrote to friends and Dagny's family.[56] Seldom able to tell the truth and now driven to discredit Dagny, he went to great lengths to tell the story to his own advantage. She remained silent. Yet they both seem to have been characters in deterioration, their emotional lives spent from too much abuse.

In early May, Dagny's sister Gudrun went to Paris, apparently to convince Dagny to go home to Rolighed. Dagny returned, and she and Zenon, already there with her mother, stayed for half a year. Her prose-poem cycle, *Sing mir das Lied vom Leben und vom Tode* (Sing me the song of life and death), was published in Norway late in the fall. The poems tell of failure and loss.

> She had been queen in love's kingdom, for never had any man loved a woman more than he had loved her.
>
> And now he was dead.
>
> Never more would she read in his eyes that she was the sun round which the world turned. Never more would she feel the fragrance of the flowers his love bred all about her. The flowers were now withered and death's bony hand had torn the queen's crown from her head.

As in the early 1890s, Dagny and Ragnhild spent some time together in Christiania, but they both felt times had changed. In October Ragnhild wrote to her husband Helge:

> Yes, we're actually here in Xania now and it's rather strange—not at all like it was in the days of our youth and not many of our old friends either. Were at a Bodega with Bille on Monday and then met Wilhelm Krag briefly, and tomorrow we're going to Hedvig's with him and his wife. We've been with Maya Vogt a lot and she's her old sweet, kind self. Munch isn't here—[57]

And four days later:

> . . . Maya and Dagny and I hung out together a lot, and since no one else wanted to treat us I, of course, had to put on the treating-trousers and hold an elegant soupé at Grand for Maya, D. and myself with good food and fine wines that cost a lot of money.[58]

In early December Dagny wrote Munch from Rolighed:

I've got a big favor to ask you: won't you send me a couple of your lithographs, for example Madonna and especially "the scream"? You've promised them to me and I don't own a single etching, not a single lithograph of yours. You would be so fantastically kind, if you would. I ask you so boldly because I know that if you don't want to send anything, then you simply won't.

Ragnhild and I were in Christiania a month ago and we so wanted to meet you. We telephoned to Holmenkollen, Grand, Åsgårdstrand, but in vain, whether you kept yourself hidden on purpose or whatever.[59]

She wrote again once she had gone to Warsaw:

Thank you for sending those lithographs I asked for! I'll be so terribly glad to get them—actually the request was in great part an excuse to hear a little from you personally. Everyone said you were sick, absolutely shy of people and impossible to be around and all the attempts Ragnhild and I made to get together with you in Christiania were fruitless. . . . Christiania is an impossible place right now; they all behave like children. I was home in Norway for over half a year, but hardly 14 days in Christiania.[60]

According to Ragnhild, Dagny remained at Rolighed, waiting for Stach to send word of his plans. "She waits daily for a letter, but no letter comes."[61] But they did decide to reconcile. First Dagny planned to leave for Poland in October, then December. Finally in February she and Zenon joined Stach in Berlin. They traveled first to Kraków, and in March they all moved to Warsaw. Iwa was still in Lemberg.

Just before they left Kraków, Dagny wrote assuringly to her mother that all was well.

We're staying here in a hotel now and as soon as Zenon's passport is issued, we'll leave the same evening for Warsaw, where our new home is already waiting for us.

I am endlessly happy to be home again with Stachu. . . .

Mama, you can really be happy with us: it's beginning—no it's already going remarkably well for us economically! . . .

And you can simply not imagine what glorious things he has written now, since he's well again. Three new plays that are now going to be performed all over Poland, a novel [*Synowie ziemi* (Sons of the soil)] that is coming out in Przesmicki's new journal. Everyone is on their knees to him.

He's worked so hard during this time that it's completely super-human! Finished and improved the new German editions. . . . Taken care of all those masses of corrections. Written all the glorious new things as well as his lecture which he is going to give in Warsaw as soon as we arrive!

If that isn't impressive, then I don't know what is.[62]

But all was not well when Dagny, Stach, and Zenon got to Warsaw. Stach had not arranged for housing. They moved into a single room in a crowded pension. He was apparently more deeply than ever involved with Jadwiga Kasprowicz and seldom in Warsaw, saying he was sick and unable to return to Dagny and Zenon. Stach's novel, *Synowie ziemi*, about which Dagny had written so proudly to her mother, was in reality Stach's vitriolic attack on Dagny and their marriage. It had been coming out in serial form in the journal *Chimera* since early January. As Stach had once worshiped Dagny in his writing, he now reviled her. Everyone knew who the main characters were intended to portray. Though publication of the installments was finally stopped, Dagny had been the victim of a wicked display, and she was deeply wounded.

Yet publicly she was loyal to Stach and forever "the Lady." Sometime early in the spring of 1901, a Warsaw journalist met her and Stach walking on the street.

Przybyszewski promenaded with a tall blond. She was stylish and beautiful, with hair that formed a gilded halo around her face. The blond held Przybyszewski under his arm. When she saw me, she let go of her husband's arm, stopped in the middle of the sidewalk, lifted up her dress and curtsied mockingly. The people around us stopped. Then she took her husband's arm again, and they walked on. It was her ironic way of thanking me for a newspaper article, in which I criticized Przybyszewskiism. But she was so charming, and the entire happening took place on such a beautiful spring day, when the sun shone so enchantingly clear, that I remember everything as a beautiful and poetic picture.[63]

Dagny's charming, proud presence belied her situation. In retrospect, the discrepancy was sadly disturbing. As the weeks wore on that spring, people began to see her as a haunted soul, shrouded in black.[64]

In late April Dagny set out on her final, bizarre journey. Without passports, she and Zenon left Warsaw for Tiflis in Russian Georgia, traveling by train over a thousand miles through Russia with a young man named Władysław Emeryk. A Pole of Russian extraction and son of a wealthy businessman, Emeryk owned a salt mine near Tiflis. Only Emeryk knew at the time that the mine was on the verge of bankruptcy. Earlier in Kraków and now again while home visiting in Warsaw, he had lavished money on his poor artist friends, in particular Dagny and Stach. Sensitive, idealistic, and emotionally unstable, he was said to have adored them both to excess.

The circumstances of Dagny's departure are unknown. Some said that Emeryk was providing Dagny and Stach with a way out, that Stach was to follow and they would then be together again in an environment far from all the pain they had suffered in Poland. Others said that Stach, never intending to follow, used Emeryk to be rid of Dagny. Ragnhild wrote to her husband, Helge, that if people inquired, it happened this way:

> Stachu, Dagny and both children were going to live in the Caucasus for a couple of years, at the invitation of the elder Emeryks, but when Stachu still had to stay in Lemberg another month for his work, and Dagny did not want to go to Lemberg and was reluctant to stay alone in Warsaw, she decided to leave, with the young Emeryk as her escort, his parents having assured Stach that he could safely entrust his wife to his care.[65]

Dagny, Zenon, and Emeryk traveled for three weeks, arriving in Tiflis on May 18. As if she were simply a tourist on an exotic trip, she had sent picture postcards along the way to Ragnhild in Stockholm, some of which Ragnhild did not receive until after Dagny's death.

> [From the train station in Warsaw, April 26, 1901:] Beloved! Next station Tiflis! Your own, own Dagny. [Stach, who had accompanied her to the train, added in his own hand:] Skål! Stach!

> [From Kiev, April 28, 1901:] A thousand greetings from one of the most beautiful cities I've seen! Will write a letter from Rostoff on the Asiatic Sea! Your Dagny

[From Tiflis, May 22, 1901 (Dagny sent at least six separate cards in tandem. Only four have survived.):]

I. Will write soon! Look how beautiful it is here! Address: Emeryk, Grand Hotel, Tiflis. Dagny

II. Card I is just the view from here, but as . . .

III. you see here the mountains are much higher around the city! Your own Dagny. Long terribly to hear from you.[66]

At the same time, a much more desperate Dagny was sending telegrams to Stach in various cities in Poland, asking for the passports he had promised to forward. She was a woman literally wiring from place to place for proof of who she was. In her last letter to him, supposedly sent the day before Emeryk killed her, she wrote, "I'm about to lose my mind. Not a word since a month ago. I have telegraphed to Kraków, to Lemberg, to Warsaw. No answer. . . . I am dumbfounded, completely dumbfounded."[67]

Right up to the end Dagny kept her worlds strangely separate. Dagny, the loving sister, and Dagny, the confused wife, seemed to have had little to do with each other.

Her mother sent her a letter on June 2, 1901, three days before she died. Minda Juell was anxiously trying to reach her daughter. "Your birthday is nearing, my beloved child, and I send you my warmest good wishes for your new year. Hoping that this letter will reach you, though I have no definite address, so I'm in fact sending it out into the world on a wing and a prayer. God grant that your new year will be a blessed year for you, my dearest Dagny. . . ."[68]

Dagny never received her mother's good wishes. Shortly after noon on June 5, 1901, three days before her thirty-fourth birthday, Emeryk shot her, and then himself. Both acts were premeditated. Emeryk had left several sealed letters, written in the days prior to the tragedy, explaining in particular to Stach and the five-year-old Zenon that he had to take her life. To Stach he wrote, "I'm killing her for her own sake." To Zenon, "She was not of this world, she was far too ethereal for anyone to understand her true nature."[69]

Dagny was buried in Tiflis on her birthday, June 8, 1901. As complete as the symbolism was, so incomplete was her life.[70]

4 : THE ARTIST

It is really a curse that if you've once started to write, it is impossible to stop. First comes one theme and then another and so it continues. My books have not yet been published in Norwegian, otherwise I would have sent them to you a long time ago.
[Dagny to her friend, Margarete Ansorge, June 12, 1899]

I have no literary ambitions . . .
[Dagny to her publisher, Arnošt Procházka, May 23, 1899]

As myth, Dagny became superhuman, creator and creation at one and the same time. As a woman she wanted to be many things, but above all, perhaps, an artist. She studied the piano, she wrote, and she lived the life of the *bohême*. She dressed in slender black gowns with yellow sunflowers and long black boas. She wore her hair free and parted in the middle. She held court in the taverns, dancing, drinking, smoking, and talking with the men. Yet ultimately only the costumes and the company came easily to her. The power she wielded as a mythic presence was crossed by the powerlessness she experienced as a woman attempting to express herself through her music and her writing. Hers was still a nineteenth-century man's world, where myth was one thing, reality another. Her efforts to function as an artist in her own right reveal the tragic failure of the myth to translate into life.

Alfred Wysocki remembered visiting Dagny and Stach one night in Berlin.

I've always liked music, and after dinner I asked Dagny to play. She resisted for the longest time, but finally gave in. I noticed later that Przybyszewski was jealous of his wife's music, which clearly brought back uncomfortable memories to him.

. . . When later at my urging she began to play a piece by Chopin, she didn't get farther than a few bars when Stachu said something to her in Norwegian. She got up at once, sat down in the sofa next to me and explained that Stach himself would play Chopin.[1]

Wysocki's story of Dagny being silenced by Stach when she began to play *his* Chopin, might be the metaphor for her struggle to compete in a world where men considered art their territory, and women only hesitantly dared to challenge them. Stach's piano playing, for example, was a very public phenomenon and greatly praised. Munch's remembrance of him from the *Schwarze Ferkel* days was typical.

I still see him, as he sat there in the corner of the sofa of that little wine house in Berlin, slouched and with feverish eyes, talking hoarsely and slowly as if he was giving a monologue about himself. Then he could suddenly jump up in ecstasy, and run over to the piano so fast that he seemed to be following an inner voice calling to him. And in the deadly quiet following the first chord, Chopin's immortal music sounded through the narrow room and suddenly changed it to a radiant concert hall, to a concert hall of art.[2]

Even the people of Kongsvinger were treated to Stach's musical talents, though they seem to have responded to him with more reserve than his *Ferkel* friends. A short notice in the local newspaper in December 1895 read: "Przybyszewski's concert in the Gymnastic's Hall on Sunday attracted a relatively good house and the concert holder reaped well-deserved applause for his fine, quick and well-executed performance."[3]

Dagny's piano playing remained private. She played for her family and her friends. She gave piano lessons to earn money both in Berlin and when she came home to Rolighed. Once in 1894 she went—or at least was planning to go—on a local concert tour in the Kongsvinger environs with her sister Ragnhild and a friend. The only notice, however, was in Ragnhild's letter to her husband Helge, ". . . actually we're going out on a tour—Lubben and Dagny have asked me to do it for so long that I really can't say no, and naturally it will be fun and good to earn some money too. It will be a tour of 14 days at the most and we're leaving sometime next week."[4]

PLAYING CHOPIN

Dagny achieved greater success as a writer than as a musician, but she struggled equally in that role to "play Chopin." By the time she died, three of her plays had been published, *The Stronger* in her native Norwegian, *When the Sun Goes Down* and *Synden* (The sin) in Polish, and the last also in Czech; and her prose-poem cycle, *Sing mir das Lied vom Leben und vom Tode*, first in Polish and then in Norwegian. Her death in 1901 shocked the public and in Poland aroused the public's interest in her works.

In Norway people took note of her scandalous death but paid no further attention to her writing until the 1970s, when there was increasing interest in women authors of the past. Her cycle of lyric poems, *Digte* (Poems), was published in 1975, the short story, "Rediviva," in 1977, and a collection of three plays, *Synden og to andre skuespill* (The sin and two other plays), in 1978.

The first known mention of her as a writer was made by Bengt Lidforss in a letter to Strindberg, dated February 6, 1894. "Juel has now chosen her occupation, and seized the pen instead of the prick. She's writing short stories about love, whoring, murder and other depravities, and the saddest thing of all, Poland [Przybyszewski] says it's good. But deeper in animal baseness one can hardly sink and then the only resort is to retreat upward or die in the muck."[5] Lidforss confided that Dagny had promised to show him her manuscript. He wondered if Strindberg would like to see it.

Connecting Dagny to whoring was a tactic consistently used against her by the men she provoked. In retrospect it was the perfect strategy for limiting her power. She challenged these men on sacred battle ground, threatening the primacy of their closely guarded creative and sexual authority. Two of the men most captivated by Dagny and two of the most sorely wounded were Lidforss and Strindberg, who conducted what can best be described as a hate campaign against her in their personal correspondence of 1893–94. As Strindberg's friend, Adolf Paul, wrote: ". . . he hated her like sin, all the while he must have loved her."[6]

Dagny could only have added insult to injury when she decided to take up the pen herself. That there existed in the nineteenth century a near-literal connection in men's *and* women's minds between creativity and male potency has been convincingly demonstrated by, among others, Sandra Gilbert and Susan Gubar in *The Madwoman in the Attic* (1979). "Male sexuality . . . is not just analogically, but actually the essence of literary power. The poet's pen is in some sense (even more than figuratively) a penis."[7] Gilbert and Gubar contended that literary authority, like sexual authority, was considered so exclusively male, that any woman who attempted to achieve it was considered not only "intrusive" but "absolutely unredeemable: no virtue can outweigh the 'fault' of her presumption because she has grotesquely crossed boundaries dictated by Nature."[8] Bengt Lidforss proved their point as well as anyone possibly could with his insinuation that Dagny, like an animal, would be dying in the muck, all because she decided to try her hand at writing.

Lidforss was less incensed, though still exceedingly condescending of the fact that Dagny had also started writing her memoirs: ". . . she mustered up her courage and read the beginning to me." He conceded that her style was sincere. "It really seems to be written straight from the heart, simple and unaffected; the poor devil loves her Stachu absolutely incurably, it seems." Lidforss must have considered memoir writing a more appropriate literary activity for a woman than short stories about love, infidelity, and murder, apparently depraved subjects in his mind unless, we must suppose, in the hands of men. For what could he have thought his friend Strindberg wrote about? Unfortunately, Dagny's memoirs have not survived.

It is quite apparent from Lidforss's letter that he was agitated not only because Dagny had literary ambitions, but because she had literary connections as well. He referred to his translation of an article by Strindberg on immortality which he had submitted to the editor of *Freie Bühne*, Otto Julius Bierbaum. Lidforss attributed Bierbaum's lack of interest to Dagny's influence with him, though Lidforss's method was once again to ridicule her rather than to acknowledge her power. He suggested that she had not understood the meaning of the article.

Lidforss's letter indicates the prejudices Dagny faced and the ways they were made manifest. She was open, trusting, and anxious for a response.

He reacted with duplicity and ridicule, directed in this particular letter not only toward her but toward Stach, who encouraged her in her ambitions. Lidforss appealed, too, to the mutual fears of his colleague, Strindberg, solidifying the bonds of this brotherhood whose main aim was to assure each other that "Juel" was "no good."

On the other hand, at least at this time, Dagny seems to have had Stach's support. He was the spiritual force of the *Schwarze Ferkel* group and the man whose opinion must have mattered the most to her. He obviously encouraged her privately. He boasted of her writing publicly, to their friends, and on occasion to his parents. His backing of her writing also took a more active form. In December 1897, he wrote to Arnošt Procházka, editor of *Moderní Revue* in Prague, asking him to publish three of her plays. "I have a very big favor to ask you. My wife has written three little plays, fully perfected in their way. I speak not as a husband, but as an artist."[9] He negotiated with Procházka for publication of *The Sin*. It was also undoubtedly through his influence that Dagny's works were published in Poland, initially all of them in *Życie*.

Supportive though he may have been, however, Stach primarily thought of his wife as the force behind his own pen, not the wielder of her own. In the preface-dedication to the posthumously published collection, *When the Sun Goes Down*, he presumed to be passing on Dagny's legacy rather than she, as the author of her own works. "To my children, Zenon and Iwi, I pass on your mother's legacy," he wrote. He left no doubt that it was in reference to himself and *his* creativity that her significance lay.

> She grew up in wealth and luxury. For a dozen years she was given the opportunity to test herself on need and difficulty, because she shared her life with an artist, who had to fight to survive.
>
> A highly cultured woman with an unusual and artistic intuition, intimate with my unexpressed creative intentions, the one person who knew the entire depths of my creative power and who lured from my soul what was still unconscious to me. That was your mother.[10]

In Stach's eyes there was only one "Artist." Dagny's role, he made clear, was as his muse, not his equal.

Much earlier during their first year together, he had written to Adolf Paul about Dagny's unusual inspirational powers. If the pen is the supreme metaphor for male literary creativity and authority, his choice of metaphor for her genius is the pen's opposite, a force without form whose meaning is derived from its service to his creator "soul." "Much in my soul was written with invisible ink. It only needed heat to be visible."[11]

Dagny seemed to vacillate between knowing she could be, and knowing she was not, as creative as Stach and their artist friends. She was deeply ambivalent about writing. Though she wrote throughout her adult life, she did not seem to know whether to admit to having literary ambitions or not. The first mention she made of her writing, in the correspondence that has survived, was in a letter from Berlin to her sister Ragnhild, around the New Year, 1896–97. She said that her play, *The Stronger*, was going to be published in the Norwegian journal *Samtiden*. Her reaction was a mixture of excitement and surprise, for she had not submitted the play for publication herself. "Think, my little drama, 'the stronger' is appearing in the next issue of Samtiden. Do you get Samtiden? I suddenly got a letter from Aunt Birgit, who apparently has shown it to Gerhard Gran. It was a complete surprise to me, it wouldn't even have occurred to me to send it out."[12]

Dagny's surprise that her play should be taken at all seriously is curious, for she had submitted it to the Christiania Theater in January a year earlier.[13] She may, however, have submitted it more in the hope that it would bring money than artistic recognition. She and Stach were in Copenhagen and trying to get to Berlin. For lack of money she returned to Rolighed for several months. The theater's rejection of her play may have convinced her not to take it seriously herself. But then her very choice of a title is again curious. Surely she knew that Strindberg had written his one-act play of the same name in 1888–89. Was her own play meant as a challenge to him, at the same time as she could only think of it as her "little drama"?

She did not grow less ambivalent over the years, though she enjoyed some success. In 1898, *The Sin* was published in the Czech literary journal *Moderní Revue*, as well as in the journal's book series. The prose-poem cycle, *Sing mir das Lied vom Leben und vom Tode*, was published in *Życie* in 1899. In June of that year, Dagny wrote to Margarete Ansorge, saying that she wished she could send her her books and also that she was working on a new play. Writing seemed to preoccupy her. She called it a "curse." "First comes one theme, then another, and so it continues."[14] Yet just three weeks earlier she had written to her Czech publisher, Procházka: "First my heartfelt thanks for the nice remuneration for my dramas, which pleased me greatly—but even more for the friendly words which you once wrote about them in a letter to my husband. I have no literary ambitions, but I place high value on your judgment. And I know that you say only what you mean."[15]

Dagny was far more assertive as a cultural agent on others' behalf. She was, of course, one of the driving influences behind *Pan*, the exquisite, short-lived *art nouveau* journal that featured the works of the most progressive artists of the time, among others, Arnold Boecklin, Richard Dehmel, Arne Garborg, J. K. Huysmans, Thomas Kittelsen, Max Klinger, Maurice Mæterlinck, Friedrich Nietzsche, Novalis, Sigbjørn Obstfelder, Dante Gabriel Rosetti, Paul Verlaine, Gustav Vigeland, and James Whistler. Dagny translated Stach's novel, *Unterwegs/On the Way*, from German to Norwegian,[16] Obstfelder's short story, "Liv," from Norwegian to German for the fall issue of *Pan* (1895), and Karl Gustav Tavastjerna's novel, *I forbund med döden* (In league with death), from Swedish to Norwegian (1894). In connection with Tavastjerna's book, Ragnhild inadvertently captured a picture of Dagny working intensely in the service of others versus Stach working intensely for himself. She wrote to Helge from Rolighed: "Stachu is fantastic—is almost finished with a 300 page long novel and has many irons in the fire. . . . Dagny is also overcome with colossal diligence and is right now working on the last chapter of Tavastjerna's newest book, so I think things are beginning to brighten for them" (June 13, 1894).[17]

Dagny took a particular interest in the work of her friend Munch. During her last spring in Warsaw she was trying to arrange an exhibit for him for the coming fall and to negotiate the sale of his works. In her two last letters to him from this time there is almost no hint of the tragedy unfolding in her own life, only the following melancholy note:

> Things are going well for us at the moment in so far as Stachu is the world's most famous poet in Poland right now and beginning to earn a little money, in Germany his books are in their second printing, but actually we are rather sad people. Things were better in Louisenstrasse. As a matter of fact, if you came, we would drink schnaps and smoke cigarettes and have fun.[18]

In relationship to Stach, Dagny seemed not only to accept with enthusiasm but to indulge in her secondary roles as his editor, agent, translator, muse, and handmaiden. She was always fiercely loyal to him as an artist. Even during the last months in Warsaw when they were so estranged, she had publicly chided the newspaper journalist for criticizing Stach's ideas, curtsying to him on the street in mock appreciation of his attack on "Przybyszewskiism." Several weeks later, her life falling to pieces, she was trying to convince Stach to change publishers. He was in Lemberg preparing one of his plays for production and Jadwiga Kasprowicz was with him. Dagny was alone with her son in Warsaw. In a letter taken up completely with Stach's professional future, she wrote, at a time when her own future was as precarious as it had ever been:

> First: Send me *immediately* an original *manuscript*—you understand, manuscript, not printed—of "Stoly runo." Sacsjewski has influence, he knows the conditions and he is your honest friend! His wife is sweet, smart, pretty.
>
> Now, further: Fischer is an absolute, known swindler and Sacsjewski says that the prices he paid you are miserable. Gebethner and Wolf want—positively—to take you completely into their hands. . . .
>
> Please, Stasiu, do it right away and you will not regret it. . . .
>
> And then Stasiu come back to Warsaw soon! You are absolutely needed here!
>
> It is infinitely sad and gloomy here! And it is snowing and terribly cold! Sad, too sad! And why do you never write when you will return?[19]

Dagny had long gone to considerable lengths to help Stach get publishers. In the summer of 1894, for example, when they were both home in Norway, she tried to use her influence with Lars M. Swanström, head of the Christiania branch of Gyldendal Publishers. In an effort to convince him to publish a new book by Stach, she had shown him a private letter from the Norwegian writer, Arne Garborg. Garborg had written in praise of Stach's earlier novel, *On the Way*, which Dagny had translated. To her embarrassment, Swanström printed the letter in the newspaper, *Verdens Gang*. She immediately sent an apology to Garborg:

> It is partly my fault and partly a misunderstanding on Mr. Svanström's [sic] part. I gave him an indefinite "yes," when he asked my permis-

sion to do it. I did it mostly out of irritation, because Svanström would not accept a new book by my husband, because not a word is being written about this one, but right away the next morning I saw how tactless it was to misuse a private letter in that way and went down to S. to get the letter back. I got the letter but didn't see Svanström and I see from *Verdens Gang* today that I was too late anyway.

My husband is terribly upset and asks me to convey his apology to you.[20]

A year later, in the late summer of 1895, Dagny was prepared to jeopardize her own health and the health of her unborn child to bolster Stach's impoverished literary career and their impoverished circumstances. More than eight months pregnant and at home at Rolighed, she was planning to go to Copenhagen to search for a publisher. Ragnhild, who was also home at the time, wrote to her husband Helge: "Dagny and Stach are so desperate again they're completely crazy and it's terrible to watch. Aunt Henrikka *must* absolutely have her money back, and they don't see any solution at all, so Dagny has this mad plan to travel to Copenhagen to look for a publisher. But that is insanity for her now. . . ."[21] Dagny's sisters protected her by devising a complicated plan to lend her money while concealing the source.

Dagny may certainly have always had an ulterior, monetary motive in attempting to secure publishers for Stach, and she may also have gained a modicum of control over him as his professional advisor. But there was also something obsessive and self-destructive about her dedication to him. Ewa Kossak often portrayed her as a woman who built an altar to Stach and his art, painting a picture, for example, of masochistic devotion in the wake of Marta Foerder's suicide. Kossak pointed out that it was at this time that Stach wrote the long poem, "Am Meer" (By the sea): ". . . which later, during the time in Kraków, was dedicated to 'my wife' and illustrated with the fantastic portrait Wyspiański drew of Dagny. It is the tale of a white slave from the North, captured by the king of the South, who loves her so much that he becomes her slave."[22] Kossak did not know that Dagny, too, was writing poetry at this time, poetry that reveals a woman so alienated from her world and herself that she exists only in scattered bits of body and soul.

In a prose poem probably written sometime later, Dagny, in fact, told of a woman who loses her soul when she builds a spiritual altar to the man who had loved her.

Then she genuflected in memory of him, in memory of his great love. She built a temple to him in her heart, and all her dreams, her pain, her longing she let billow like frankincense around his portrait . . .

("Sing mir das Lied vom Leben und vom Tode")

So aware as a writer that such self-annihilating devotion was a danger, Dagny seemed nevertheless to court it in her relationship to Stach as a man and as an artist. Their good friend from Kraków, Boy-Żeleński, remembered that she was interested in every detail of Stach's career, every novel, every poem, every article he wrote. Since she did not read Polish well, she insisted that everything be translated for her.[23] Boy-Żeleński remembered, too, that when Stach was writing Dagny kept their house as silent as a church. When he finished, she let it fill up with laughter.[24] Stach accepted her devotion as his due.

Although Dagny enjoyed near mythic status among her contemporaries, historical and psychological factors mitigated against her assuming that she was an artist on equal footing with those she inspired and helped. She had no permanent home, little money, and little peace of mind. She was torn between her many roles as artist, wife, mother, daughter, sister, celebrity, and muse. Her marriage to Stach, fulfilling as it may have been at times, was marked by separations, scandals, and betrayals. As a writer she received little encouragement, succeeded in getting very few things published, was ridiculed, at least by some, for her literary presumptions, and ignored by most as a creative person in her own right. Stach, her greatest support, was a narcissist who could conceive of only one artist—himself.

Yet Dagny also had an unnamed demon that waged war from within. It was the part of her that rushed to submit to Stach's emotional tyranny, the part of her Ewa Kossak called her "somnambulent psyche,"[25] the part of her that preferred to drift in spooky silence, and the part of her we are unable to reconstruct.

If we compare Dagny to her youngest and favorite sister, Ragnhild, we must suspect that she lacked some inner conviction that would have allowed her to assert herself more aggressively as an artist. Ragnhild was nearly five years younger than Dagny. As early as her teens she had decided to become an opera singer, studying initially in Christiania with Erika Nissen, the Norwegian pianist of European fame. At the age of twenty she went to Paris to study, first for several months in the winter of 1891–92, then again the following October for a period of eight months.

Both Ragnhild and Dagny became secretly engaged in the spring of 1893. Ragnhild, only twenty-two years old, suffered deep conflict about giving up her singing career. Prior to her marriage in November 1893, she went on tour with Nissen down the west coast of Norway, and in Bergen she sang for Edvard Grieg. Her letters to her fiancé, Helge Bäckström, reveal both anger and anguish at the possibility of giving up her artistic aspirations.[26] She did finally choose marriage and motherhood, but she had shown a conscious determination to be an artist that Dagny had not.

When Munch painted the early portrait of Dagny and Ragnhild, *Two Music-Making Sisters,* he had Dagny sitting at the piano with her back solidly to the viewer, and Ragnhild standing at her side, face-forward and upright. Perhaps Munch understood something already then about that part of Dagny that simply turned away from life.

It was, of course, Dagny and not Ragnhild who remained the artist. But had Dagny had her sister's inner conviction, she might have become a greater writer, even in the face of the severe limitations her times and circumstances placed upon her. Dagny seems, in fact, to have used Ragnhild as the inspiration for one of her prose poems in which a woman painfully strives to create.[27]

> She stands at the piano and sings.
> He sits leisurely back and listens.
> She stands and sings, inward turned, drowning in this one single feeling that lifts her soul into the clouds, into the sun. Time and space fade into a dawning mist, past and present meet in a bluing crest.
> And the melody lifts its bleeding wings and flutters enrapt into space, searching, searching, and turning back with a sigh.
> And again it raises its wide wings, and light as sundust flies up to the stars and sits among them, itself a star.
> And now the melody lifts its broad wings and majestically sails out

Edvard Munch's To musiserende søstre, *probably 1892.*

over the wide, wide sea, over high hills and mountain crests, higher,
higher, reeling oblivious—ah, it's flying into the sun.

("Et la tristesse de tout cela, mon âme")

BLACK MIRRORS

Dagny wrote too little to have become a major writer of her time.[28] Yet
her plays and poems are at once links in the literary chain of the 1890s
and dark mirrors into the heart of this very intelligent, very conflicted,
and ever so silent woman. She wrote quintessentially *fin de siècle* works,
exotic literary flowers that seemed to grow from the darkness of the heart.
A spiritual sister of Baudelaire, Verlaine, Knut Hamsun, Sigbjørn Obstfelder, Ola Hansson, Strindberg, and Przybyszewski, she was haunted by
the moods of the soul and dreamed of conjuring forth its secret truths. She
was experimental, searching for the perfect form and the perfect language,
be it in the prose poem, in lyric poetry, or in the anti-naturalistic drama.
In order to convey the very essence of a mood, she pared her language
down to a minimum, heightened her imagery, and developed a supremely
sensitive, self-absorbed poetic persona. When she looked into the anxious
soul of that persona she saw longings for inner harmony transformed into
pathological obsessions with love, beauty, erotic power, fate, and death.

Dagny's writing is daring in its themes, its imagery, and its techniques.
Her heroines make bold, if often criminal choices, they cross sacred boundaries, and they accept the tragic consequences. Her landscapes are gothic,
full of dead spirits, rare flowers, cold dark tombs, and bloody rivers. Her
techniques are expressionistic, designed to project a dark, internal world
into the light.

Yet her bold style is made to serve far more fragile feelings, all of them
manifestations of anxiety. The myth of womanhood she inspired suggested
a world of unlimited promises and possibilities, changing definitions, and
new modes of behavior. As a writer she was preoccupied with the under-
belly of the myth. She wrote about the near madness suffered by a woman
trapped between one identity and another, one world and another, one life
time and another. The myth celebrated the integration of the intellectual,
the spiritual, and the sensual in one woman. Her works probe the schizo-

phrenia experienced by a woman who seeks to know and be herself in all her glory, human, demonic, and divine. The myth suggested that there were no limitations. Her works are like prisons from which she cannot escape. The myth promised freedom. The writer revealed a world in which she could barely breathe.

The striking, unsettling similarity between the woman of the myth and the woman of the works is that they are both utterly alone. They are back sides of each other, the one dancing self-possessed in the phosphorescent light, the other fleeing through dark landscapes in search of herself.

Dagny's poems and plays are like the black mirrors used by the artists of the nineteenth century to read the mystery of their own image. "The blackness, the longer one gazes into it, ceases to be black, but becomes a queer silver-blue, the threshold to secret visions. . . ."[29] They are, indeed, the legacy she left of who she was and what she saw. Hers was a frightening world.

5 : THE PLAYS

want to tell my life's strange story. Perhaps not everyone will find it so
strange. Perhaps the same thing has happened to others.—But I have
never heard of it, and therefore I think I am the only one who looks
this terribly tragic, mysterious fate in the eye." So begins the short story,
"Rediviva,"[1] Dagny's first known work, which she dated Berlin, December
1893.

The "strange story" tells of a man and a woman who at first meeting
know they must live out their lives together, despite the other woman to
whom the man belongs. They kill her, not with a dagger or a bullet, but
by willing her dead: ". . . we simply knew with smiling certainty that she
must and would die—she stood in our way—everyone had to understand
that—we did not need her—no one needed her, and so we let her waste
away and die." The ruthless lovers feel singled out by happiness, until one
day the dead woman returns to haunt her living rival. "And she never left
me after that—every night—every sleepless, fright-filled night she lay by
my bed." The dead woman becomes her destiny, while her lover remains
unknowing and thus unmoved by her tragic fate.

The events of this story, the coming together of the destined lovers, the
death (physical or psychological) of the socially legitimate lover at their
hands, and the haunting consequences, comprise the dramatic nucleus of
each of Dagny's plays, *The Stronger*, *Ravnegård* (Ravenwood), *The Sin*, and
When the Sun Goes Down.

Written in December 1893, "Rediviva" not only anticipated the plays, it foreshadowed the actual events of June 1896, when Stach's mistress, Marta Foerder, committed suicide. Stach had also told the tragedy in his play *Das grosse Glück/For Happiness*, written between 1894 and 1896, but *not* before Dagny had done it in 1893, just four months after they were married.[2] We might speculate that marrying Stach and replacing Marta, who had already born him two children, made Dagny deeply anxious, prompting her to write "Rediviva." We might also speculate that she wrote *Ravenwood* and *When the Sun Goes Down*, both of which contain the death/ murder of the first woman, partially in response to the suicide. During the summer of 1897, when Dagny was pregnant with Iwa at Rolighed, Stach said that they were both writing long into the light nights. It was that December that he wrote to Procházka that Dagny had completed three plays, probably *Ravenwood, When the Sun Goes Down*, and *The Sin*.[3] *The Stronger* had been written earlier, prior to January 1896.

It would be a mistake, however, to interpret Dagny's tragic formula literally. She did not write realistic plays about three people involved in a love triangle. She wrote mythic plays about the internal drama of one woman, a woman larger than life, who surrenders her innocence in favor of a darker, more demonic persona closer to the source of her power as a woman. Fundamental to the "action" of each of her plays is the slaying of the inhibiting inner angel. The model she used was herself and the myth she engendered. As a playwright she created a woman who challenged the traditional notions of feminine identity at the price of severe internal anxiety and external ostracism. She used the triangle to symbolize the painful, incomplete rite of passage of the passionate woman seeking self-knowledge and fulfillment. A friend of Dagny wrote to Ragnhild several years after Dagny's death: "I remember that Dagny once said to me: 'Everything that we experience of good and perhaps most of bad contributes to our development: and the intention must be that we shall reach completion.'"[4] Neither Dagny nor her characters ever did.

The publication history of the plays is itself indicative of her struggle for serious recognition.[5] *The Stronger* was accepted for publication in *Samtiden's* issue number 7 for 1896, the only play to appear in Norway in her lifetime. *The Sin* was the next to be published, accepted by Procházka to appear in Czech translation in *Moderní Revue* in issue number 9, 1898. There was also talk of performing it in Prague, but no production materialized, save for a reading of the Czech translation at the city's intimate theater, Intimní Volné Jeviŝte (The Free Intimate Theater).

In 1899 *The Sin* and *When the Sun Goes Down* were published in the Polish journal *Życie*, edited by Stach. He translated the plays and undoubtedly made the difference as to whether they were published or not. He always acted out of self-interest, however, and must have deemed the plays advantageous for *Życie*. Though estranged from Dagny at the time of her death, he availed himself of the notoriety, writing the preface-dedication to the small, posthumously published collection of her works, also called *When the Sun Goes Down*, and he translated *Ravenwood*, which appeared separately. Both the collection and the single play appeared in 1902. Stach owned the rights to the plays and permitted *Ravenwood* to be performed in Kraków that same year. When Polish writer and actress Gabriela Zapolska tried to initiate a second production in 1911, he refused to allow it, supposedly heeding the wishes of his second wife, Jadwiga, who was said to have been jealous of Dagny long after her death.

In 1899 Dagny had written to her friend, Margarete Ansorge, to explain that her books had not been published in Norwegian. She would have had to wait, in fact, until 1978, when the small publishing house, Solum Forlag A/S, published *Synden og to andre skuespill av Dagny Juell* (The sin and two other plays by Dagny Juell).[6] Ole Michael Selberg wrote the introduction, one of the very few serious treatments of her work up to that time. He traced the history of the plays, analyzed their literary origins, and interpreted them in the framework of the 1890s. Yet what Selberg gave with one hand he took back with the other. Intentionally or not, he ultimately traced everything about Dagny's literary endeavors, her inclination to write, her choice of material, and her philosophy of life back to Stach. He assumed that she wished "to express herself in the same medium as her husband," and that she derived her central dramatic thesis, the dual nature, restorative and destructive, of erotic love, from his thinking.[7]

Selberg was by no means wrong to establish a thematic and philosophical relationship between Dagny's writing and Stach's. Undeniably it exists. But her writing shares concerns not only with Stach but with many of the major writers of the 1890s. It is a very different thing to say that she wrote in concordance with the writers of her time than to say that she wrote like her husband.

THE REJECTION OF INNOCENCE

Dagny was a revolutionary playwright. Just how revolutionary she was can best be gauged by comparing her to other women writers of the 1890s.[8] By virtue of her choice to write plays and poetry, not prose, she had already aligned herself with the literary avant-garde, made up primarily of men. By virtue of her choice to write expressionist plays about erotically driven women she stood virtually alone.

Norwegian women playwrights of the *fin de siècle,* such as Hulda Garborg, Laura Kieler, Anna Munch, Alvilde Prydz, and Amalie Skram, tended to rely on conservative forms to convey an essentially feminist message. They wrote in the style of the realistic *tendens* genre of the previous decade, for they had a "problem to debate,"[9] women's precarious position in a male-dominated society. For them the roots of the problem lay in the disparity between women's and men's ideals, on the one hand, and women's inability to assert their ideals on the other. Women, they suggested, innately had the superior value system, men had the power. They fashioned heroines who attempted to assert the validity of their own ideals, independent of and as a challenge to male dominance. Structurally this usually meant separating the heroines from their lovers. The more progressive writers empowered their women consciously to make the love relationship secondary to self-fulfillment, going their own way in an attempt to realize themselves. Few of these women playwrights of the 1890s thought so clearly or felt so resolutely about this very complicated issue, however. Often they accomplished the separation only by means of the death of their heroine, after she had been abandoned by her unfaithful lover. But in either case they made their point that it was deadly for women to derive their identity from men. The radicalization of women writers throughout the last three decades of the nineteenth century can in one sense be measured by their increasing tendency to distance themselves from the romantic love cult which equated a woman's worth with a man's desire for her.[10]

In part to emphasize the necessity and the desirability of a self-determined female identity, these playwrights intensified the difference between female and male behavior in favor of the woman, idealizing her and exposing him. She was the original, innocent daughter, constant, loving, and altruistic; he the seducer, lying, manipulative, and egotistical. Even those few writers who attempted to portray women who were capable of "bad" behavior insisted that these same women were intrinsically innocent.[11] The myth of innocence, in other words, remained absolutely fundamental to their definition of a woman.

Not surprisingly, the issue of a woman's erotic identity engendered great ambivalence. Traditionally, female eroticism was a tabu subject, in as well as outside of literature, and these writers could only have been beginning to wrestle with it in the privacy of their own lives. Their plays show them clinging to a myth of innocence that would have been severely threatened by any assertion of female sexuality. In addition, in the public debate about women's independence from men, it may have behooved them tactically to de-emphasize sexuality, to ensure the woman moral superiority.

At the same time, in attempting to come to grips with a new identity for women, it was obviously becoming increasingly difficult to deny an essential, if long repressed aspect of their natures. Ambivalence runs like a red thread through these writings, often surfacing in split characters, the sexual side of the heroine displaced onto minor players or, indeed, onto the man from whom she was trying to free herself. Although these writers intimated that women were capable of sexual as well as spiritual love, they tended to confine the former to an assertion. The protagonist, for example, could be married, or have been married, or be living with a man, always an artist, in a "free" relationship. Symbolically, however, they kept their heroine a virgin and viewed her as man's potential victim.

Dagny, also profoundly concerned with the problem of identity, chose diametrically opposed means to grapple with it. She embraced once again the cult of love. But in one stroke of the pen she modernized it, internalizing it and replacing romantic love with passion. She literally put eroticism on the stage in the form of her mysterious, magnetic, brooding protagonists, driven by their instincts and the heat of their blood.

In effect, she reached backward in time to an old paradigm but used it to accomplish things quite revolutionary. She asserted female sexuality. She portrayed women who were equal to men. Rather than idealizing her women, she insisted on their right to be both good and bad. She wrote leading parts for women who defied sexual tabus, and who committed crimes. Ultimately she was the only Norwegian woman dramatist of her time definitively to abandon the myth of female innocence.

Paradoxically, she did it through the romantic love paradigm, from which most women writers were struggling to free themselves, albeit with the greatest ambivalence. Their difficulty is understandable, for the love paradigm, in its purest, platonic form, symbolized the very myth of innocence to which they still firmly held. The union of two soul mates, preordained by God, was contradictorily and simultaneously a sign of a woman's fulfillment and her innocence.[12] It was, if you will, a way of achieving adulthood without a fall from grace.

Dagny, in effect, used the paradigm to destroy the myth of innocence for which it traditionally stood. Her women are driven not by spiritual but by sexual love. They are indeed predestined, not by God, but by urges deep within. Fulfillment of the love relationship means the loss of their innocence, and though they must suffer, ultimately they neither repent nor regret the loss. Dagny accepted the psychological consequences of female autonomy.

THE SUFFERING FEMALE SOUL

If Dagny broke radically with the traditional notion of female identity, she found an equally radical new form in which to express herself. Unlike other Norwegian women writers of her time, she sought to expose the suffering soul, not the unjust social arena. In this she had more in common with the male dramatists of the decade, like Ibsen and Strindberg and certainly Przybyszewski, seeking to tap into the primitive regions of the psyche, to bring to life the inner drama ensuing from a rejection of internalized social and ethical norms in favor of the more vital if more sinister impulses imprisoned in the unconscious.

Both Ibsen and Strindberg saw passion at the root of the instinctual drive, but they then followed its diversions and perversions into substitute drives for power. Ibsen, for example, created the fascinating Rebekka West of *Rosmersholm*, who usurped her mistress's power and then led the faltering Rosmer to their shared suicide. Strindberg created Henriette of *Crimes and Crimes*, who wreaked havoc with her erotic power and was then banished from the "kingdom." For Dagny passion remained a naked drive and *the* central theme of her plays.

In Norway she stood closest perhaps to Gunnar Heiberg. A member of the *Schwarze Ferkel* circle, in 1894 he published his drama *Balkonen/*

The Balcony,[13] in which he asserted the inevitable right of erotic love to triumph.

Dagny also stood close to her husband, for whom sexual love was the surest, albeit most painful conduit to the unconscious. But whereas he elevated sex to a satanic religion, indulging in a wordy emotionalism, she distilled eroticism down to a single, powerful impulse flowing through her protagonists and the lines of her plays. Her intense, but spare style reflects the emotional concentration of her texts. Stach, excessive both in style and mood, as a translator sabotaged his wife's plays, which were structurally and emotionally refined to reveal an internal world of inevitable tragic action and inevitable pain.

Compared to the works of Heiberg, Ibsen, Strindberg, and Przybyszewski, Dagny's plays are radical distillations, both thematically and stylistically, of the internal conflict between ethics and instincts, ego and id, the battle taking place within one single character rather than among several. Ibsen, like Dagny, had, for example, long been interested in the angelic/demonic dichotomy in his women characters, but not until his last play, *Når vi døde vågner/When We Dead Awaken*,[14] did he really begin to strip it down to its symbolic, psychic content. Anticipating that play and the later plays of Strindberg, Dagny wrote truly expressionist plays. She achieved what Sigbjørn Obstfelder envisioned when he wrote about his play, *De røde dråber* (The red drops): "One might think that the dramatic conflict is that which takes place between [the protagonist] and [the characters who surround him]. This is not the case. What happens dramatically to [him] happens only in terms of himself. And that is what should be new and crazy or new and good, and for a good actor, the interesting task."[15] Whereas Obstfelder ultimately failed to translate his theory into real theater, Dagny did not.

To this end her sets are deep, amorphous spaces, and her characters, boldly drawn, haunt them like shades from a nightmare, all of them the various warring faces of the tormented dreamer. Save for *The Stronger*, they reject any realistic dimension, and even that play strains against it. *Ravenwood* invites us to read it as if it were a sinister fairy tale. The set resembles a dark cave or tomb, and there is early talk of princesses and trolls. *The Sin* and *When the Sun Goes Down* tell us to read them as if they were dreams, their protagonists lying down much of the time, dressed in white gowns, curled up like children trying to hide from themselves. And if the characters and sets are the stuff of nightmares and dreams, so, too, is the action, propelled forward by large visual images rather than sophisticated dialogue: exotic flowers thrown into the fire, a woman dressed like a white flame, black birds of death flying just beyond the reaches of the stage.

The cast of characters is virtually the same in every play. The strong, troubled protagonist is torn between her fatal, demonic lover, the voice of her repressed passion, and the agents of innocence, a husband, a sister/ wife, an old aunt, the internalized voices of traditional morality. Together they act out the same set of events time and again. In *The Stronger*, Siri abandons Knut, her husband, for Tor, her previous lover. She knows that leaving her husband will crush him. In *The Sin*, also about two men and one woman, Hadasa deceives her husband, Miriam, by sleeping with the seductive Leon, then takes the life of Miriam to spare him the pain of her betrayal. In *Ravenwood*, Gunhild and Thor, unable to remain apart, cause the death of Sigrid, her sister and his wife; and in the parallel play to "Rediviva," *When the Sun Goes Down*, Ivi struggles with the dead woman she and her lover, Fin, have destroyed.

Every play contains a ritualistic murder of the innocent part of the soul, preceded, accompanied, and followed by great internal suffering for the protagonist. Her suffering is ever-present, ever-felt on the stage. Yet the meaning of the murder, or the loss of innocence, is potentially ambiguous, like dream content containing the possibility of multiple interpretations.

Innocence may be interpreted as a spiritual and psychological good. Thus the protagonist, having slavishly submitted to her powerful, instinctive, libidinous drive, is doomed to destroy a fundamental part of herself. She is a lost soul. Passion is at once essential and evil, and great suffering will be visited on the one who gives herself up to it. Ewa Kossak, in her brief allusion to Dagny's writing, interpreted all her works within this fatalistic context. "The deepest love, Dagny reasoned, is that which leads to destruction and annihilation and there finds its fulfillment. It was this love that tempted her. She considered it to be the only feeling in the world worth experiencing."[16]

Ole Michael Selberg read the plays in much the same way, detecting at their heart Stach's Schopenhauer-influenced philosophy of amoral determinism. Driven to love whom we must, rendering moral categories inconsequential, we are nevertheless responsible for our "good" and "evil" actions. Doomed to live according to one law, we are doomed to be punished according to another. "For both [i.e., the Przybyszewskis] tragic situations arise in the intersection between the two naturally given necessities—the ethical law's merciless demands and the instincts' overwhelming compulsion."[17]

All of Dagny's plays can be interpreted in view of this principle of fatal convergence, in which submission to "the instincts' overwhelming compulsion" is paradoxically the way to discover and to destroy oneself. As a consequence of this interpretation, however, her protagonists must be viewed as slaves to their destructive passion. And, indeed, sounds of this deadly determinism are heard throughout the plays. In *The Stronger* Tor says to Siri: "Oh, how you long to feel my foot on your neck again." Fin reassures Ivi in *When the Sun Goes Down*: "She had to die. It was our happiness that she walked into the sea. Your good angel led her, Ivi. Now she is out of the play." And Gunhild in *Ravenwood* cries out at the very end: "No one is guilty but fate. Woe, woe to the day I was born into the world!" According to this interpretation, Dagny's revolutionary assertion that a woman has a powerful sexual identity is crossed by her counterrevolutionary assertion that it is by definition destructive and that she can fulfill it only through masochistic submission of herself.

THE JANUS HEAD

There are, however, compelling reasons to treat these plays like a Janus head, as with everything about Dagny; to turn them around and interpret them in a psychologically more subversive, more modern, and more positive way, restoring meaning to the killing ritual and independence to the protagonist. There are simply too many signs of defiance in these plays, from the submerged energy that gives them life to the many metaphors they contain of the struggle for freedom, to confine them to a nihilistic interpretation that itself stems from the *fin de siècle*.

Innocence may be interpreted as a spiritual and psychological evil. Rather than plays about the submission of the self, they may be understood as plays about the assertion of an essential part of the self. They may be read as ritualistic soul dramas about the killing of the "false" or the "good" ("innocent") self, reared and so valued by society, so that the "real" self, repressed by society, might survive. Long before Virginia Woolf called for it, Dagny herself wrote about "killing the angel in the house." She knew as well as Woolf, however, that angels do not die unavenged.

For Dagny passion was the metaphor for the source of a woman's identity and the seeds of her power. Passion was mysterious, even spiritual, yet unknown and so dangerous. Her heroines interpret it as their truest, but most perilous impulse. They heed it as if they were martyrs in the cause of their own fulfillment. Thus, in *The Stronger* Siri leaves her "good" but jealous husband for a man from her past who knows and accepts her dark side. He says to her: "[Your husband] believes you're good. That's his misfortune. It's too hard for you to be good. It tires you, it feels like an unbearable yoke to you. . . . I know your poor, evil soul, and I love it." And in *The Sin*, Hadasa, the beautiful woman in white, commits adultery, what her "good" husband calls the sin against the Holy Ghost (i.e., the sin for which there is no forgiveness in Catholic doctrine). She makes love to a man who seduces her with his dream and who understands hers, a dream of a black velvet abyss. It is as if the true selves of Dagny's women are kept alive in these dark dreams. It is where their fires burn, their flowers grow, and their stars shine. And they will cross society's sacred boundaries to tread into their even more sacred inner ground. Once there they will repeatedly kill the "good" self, the self molded by society's agent—the mothering aunt, the nurturing husband—to exist for the pleasure and well being of others.

The scenario is most complete in *Ravenwood*, whose cast of characters includes the dark, silent, inward-turned protagonist (the imprisoned self), the light, talkative, outward-turned sister (the socialized or "good" self), the lover to both, and the old, mothering aunt. Gunhild, the dark sister, is shunned by Aunt Åse, who thinks of her as "supernatural" and "sinister"; Sigrid, the light sister, is loved by the aunt as "the ray of sun that shined gold on everything and everyone." Gunhild lives like a prisoner in her own dark house, unable to speak save through the strange flowers she grows in her private greenhouse. But Sigrid recognizes who she is: ". . . whatever you touch doubles in value. You are like moonlight. You beautify everything." The aunt, however, denies her value and Gunhild takes her revenge, claiming Thor for herself, driving her "good" sister into death.

In *The Sin*, a counter piece to *Ravenwood*, the beautiful Hadasa is dressed in white silk, like the pure white fantasy in which her "good" Christian husband Miriam envelopes her. He demands that she relinquish herself entirely to him, attempting to convince her that herein lies her power. "Do you think a woman has power, real power, when she does not give everything?" Hadasa answers with words he does not understand, but which her dark lover implicitly did. "I once dreamed of a deep, black velvet abyss full of flowers shining like stars and moons . . . flowers on tall glowing stems. . . ." She would break out of her white prison. She would tap into her own dark source of power. He denies her that and she poisons him.

TENDING THEIR DARK INNER GARDENS

Twentieth-century psychologists, like the Swiss psychoanalyst Alice Miller, have formulated what writers have known and attempted to express for a long time, that children in our society, brought up to be "good," "have all developed the art of not experiencing feelings. . . ." "The true self cannot communicate," says Miller, "because it has remained unconscious, and therefore undeveloped, in its inner prison. The company of prison warders does not encourage lively development."[18]

But Gunhild has tended her "inner prison," her dark greenhouse full of exotic flowers. She says to Aunt Åse that they speak for her.

> Do you see the ones that look like fever blotches on a sick woman's face? And those that look like frost flowers on the window pane. . . . my soul's big speckled birds! They would love to fly to another world where space goes on forever . . . , but they sit so tightly on their stems, they're bound so tightly to the earth, and they're suffering. Can you see that all my flowers are sorrowful? I've nursed them all in my greenhouse. . . . Don't you think that's better than all those words?

And once again it is Sigrid, Gunhild's sister soul, who recognizes their value. "If you understand Gunhild's flowers," she says, "you understand her very heart and soul."

The pattern of the "killing" of the "real" self, the world of Gunhild's flowers, has been endlessly repeated, particularly for women, in life and literature for hundreds of years. Dagny reversed the pattern in her plays, "killing" again and again the "false" self, Virginia Woolf's "angel," Aunt Åse's "ray of sun." Her heroines are all in prison, be it manifested in bourgeois houses, gloomy mansions, white gowns, sickrooms, or silence. But they long to break free, and images of their longing abound. The door of Siri's house in *The Stronger* is always open to the sea. Gunhild speaks of her flowers straining to be free of their stems, and of liquid fire bursting through the crust of the earth and flooding the world. Hadasa, by virtue of the associations made by her lovers, changes from a woman dressed in white silk to a mermaid, a silver arrow, a star, and finally a white flame, as if she shot up from the sea, through the heavens, and was transformed.

But Dagny understood that she, or any woman, would pay dearly for daring to destroy what society has wrought. Aunt Åse brings down a curse on Gunhild.

> The last words you will hear from my old mouth that so often sang you to sleep when you were an innocent angel of God . . . I curse you! I curse you for all eternity! May your bewitched hell-flowers cloud your mind and soul with their poisonous breath, so that you will never more see the light and the sun! May you sink into the madness of depression.

The curse is all the more terrifying, since it, too, is spoken by one of the dreamer's own voices. She is internally rent asunder, her innocent persona dead, her passionate persona condemned by her punishing demon-conscience.

The curse is madness, and none of Dagny's protagonists escapes it. *When the Sun Goes Down*, the play that thematically brings the cycle of plays to a close, is, in fact, a portrayal of the visitation of the curse on the heroine, Ivi. The scene is a bedroom. Ivi, dressed in a white nightgown, is lying on her bed, desperately struggling with the memory of a murder. As in *Ravenwood*, the lovers, Ivi and Fin, have driven the other woman into the sea. "Your good angel led her," Fin tells Ivi. But she has grown fearful of Fin, the voice of her passion, who cannot feel her fear. He accuses her of not loving him enough, if she can be so afraid. She begs him to stay with her, trying all the while to reassure him that her love is still strong, but he leaves her so that she might sleep. She is left to lie there, "dying of anxiety," struggling with the ghost of the dead woman, who presses against her chest and breathes poisonous air into her face. She is left alone and torn apart, beleaguered by the warring internal voices of the angry, rival woman and the passionate lover. She has no safe, internal space in which to hide. Dagny appropriately portrays her as a helpless little girl afraid of the dark.

All of Dagny's women have committed the same crimes. They have dared to be women. They have rejected innocence, rejected being "good," rejected being children. At the same time, just as Ivi both embraces and shrinks from Fin, they love and hate, accept and deny the voices of their repressed passion. Their ambivalence is ever-present. Even as Gunhild commits herself to Thor, she sees him as a vampire. "Your thoughts always circle around me like bats around a lantern. Your blood lives only on the desire you feel trembling in mine." Just before Siri leaves with Tor, she says, "I'm afraid of you. You'll trample me." And after Hadasa has slept with Leon, she cries out, "I should love you! But I tell you: I don't know you! (Crying out) Nothing can have happened between you and me! (To him) I beg you, I beseech you: say it isn't true! Say it was a dream, a terrible nightmare." But by the end of the play she will reach for the poison and destroy the infantalizing Miriam, taking the consequences of her rebellious dream.

Dagny's protagonists are literally trapped halfway between an old identity and a new one, as she herself was. Unwilling to live with their innocence, their "false" self, they are as yet unable to live with their passion, which they interpret ambivalently as the most vital and the deadliest part of their souls. They are never, as is Gunhild's wish for her flowers, cut free, and they never truly flourish.

They are in-between creatures, afraid of what they have become, unable to be anything else. They feel in touch with their innermost core, yet they feel evil. They are filled with desire, but they lack exuberance for life. As mysterious as they make themselves, they exude emptiness as they move about the stage. Like Gunhild, they love silence, because they have too many voices at odds and none with which to speak.

They are powerful women in whom the helpless child lurks just beneath the surface of the skin. Tor says to Siri, "How I know this trembling around your mouth. Like a little child who's trying to hold back the tears. . . ." Hadasa, like Ivi, is a fragile girl afraid of the dark, who lies "curled up on the chaiselongue with her face hidden in the pillows." These are mutant women, spiritually beautiful and monstrous, powerless and helpless, terrified and thrilled by their dark inner gardens.

They have begun an inevitable journey back to themselves. Alice Miller has written:

. . . those who have spontaneous feelings can only be themselves. They have no other choice if they want to remain true to themselves. Rejection, ostracism, loss of love, and name calling will not fail to affect them; they will suffer as a result and will dread them, but once they have found their authentic self they will not want to lose it. And when they sense that something is being demanded of them to which their whole being says no, they cannot do it. They simply cannot. . . . They will not be willing to relinquish [their authentic self] again for any price in the world.[19]

6 : THE POETRY

What was she looking for? Where did she want to go in this terrible night? She did not know herself. She closed her eyes and let herself drift unresistant.
She did not know the way. She recognized none of these silent, dark witnesses of human sorrow and joy. She looked with dread into the lonely flames burning feverishly into the night, speaking of sickness—of love.
These secret flames behind high, dark walls, in the whispering green of the gardens, reminded her of something in her own life, of the fever that had driven her out into the night.
What did she want? What was waiting for her?
("In questa tomba oscura")

Dagny was as much a part of the avant-garde as a poet as she was as a playwright. She wrote both a cycle of lyric poetry and a cycle of prose poems in the tradition of the French symbolists, sharing their preoccupation with mood, mystery, music, enigmatic symbol, and the decadent spirit obsessed with death. Once again she had more in common with the men who were writing than the women, of whom so very few wrote poetry. She foreshadowed the great women poets of Scandinavia, such as Edith Södergran and Karin Boye, who would write their profound, painful verse twenty and thirty years later. In Norway she belonged to the ranks of the poets of the "Spiritual Breakthrough," including her old acquaintances from Christiania, Nils Collett Vogt and Thomas and Vilhelm Krag. She stood closest, however, to Sigbjørn Obstfelder, not only one of Norway's, but of Scandinavia's most progressive poets of the time, one of the few who can truly be called a symbolist in the tradition of Baudelaire, Mallarmé, and Verlaine.

Obstfelder had broken new ground in the poetic tradition of Scandinavia, experimenting with free verse, lyrical prose, and the application of music to the rhythms and structures of poetry.[1] Dagny was obviously taken with his writing. She translated his short story "Liv" (1894) into German for the third issue of *Pan*, and she was said to have recited his poetry at the *Schwarze Ferkel*. His sounds must have excited her. He too was a fine musician, a violinist, and he made his poems sing like soft, mourning melodies. But it must also have been Obstfelder's vision, so desperately fixed on his experiences of alienation, anxiety, and madness, that appealed to the poet in Dagny.

SING ME THE SONG OF LIFE AND DEATH
THE PROSE-POEM CYCLE

How he had loved her! His love had wrapped her in queen's robes and set a queen's invisible crown on her head, a crown everyone knew was there, to which everyone bowed. . . . She had been queen in love's kingdom. . . .

He was dead. . . . She felt at peace, relieved, almost happy. She stretched out her arms and breathed deeply, as if freed from a painful thought.

The flowers in his garden of love had grown too lushly around her, the fragrance had choked her breathing, the tendrils had wound themselves around her life, until she had felt bound, hand and foot.

("Sing mir das Lied vom Leben und vom Tode")

This mysterious flower . . .

Its fragrance filled her with a secret joy. She read her own longing in the flower's big, soft eye. She found something in it, something she had lost, a sound, a song in her soul. It sang a hymn she had forgotten.

("I tusmørket")

In her prose-poem cycle, *Sing mir das Lied vom Leben und vom Tode*, Dagny confronted the myth of the queen of love, poeticizing the nightmare of the recovery and loss of the poet's soul in the wake of her consuming attraction to the man who has adored her. The four poems tell of her inner struggle to find the seeds of herself. The critical tension lies in the vacillation between her desire for self-definition and her pathological need for definition in terms of another. Time and again she is overwhelmed by a sick longing for her lover, spelling her spiritual death. Yet occasionally, briefly, she turns to herself and experiences moments of inner harmony and creativity that fill up the emptiness within her.

The theme of the tragedy inherent in the myth of the love goddess was obviously a personal one for Dagny. She chose to write about it in the form of the prose poem, the genre favored by the poets of the *fin de siècle* for its freedom of form, which they hoped would allow them to express the intense moods and magical language of the unconscious. Baudelaire had written: "Who of us is there who has not, in ambitious moments, dreamt about the revelation of a poetic prose, musical without rhythm and rhyme, sufficiently supple and sufficiently flexible to subordinate itself to the lyrical rapids of the soul, the fluctuations of the dream, the spasmodic springs in consciousness."[2]

Dagny's poems are precisely similar to dreams or nightmares, abstracted from the constrictions of time and place. To emphasize the lack of specificity, she gave literary mottos to each in a different language: the first, "Sing mir das Lied vom Leben und vom Tode" (Sing me the song of life and death); the second, "Et la tristesse de tout cela, oh, mon âme" (And the sorrow of it all, oh, my soul); the third, "I tusmørket" (At dusk); the fourth, "In questa tomba oscura" (In this dark tomb). To achieve her form she relied on the structural patterns of music—a statement, repetition, and variation of the theme—rather than the traditional patterns of prose. Mood rather than story is the essence of the classical prose poem, as it is the essence of hers, anxiety relieved by fleeting calm, melancholy briefly interrupted by joy. The vision is narrow, the concentration on the self absolute, intensifying the obsessive, anxious mood of the poems.

The poems were first published in Polish translation in 1899 in *Życie*. A year later they appeared in Norwegian in *Samtiden*.[3] After Dagny's death the poems, along with *The Sin* and *When the Sun Goes Down*, were published in Poland (1902) in Stach's translations.

When Dagny wrote them is unknown, though they seem to have been inspired by the Berlin years and the reputation she then enjoyed as "queen in love's kingdom." She took the title of the cycle from the refrain of a poem by her friend, Richard Dehmel. Called "Das Trinklied" (The drinking song), the poem was published in the first issue of *Pan* (April–May 1895). She slightly altered Dehmel's refrain, "Singt mir das Lied vom Tode und vom Leben," most likely to emphasize the power of death over life. Dehmel's poem is a plea to celebrate life before it comes to an end, Dagny's a mournful cry that death is so ever-present.

It seems likely that she wrote the poems during the winter-spring of 1898, when she and Stach spent some weeks in Spain, having left the children at Rolighed. They had first gone to Paris, but found themselves with neither money nor prospects until the Polish philosopher, Wincent Lutosławski, invited them to his home in the little fishing village of Playa del Mera on the west coast. They stayed with him and his family from February to early March. Dagny wrote to a friend from Playa del Mera: "Silence reigns everywhere, which makes it easy to work. Stachu is more productive than ever. I have myself written some small pieces."[4]

There is a further, perhaps coincidental circumstance that links these poems to Dagny's time in Spain. Lutosławski recounted that he and Dagny had long discussions on the nature of love. She tried, he said, to convince him that centuries ago she had been destined for Stach. Lutosławski rejected the notion of predetermined love as nonsense. To convince Lutosławski of Dagny's sincerity, Stach told the following story. One day the two of them sat on a precipice in Filtvedt overlooking the Oslo Fjord. Stach suddenly asked Dagny to throw down a piece of family jewelry she always wore, as a sign of her eternal love, and without hesitation she threw it into the fjord. Lutosławski said he thought her a fool. When Dagny and Stach left Playa del Mera, Lutosławski gave her a copy of Dante's *Divine Comedy*.[5]

These poems appear, indeed, to be about an obsession with fatal love, but they are far more profound than that; and they were certainly not written by a fool. They are complex, lyrical reflections, riddled with contradiction, on the search for the "lost" self. Dagny sees her poet as destined to search for her soul in a fatal lover, ultimately driven "like a ship at full sail," unresisting and docile. She also sees the lover as destined to fail her. He will consume her, misinterpret her, trick her, but he will not reveal her

to herself. Although she clearly defines self-definition as life-giving, definition in terms of the other as life-threatening, she makes no overt authorial
appeal for resistance to the fatal course of the other. Her poet's sense of self
is too frail. Yet her appeal is there all the same in her persistent, if fragile
presence, in the very theme of psychic frailty, and in the beauty of the few,
fleeting images of self-definition, when her poet stops running toward the
darkness, looks into herself and sees the sun. The sum of these images is
the critical, contrary, underlying text of *Sing mir das Lied vom Leben und
vom Tode*.

The first poem, bearing the motto of the entire cycle, also contains the
themes that will be restated in variation in the other three. It opens with
a startling image, a woman sitting staring down at the corpse of her lover.
Her state of mind is equally startling, for she is "at peace, relieved, almost
happy." Though he had made her a queen in the kingdom of love, his
love had nearly killed her. His flowers had choked her, their tendrils had
bound her hands and feet. His passion, which she could not return, had
humiliated her. His jealousy had imprisoned her in ivy-covered walls. She
awakens as from a nightmare, and in a gesture of liberation, stretches
out her arms in well-being, dispelling the images of imprisonment and
suffocation.

Time passes and many men wish to know her, but she is enjoying the
pleasure of her own feelings unconfined and seeks a definition of her own
making, rejecting traditional, romantic, male definitions of female worth
and beauty.

> She wished for no eagle, whose proud wings could fly her to the
> clouds, nor for a nightingale to sing her beauty's praise. She would fill
> her life with the rainbow colored cobwebs of her own dreams.

But the longing to find resolve in the overpowering other is too strong,
and she begins to search in men's eyes, until one day a glance brings her
to her knees. The dead man has come back to claim her. His eyes fill her
with terror and she resists, but he is too powerful. He returns as a glance,
then a voice, then a heartbeat that invades the wind, the sea, and finally
her own body, clutching at her from within and without.

> How it throbbed, this great, inscrutable heart that had beat only for
> her! She heard it in the sea, in the ground under her feet, in the great

black mountains. And now she heard his sick heart full of love throb inside her own. And she felt him put his long arms around her and press her to this heart that could not die for it was so full of love.

The "rainbow colored cobwebs of her own dreams," perhaps too fragile from the start, are replaced by an internal altar to her dead lover. From queen to supplicant, she now offers up to him. "She built a temple to him in her heart, and all her dreams, her pain, her longing she let billow like frankincense around his image." Her heart is replaced by his heart. The ending is far worse than the beginning, for the imprisonment of her soul has led to the replacement of her soul, with not a trace left of her *self* and her beautiful cobwebs.

The prose-poem cycle as a whole repeats this same pendulum movement between rejection of the other, assertion of the self, and a helpless return to the other, each subsequent poem taking an image from the first and elaborating upon it, enlarging it like a photographer would a mysterious detail on a negative. The second poem, "Et la tristesse de tout cela, oh, mon âme," is the shortest, sparest, most powerful, and consequently the one around which the others must turn. From the first poem it takes the linear image of liberation—the woman stretching out her arms to the winds—and magnifies it into an attempt to fly into the sun. The woman is standing at a piano singing. A man sits back and listens. She is turned inward, immersed in her own creative effort to break through the clouds with her song. The effort is painful. "And the melody lifts its bleeding wings and flutters enrapt into space, searching, searching, and turning back with a sigh." But finally she succeeds and her song touches the sun. She stands there, feeling pale and naked, afraid that she has too honestly sung of her pain and her longings that go far beyond the man who sits listening to her. But he has noticed nothing of her spiritual flight. He comments unaware, "you have sung brilliantly, . . . you have never taken high b so well before."

This short poem in relation to the other three is the most complex and contains a strength they do not. Unlike the others that take place in stormy landscapes, lush flower gardens, and dark tombs, "Et la tristesse" is anchored in a simple reality, a room with a piano, a woman singing, a man listening. The woman is erect and active, striving to create, unlike any of the other variations of herself in the cycle. The image of her song flying into the sun with bleeding wings has no counterpart in power or importance,

Dagny allowing it to dominate the poem completely. At the same time, the woman's experience of pain and isolation, deriving from her creative attempt, is intensified by her sense of exposure. We in turn feel a sympathy for her which we never do for the women of the other three poems. "Et la tristesse" raises the question that quietly reverberates to the end of the cycle. Is it too painful for the woman to seek self-definition? Does it spell a death of another kind?

The third poem, "I tusmørket," momentarily sustains the theme of "Et la tristesse," though the poet has assumed a more passive mood. The woman sits with her mysterious flower that sings the lost song of her soul, the "hymn that she had forgotten." Dagny then reintroduces, however, the theme of the need for the fatal lover central to "Sing mir das Lied," developing the image of the suffocating flowers to tell once again her tale of spiritual death.

Sitting securely with the flower of her soul, the poet reminisces about the many flowers she had known before she found her own. As she describes them in turn she reveals a growing attachment to the macabre and the decadent. When she was young and innocent she had loved the flowers for their adorning colors, like jewels, "gold in her hair, red on her arms, blue and white . . . tulips, violets, lilacs." But they had not moved her soul. Then she had loved the roses, which were dearest to her when they were dying. "She enjoyed watching the leaves grow yellow at the edges. She filled both hands full and let them fall, one by one." Her love of death intensified, and she longed for secret flowers "that no sun had shone upon, dangerous flowers, carrying poison in their veins, numbing and incomprehensible." One day she found "a dark and fatal plant with furry leaves and melancholy bells of color taken from heaven and earth." Retreating from the sun and from the woman in "Et la tristesse," moving toward the woman in "Sing mir das Lied," she took the flower home and built an altar to it, as she had built an altar to the image of her dead lover. But the flower withered like all the others, and she threw it into the street, resolving to have no more flowers. As if in revenge for her rejection of them, they threaten her life, as had her lover's flowers in "Sing mir das Lied."

> . . . they grew up everywhere, they crowded around her, fluttered around in her parlor like birds of a thousand wings and a thousand colors. Radiant lilies licked her with burning human tongues, orchids,

chrysanthemums, cacti, oleander . . . brown, yellow, mysterious red, blue like the fairy tale's glowing grotto. The fragrance bewildered her . . . now she saw the whole flower flock stride toward her . . . they pushed at her, pressed against her, they breathed their awful breath into her face . . . she was choking . . . she was choking . . . oh!

But then, just as she had temporarily awakened in the first poem from the nightmare of the dead lover, she awakens again with her own flower, which is transformed into the symbol of her self, a star shining over the miracle of her birth, "the star over her soul."

The star disappears, however, and the nightmare returns in the fourth and last poem of the cycle, "In questa tomba oscura." Once again Dagny elaborates on an image from the first poem, this time the poisonous, internal altar at which her poet will meet her death. In every sense the poem is a retreat from the active, creative woman of "Et la tristesse." The space imagery is enclosed and womblike, the poet moving first into a large vault, then down a narrow corridor lined with the "living dead," then into a tomb, as if she were literally shrinking back into the darkness of the womb. There is no sun, no flower, no color, save for the blood red question burning in her soul. "Who is she?" She has no goal of her own, letting herself be driven "like a ship at full sail." "What was she looking for? She did not know herself. She closed her eyes and let herself drift unresistant."

She has no control over herself or her environment. The scenes change suddenly, without warning, from a dark, windy street to the vault to the corridor, and finally to the tomb, where she finds the dead man lying on a bier, copper-green light billowing around him like her longing had billowed around the altar in her heart. She looks into his face and knows that only he could have given her the answer she seeks. But his mouth is silent and his eyes are closed. Then he tricks her. He stands behind her "with big, living, burning eyes." Frightened yet so greedy to know who she is, she whispers to him, "The answer, the answer, give me the answer now!" But his face stiffens and his cold hands clutch hers, "as the storm once again sang its wild psalm of death around her and the black night covered her up forever."

The remarkable, if appalling aspect of the prose poems is the poet's diminished sense of self, which is Dagny's relentless, underlying theme. These are not really poems about love. They are poems about an inner image so frail that at its strongest it is only a song flying into the sun, the eye of a dying flower, or cobwebs of dreams. The poet's overwhelming experience of herself is either as empty or invaded. The dead lover is in essence a metaphor for the horror of all she is not. In the lyric poems the "lover" disappears, as Dagny's poet confronts the nightmare of the shattered self, but now without the romantic framework of the prose poems.

"MUSIC BEFORE EVERYTHING": THE CYCLE OF LYRIC POETRY

In a place sunlit and far away
My pale dead meet in festival
Their moon-sick faces giving birth
To a new and lasting peace for them and me.

Once we sailed together on the river
On the river where life's riddles burned
Together with me they were doomed to command the voyage
To the bottom where the river sailed to the sea.

Now in a land sunlit and far away
Bathed in sun I sit watch
And feel the power in my heart

To bewitch unto the pain of oblivion
In a festival dance around the old fire,
A world brought home from Lethe's shore.
("På et fjernt og solbeskinnet sted") (Unpublished)

Dagny wrote a cycle of thirteen lyric poems, which she called simply *Poems*. They were not made public until 1975, when Martin Nag published them in *Samtiden*.[6] A fourteenth poem, "In a place sunlit and far away," was given to me by Dagny's daughter, Iwa Dahlin.

The cycle bears the motto, "De la musique avant toute chose" (Music before everything), from Paul Verlaine's program poem "Art Poétique." Symbolist in spirit and intent, Dagny's poems sing of the pain and alienation that reverberate through the surreal landscapes of the poet's spirit. Her kinship to Obstfelder is particularly evident in the sensual rhythms and dark moods of these poems. She shared, as did he, the French poets' belief that music held the key to a more original, psychologically truer poetic language. She also shared their obsession with death, dreading its oblivion, longing for its secret wisdom and its peace. As a poet she expressed an unrelieved fear of living, like a child who feels she has committed some unforgivable sin. Punishment awaits her at every door.

> When the storm hurls itself around the house—at night—
> And the door opens wildly:
> I see fear standing in the doorway—
> Gray-haired—without mercy . . .
> And I do not own the sword that
> Can cut off its head!

> When the moon, sick with revenge, sneaks in
> The house—at night—and the door opens
> Wily and long:
> Then in the doorway I see a hand
> Stretched out—long—dead . . . and I dare
> Not, dare not shake it!

> When the sun shrieks in the sky
> —In the daytime—and spits its gold coins
> Into the living room:
> Then the door opens wide and I
> See that the doorway is like the jaws of a beast.

Dagny's unpublished poem, "In a place sunlit and far away," might be the epilogue to the thirteen poems of the lyric cycle. The poet, warm, calm, and powerful, looks down from a sunlit land beyond life, safe from the anxious landscapes of *Poems*, watching her fellow dead dance around "the old fire," as if it were a burnt offering to some greater god. Together they are bringing about "a new and lasting peace" in this fantasy of death and freedom from fear.

Dagny probably wrote the poem cycle in late 1896, early 1897, when she and Stach, without money and abandoned by their friends in the wake of Marta Foerder's suicide, were living in Nieder-Schönhausen on the outskirts of Berlin. Just before Christmas Dagny had written Ragnhild, congratulating her on the birth of her second child: "I think it's such a wonderful feeling to lie there with your baby beside you." Dagny must have been very pained, because she was separated from her own child, then only a little more than one year old, whom she had left at Rolighed with her mother and her sister Astrid. Perhaps in thanksgiving for her care she dedicated the poem cycle to Astrid. At New Year's she wrote to Ragnhild: "Oh God, how I long for Zenon! Astrid writes so many wonderful things about him. Still 3–4 months and then—and then—hurray!"[7] She almost seemed to be grieving for him. Stach wrote in February that she was composing "long hymns to our little son who is in Norway and just beginning to talk. . . ."[8] One of the poems of the cycle is dedicated "To Zenon."

> Sleep! Sleep!
> The angry voices grow silent.
> As if the day had spoken far too many words,
> .   .   .   .
> Soon the angry voices will rise, . . .
> Waking storms in your golden kingdoms:
> Then the storm will open your frightened eyes. . .
> Sleep long!

In her Christmas letter to Ragnhild, Dagny had written about the peace of Nieder-Schönhausen. "In the main there are only villas here, widely spread out, with surrounding gardens and wonderful avenues of chestnut and lime trees. I have never seen such trees. And so still, so still, so still."[9] Stach too wrote to family and friends that he and Dagny were living serenely, far from other people, playing cards and drinking toddies at night. Yet she could hardly have known much peace of mind. The scandal had cost them their friends. They had no money. Stach was drinking to excess. She was separated from her son. And she was pregnant for the second time. "So still, so still, so still," she had written, as if she wished to withdraw into some soundless scene.

Several of the poems call for a similar silence to descend on the poet's anxious world. She asks the star of her childhood to sink back into her heart and the child to sleep for a very long time. In one of the most moving poems of the cycle, the poet admonishes her listeners to be silent as she watches herself die.

> Be still! Be still!
> The stars are singing a mysterious song

About one who's walking for the last time
Through the rose garden . . .
    Be still!

    Be still! Be still!
Do you see the smoking, flickering candle?
Do you hear the snow falling in my heart
So hushed?
So hushed . . .

    Be still, oh, be still!
I hear a loved voice calling . . .
Do you see all the stars falling
Over my life?
    Be still . . .

The poems that speak of sleep and stillness are ominous resting places
in this cycle that mourns the anxiety of life's journey. Time passes relent-
lessly, ever-present like a snake slithering along the horizon, destructive as
fire touching butterfly wings.

The wind chases dust gray butterflies
Across the sky's deep golden ground.
I see them flocking round the sun's red sphere.

I see them burn up the very second
Their thin wings are illumined,
Then charred, they're spread over the heav'ns murky floor.

Now only a copper-green, poison fly
Clings to the sun's giant rose
Fading slowly over the horizon's arc.

And the evening wind cries at my ears.
When the sun sank, the shadows grew so long . . .
What is hammering in the quiet of the night?
What makes my heart so afraid?

The poet sees life taken from her even as it is given. Yet even more
alienating than the brevity of her time is the fact that she is the only witness to her having ever been. She is completely alone. There has never

been a lover to consume her. Nothing marks her passing but her own self-consciousness. She sees herself as a by-product of forces unaware. She exists no longer than a lyrical image, living and dying, her golden hair graying, in two short lines of a poem.

> Hot winds sweep through the valley of the night,
> A thousand wild eyes quickly tremble,
> The sleeping earth moans anxiously in its dreams.
> Feels the kiss on its will-less mouth.
>
> All the golden leaves in a whirl!
> The last dance . . .
> My golden hair: a wreath of fire!
> And soon so pale . . .
>
> The earth opens its wide womb
> And seething floods flow forth:
> Glowing flowers
> Grand as rainbows,
> Blood and fire!
> With terror's might
> Raise their arms toward the shining stars.
>
> Gentle winds sweep through the valley of the night,
> A thousand golden stars quickly tremble,
> The sleeping earth smiles calmly in its dreams,
> Feels the kiss on its closed mouth.

The poet captures her conscious self only in the single use of one personal pronoun and a fleeting reference to her golden head of hair. The nature that conceives her, gives her life, and envelopes her again is oblivious to her. Yet at the same time, she is the issue of the earth's surreal orgasm/birth, just as she is the earth's sister spirit, her flaming hair a parallel to the earth's floods and flowers, blood and fire. By virtue of association she shares the earth's surge of power, ecstacy, and rage at being quickened to life, then passed over by the forever blowing winds. But her identification with the earth remains by virtue of association only. The two are never united. She is a golden head of dying hair. The earth remains a dark, magnificent body. The one never knows the other. Dagny seems to raise her own arms up in fury toward the sky, protesting a world in which she has never been allowed to be.

Her poet is trapped in humanless landscapes where she is condemned to go looking for herself. When she catches a glimpse of who she is or might have been, she speaks in intrinsically female metaphors of natal fluids and blood. In the poem "Two strong, pale hands," she sees herself schizophrenically divided, the one self on a mountain top lighting a signal fire, the other "the bloody memory" of who she is, powerfully swimming toward the fire she has lit. There is madness in the memory but she welcomes it, as it holds her tight in its magnificent, gentle hands, and her heart breaks.

In "The river flows dull and dead," one of the few poems in which the poet commands her landscape, she presides over it like some giant priestess in the throes of menstrual pain. She straddles a river "full of dirty, clotted blood," on which sails a boat with a flame red sail. A bat, a "friendly spirit," hovers over the mast. Dressing herself in the bat's colors, she puts on the "gray hood" of night and makes her way through the dammed-up valley. She empties fresh blood from her chalice into the river and it begins to flow free.

The release of the flood of her power triggers a series of fantasies of who she is. She nods in collusion to the bat, her "gray sister," who makes her think of her nightmare, the "child of her pain." Its claw seems to touch her, and she thinks of its black wings that ensnare her dreams as if they were flocks of birds. She imparts to this sinister, sisterly creature her fantasies, her dreams, her spiritual and intellectual self. Yet she remains forever separated from her. The poem ends in a mad, schizophrenic image, the gray sister staring into her mind, which is nothing more than an empty cavity, as they both stare into the sun that pours "its golden flood/Over the river's blood." Looking into the sun can only mean death for this female priestess forever separated from herself in life.

The poems of the cycle are all existential nightmares about the divided self. There is no lost lover, no soul mate for whom the woman searches. She is searching only for other parts of herself, strewn across these soul-landscapes like limbs lost in battle. She sees her twin self as a bloody memory swimming toward shore, a beast at the door, a sisterly bat full of dark dreams, a head of burning hair. Her past is separated from her present, her fear from her will, her creative dreams from her consciousness, her head from her womb. She is imprisoned with her own acute self-consciousness, watching herself die, sometimes quietly, as the snow falls in her heart, sometimes violently as the butterflies burn up in the sun.

Yet in the very quiescence of her poet Dagny also found an image of great strength. She may have lived forever fearful of extinction, but she *remained* in her poems to face her fears. It is the image of the woman— staring into the sun, standing at the open door, bearing witness to her own death—that we see even after the other images have begun to fade.

All of Dagny's works are marked by the schizophrenia so apparent in *Poems*. In the plays her heroine is torn asunder by her many voices. In the prose poems she loses herself in her projection of "the other." In the final analysis, it is this nightmare of the shattered inner image that is the quintessence of her works. If her poems and plays are the black mirrors in which she saw herself reflected, they reveal an alienated woman living in a world of fatal extremes, all of which finally came to stand for only one thing. Rebellion or passivity, passion or innocence, darkness or sunlight, snow or fire, all became metaphors of death in her hands.

Yet she faced her demons with such courage, embraced her passion with such intensity, her passivity with such longing, her fear with such wide eyes that she imbued her works with a spiritual longing for life. They lay bare the soul of a very conflicted, noble woman, who looked into herself and could not lie about what she saw. Stach's dedication in the posthumously published *When the Sun Goes Down* captured for once the most significant link between her art and herself: "Her soul was far too honest, far too daring, far too proud, and that was her tragedy. She could not bear that a shadow of falseness or hypocrisy should fall upon her. It was her tragedy that she was what her art is: Beauty and Honesty."[10]

It is a bitter, yet fitting irony that Dagny should have inspired a myth of integration and infinite mobility when she wrote of a self divided and deadly limited. Clearly she was at the heart of both, though one momentarily loses sight of the swirling solo dancer in the overwhelming darkness of her poetry.

7 : THE JUELLS

This star saw my childhood:
It shined pale over the hillside's broad forehead
Lay down like pale hands
Over the phosphor white waters of the deep.
·　　·　　·　　·　　·　　·　　·
Oh, star! Sink back into my soul!
Oh, star! Melt inside me!
("I sjælens store, dunkle sale")

Dagny was a creative, intelligent woman. Yet she compartmentalized her conflicting voices so completely that she could hardly have known who she was. As a writer she revealed that she understood her pathological, inner fragmentation. As a woman she seemed helpless to do anything about it.

How did she come to be so? What in the workings of her family might have contributed to the fact that she was at once so well and so ill equipped for life?

Dagny's poetic vision of herself as a soul rent asunder in an unknowing world clashed absolutely with the image her family projected of stability and concern. From the outside, everything about the Juells spoke of well-being. Dagny's mother, Minda Blehr, and her father, Hans Lemmich Juell, were from families with long traditions. They married and bought Rolig-

Dagny and her sisters at Kongsvinger Fortress, summer 1893.

hed, where they raised four talented, independent, and beautiful daughters. Hans was a prominent physician and a highly respected public servant. Minda thrived in her role as mother. Their daughters, Gudrun, Dagny, Astrid, and Ragnhild, were devoted to them and to each other.

Like Dagny, the Juells were very private people. They left little record of themselves, only a small number of letters and memories passed down by their grandchildren. Too few historical fragments exist to reconstruct their family dynamic in any psychological depth. But on the basis of the fragments that do exist—in particular, Dagny's limited number of letters, Ragnhild Juell Bäckström's correspondence, and letters written by members of the Juell family to Randi and Otto Blehr—it is possible to construct rough images of the five people Dagny lived with and loved the longest. Most of their letters derive from the time subsequent to Dagny's twenty-first year, which she spent with the Blehrs, but assuming that personalities and familial interactions remained relatively constant, a profile of considerable clarity emerges of the Juell family.

Life was not as harmonious as outward appearances would suggest. Yet just as Dagny's tragic, poetic persona was a real, if partial truth, so too was the Juell idyll. The single most striking fact about this family was that no one, not even Dagny, really wanted to leave it. She did not set out on her own until she was twenty-five-and-a-half years old. She then spent three of the first five years of her marriage back home at Rolighed. Her sister Ragnhild often came home after her marriage. Astrid never married and never left. Gudrun came back the least, but she often gathered members of her family around her in Lund and returned to Rolighed, as did they all, when there was a celebration or a crisis. Finally it was Gudrun who assumed responsibility for Dagny's children, Zenon and Iwa.

It may have been that the strength of the Juell family was ironically its weakness, especially in Dagny's case. While she was the woman who inspired the myth of Ducha, The Lady, Europa, and Aspasia, she was also both childlike and childish, leaving herself dependent on the generosity and goodwill of others, whether for money, love, or the care of her children. For a woman who cut such a new and independent profile, she was at the same time very much a child. The origins of Dagny's conflicted personality are certainly in great measure to be found in this family to which she remained so attached.

In her prose poem, "In questa tomba oscura," Dagny placed her protagonist at the entrance to a narrow corridor lined with portraits:

> She stood before a corridor full of such bright light that at first it blinded and confused her. And when she again opened her eyes she saw that both walls of the corridor were mounted with high, dark portraits of people, men and women, and all turned their threatening, contemptuous and sorrowful eyes toward her, and in all of these grave-sick faces she read a terrible welcome. She saw them nod their pale faces reservedly, and in these many inscrutable eyes she read: come, come nearer! You are not here yet. We only bring a greeting from the end that beckons you.

Inspired by her own structural metaphor, we might walk down a corridor of Juell family portraits. The faces would be more benevolent than those she conjured up in her poem about death, for her parents and sisters were loving and concerned people. But they necessarily gave birth to some of the internalized angels and demons Dagny struggled with so uncertainly.

Dagny herself must temporarily recede from clear view, as the primary focus rests on the members of her family. Once again, she must be seen and understood through others. Frustrating as this may be, it remains one of the abiding truths of her life. To impose a neater, more traditional story on this narrative of her life would simply be wrong. Instead the reader must fill the void and imagine Dagny at the center of her complex family.

HANS LEMMICH JUELL

Hans Lemmich Juell was the person around whom the Juell family turned. Born in the city of Hamar on October 23, 1839, he belonged to one of the oldest aristocratic families of the district of Hedmark. He studied medicine in Christiania and in 1863 moved to Kongsvinger, where within a short time he began his own practice[1] and married the young Minda Blehr. They had their first daughter, Gudrun, in 1866, their second, Dagny, in 1867.

Hans was literally a friend of both poor men and kings. His medical practice was large, reaching to Hamar and far into Sweden. He was on the road for much of the time in the care of the sick and the dying. He battled the scarlet fever epidemic in the 1870s and was instrumental in ridding Kongsvinger of cholera in the early 1890s. In 1888 he was appointed district physician. And he personally attended the king.

He was a political leader in the community, a longstanding and active member of the conservative party and its local spokesman from 1889 to 1897.

He was also his family's beloved patriarch, revered by his wife and daughters and looked up to by his relatives. Though Minda had four sisters, all of whom married, and four brothers, one of whom became prime minister, Hans assumed major responsibility for certain of the Blehr relatives, extending great emotional and economic support throughout the years. When he died in January 1899, at the age of fifty-nine, his family felt ravaged. Before they left Rolighed for good in the fall of 1901, they marked his grave with a tombstone that read:

Here lies the Friend of the People
The Man of Love
HANS LEMMICH JUELL

Hans Lemmich Juell.

Like Dagny, the man behind this exceptional social mask was both more and less than he seemed. Father and daughter were of the same clay. Physically they resembled each other, high foreheads, fine cheek bones, strong noses, lids hanging heavy over the eyes. Psychologically they were equally akin, complex and private people, in spite of their high social profiles.

Hans, like Dagny, was an aristocrat of the spirit who held hypocrisy in contempt. His letters reveal him to be a man of rare honesty. When he felt that his brother-in-law, Otto Blehr, had made the wrong personal decision in accepting the position of Norwegian prime minister to the king of Sweden-Norway, he wrote to him: ". . . I bitterly apologize that my wishes for your contentment and happiness are not as warm as I sincerely wanted them to be. Forgive me, dear brother-in-law, these words, but I cannot be a hypocrite, least of all with someone I care about" (March 6, 1891).[2]

In the fall of 1895 his honesty conspired with his paternal concern to bring him into a confrontation with the *enfant terrible* of the Norwegian art world. Munch had painted Ragnhild's portrait in Berlin in early 1894 and included it in his controversial exhibition in Christiania in 1895. Hans objected to the way Munch had rendered Ragnhild's face. He was not specific, but he was undoubtedly disturbed by the provocative look Munch had given her and the hints of witchery he had painted into her eyes, her mouth, and the shoulders of her dress. His hurt unconcealed, Hans politely asked Munch to take the portrait down.

> Forgive me that I, a perfect stranger to you, express my opinion about your works: please forgive me too that I ask you, in the name of the friendship I know exists between you and a pair of my daughters and their husbands, forgive me that I ask you to do us the great favor of removing our daughter, Ragnhild's, portrait from the exhibition! I know that both you yourself and several others with you interpret this picture differently than I do. For me it was directly painful to see my daughter's face rendered in that way; so much I ought to say when I ask such a favor of a man who in no way owes me anything. [October 10, 1895][3]

Hans objected not only to his daughter's portrait, but to Munch's lack of judgment in exhibiting a series of the "Madonna" motif which he had entitled "A Woman Making Love." The city of Christiania was not prepared to understand such a thing, Hans suggested. He understood it, but

Edvard Munch's Fru Ragnhild Bäckström, *1894.*

he was not prepared to tolerate it in public. "Several of the pictures belong in an exhibition for artists, and only if you found yourself in entirely different circumstances than those in Christiania, where they naturally call for the police, closing [the exhibition], confiscation etc. Or was perhaps something else meant entirely with these pictures of women surrounded by 'foetuses?!' "[4]

Munch immediately took the portrait down. In his diary notes he remembered meeting Ibsen at Grand Hotel shortly thereafter. "He asked about a female portrait I had just taken down from the exhibition—I told him that her remarkable Herr father had so . . . asked me to remove it that I had done so—thought this had interested him."[5]

Hans's letter is a moving revelation of his integrity as a man and a father. But it also suggests his complex outlook on life, progressive yet countered by an innate conservatism. His conflicting inclinations must certainly have affected the way he raised his daughters and the way they came to look upon themselves.

Dagny's father was an uncomfortable "pillar of the community." Professionally, he met with both career frustrations and financial difficulties, in spite of his public reputation to the contrary. In the fall of 1892, at the same time Dagny and Ragnhild were making plans to study abroad, Hans expressed an urgent desire to leave Kongsvinger and begin anew. He left his reasons curiously vague. "I would happily abandon the old nest because of so many things, but damned if I can reveal all my reasons to you," he wrote to Otto Blehr on December 10, 1892. He applied for the position of district physician in Aker, the large, working class district of Christiania. His competitors were men with more university credentials than he had, and he did not suffer them lightly. He prefaced another of his letters to his brother-in-law with: "It's not a question of finding the bacillus in the shit, but of getting rid of the shit! This can't happen with the microscope" (October 3, 1892).[6] Dagny obviously came honestly by her contempt for the academic.

It is curious that Hans should have wanted the Aker position in the first place. It paid little, which he said did not concern him, and the work was hard, given the plethora of health problems in such a poor and large district. In truth, just like his daughter, Dagny, he seemed to be looking for something to which he might commit himself in life. For whatever reason, he did not receive the appointment and continued to work with his district constituency.[7]

As the district doctor he had land and prestige, but he was actually money poor. Stach wrote of his father-in-law in the summer of 1897 when he and Dagny, pregnant for the second time, were living at Rolighed:

> This is a very strange country. No one knows here how to accumu-
> late riches, yet everyone has a life style as would a landowner of three
> villages in our country, paper money they don't have, but they have a
> wonderful life instead.
>
> I doubt if my father-in-law could put his hands on 1,000 kroner, but
> he has three servants in the house and a nanny for Zenon. [May 30,
> 1897][8]

Stach's assessment was accurate. Hans had to borrow money from both his sons-in-law, Helge Bäckström and Wilhelm Westrup, when he took sick a year later. A very proud man, he tried to put the best face on what for him must have been a very humiliating situation. Ragnhild wrote to Helge just weeks before her father died: "When he and Astrid spoke a while ago about the fact that it was too bad for you and Wilhelm having to help him with money, Papa said: 'But then they have gotten two wonderful wives from me—they have gotten the best they have from me'" (undated, but must have been written sometime in December 1898).[9] When Hans died in 1899, he left his wife nothing but Rolighed, which she was forced to put up for sale the year Dagny was killed.[10]

But as far as Hans himself was concerned, "the best" *he* had had was also his daughters. When he first wrote to Stach in 1894, inviting him to Rolighed, he wrote about the loneliness of the house with everyone gone. "Come when you want, the days are so quiet and empty here that my wife becomes quite melancholy, for me it is no problem, I travel so much and have so much work to console myself with, so time passes for me."[11]

As stoic as he may have been, Hans sounded such a sad note in his letter to Stach that one understands how deeply he too missed his daughters. If there is one thing to which all the fragments of his history bear witness, it is his grand love for his four girls. Though instinctively conservative, he raised them with a liberal hand. He made it possible for them to continue their education as long as they wanted and to choose careers in the art world. He sent them on trips to Europe, Dagny as early as the age of fifteen, when she went to Germany after her confirmation.

He treated his daughters as intellectual equals. Gudrun would often tell how shocked she was when she went to live in Lund, where society dictated that the women retired to the parlor after dinner, while the men enjoyed cognac, conversation, and cigars. She and her sisters had never been excluded from male company, and their young men friends had regularly been made welcome at Rolighed. Ragnhild wrote to Helge Bäckström, to whom she was secretly engaged, in the summer of 1893: "We have, you see, constantly had young men visiting, so it will not be strange at all [if you come]" (July 4, 1893).[12]

Hans's love for his daughters remained fiercely protective, even as they moved away. When he wrote to Munch about removing Ragnhild's portrait, she was twenty-four and had been married two years. His third daughter, Astrid, became seriously ill in 1894 at the age of twenty-five. She gradually recovered, but Hans seemed reluctant to leave her side. In a letter to Ragnhild, he wrote that he was spending all the time he could with Astrid. "Astrid and I spend the days together as much as we can. We take walks and we write together, [I] will have to leave [soon]—then our time is gone" (October 27, 1894).[13] Family lore has it that Hans told Astrid she was too frail to marry. She never did, though she had any number of opportunities and the encouragement of her sisters.

Dagny returned to Rolighed both times she was expecting a child. Ragnhild recounted a touching moment from August 1897, when Dagny was eight months pregnant with Iwa. The two sisters had driven out into the country to meet their father, who was returning home from one of his trips: ". . . and down there the three of us pitched camp and ate apple cake and drank orange juice with whiskey and water that tasted incredibly good. Papa was, as always when he has us along when he's out, charmingly sweet" (postmarked August 15, 1897). His affection for his daughters made him a vulnerable man. At Christmas time, 1896, he wrote to thank Ragnhild for an elegant knife she had sent him. "I'll never lose it, every time I use it it will remind me of my own sweetheart, Tulla!" (December 30, 1896).[14]

Yet Hans's protectiveness caused conflicts, perhaps in particular with Dagny. Two months after Zenon's birth in 1895, Otto and Randi Blehr had invited Dagny and Stach to their ministerial home in Stockholm. Fearing for Dagny's health while knowing how anxious she would be to accept the

Blehrs, Hans wrote to them: "Thank you for your continual kindness, but you *must* promise me not to repeat this invitation, when she absolutely cannot make this trip before this winter and ought not to be tempted further" (December 4, 1895). Dagny had, however, no intention of heeding her father's advice. Already in November she had written to her aunt: "We're going to Paris around the 1st of December and not coming back again for many years" (November 8, 1895).[15] Leaving Zenon with her parents, she and Stach did indeed go to Stockholm on December 15 to stay with Ragnhild and Helge Bäckström.

Dagny did not spend her time there convalescing. Ewa Kossak revealed that Dagny and Stach visited Ellen Key's literary salon, saw Eleonora Duse, and met up with their friend Max Daudenthey, from Berlin. Daudenthey told of mezmerizing parties that lasted until dawn. "In the mornings my heart felt heavy and tired, but in the evenings I longed once again to throw myself into the witches' sabbath."[16] Dagny, Stach, and Daudenthey went on to Copenhagen sometime in January. Daudenthey continued on to Paris, but Dagny and Stach were forced to remain in Copenhagen for lack of money. It was at this time that Dagny submitted *The Stronger* to the Christiania Theater, in all likelihood to see if she could finance their trip to Paris. The play was rejected, and late in February Dagny returned alone to her parents and her son. Stach went back to Berlin.

Dagny and her father undoubtedly disagreed on many issues over the years. She definitely had had a different opinion of the Munch exhibit of 1895 in which Ragnhild's portrait had briefly hung. In a letter to Randi Blehr, she wrote: "Yes, the uproar over Munch's exhibition was fantastically amusing. That's what's entertaining here in Norway, that every single person has the only, only important thing to say about art. They should really consider that Europe is always so endlessly far ahead. For that matter, they're probably better off as they are" (November 1895).

Yet Dagny—Europa—kept returning home. One of the last times she and her sisters came together at Rolighed was the summer of 1898, when their father was sick with a cancerous growth on his eye. They were all there, their husbands coming and going, they themselves traveling back and forth between Rolighed and Christiania, where Hans was first operated on and then lay recovering for several weeks.[17] Ragnhild's letters tell of the shifting moods of the sisters as their father grew worse, was operated on, and then appeared to recover. There was something movingly symbolic about the gathering of the daughters around this fallen and so beloved father.

It is striking that Dagny married someone who was her father's opposite in almost every way. If Hans was the personification of the ultimate father, Stach was the personification of the son, forever rebellious, irresponsible, irreverent, and irresistible. In contrast to Hans, Stach held both truth and tradition in contempt. Hans was conservative, Stach anarchistic. Hans protected Dagny, Stach exposed her to danger.

Had Dagny been too protected actually to know that she was in danger? Or did she court danger, seeking to deny—through Stach and the many men she gathered around her—what she most desired? Or did she find in Stach a man who, though very different, was as enigmatic as her father? Dagny seemed to lose her grip on life at approximately the same time as her father died. This may have been coincidental, given the extraordinarily debilitating circumstances in which she was living in Poland. Yet there is little doubt that the loss of her father left her vulnerable.

MINDA BLEHR JUELL

If Hans Lemmich Juell was the supreme patriarch, Minda Blehr Juell was the supreme matriarch. She gave birth to five children in five years, her first when she was twenty-one, her last when she was twenty-six. She herself lived to be eighty-three, surviving her husband and three of her children. Her only son, born just after Dagny, died at the age of one year, Dagny at the age of thirty-three, and Ragnhild of cancer at the age of thirty-seven. Minda was revered by her children, her grandchildren, and her great-grandchildren. They all called her Babsche, Polish for Grandma, the name that Dagny's son Zenon had given her.

She was born on December 27, 1845, the daughter of Maren and Albert Blehr. Originally from Christiania, her parents had settled in Kongsvinger, where her father became the county physician. They raised a family of four daughters and four sons, most of whom maintained close ties and provided a large, familial network for Dagny and her sisters.

Minda loved to recount for her grandchildren the story of the night she

Minda Blehr Juell.

Minda Juell, her sisters, and their children. Dagny is sitting to the left, holding an umbrella. Late 1880s.

first saw Hans Lemmich Juell.[18] She was just a girl of fifteen. Hans came to their home to interview with her father. It was evening, and the two men stood talking in the parlor in the glow of the fire warming the room. Minda stood watching them, unseen in the shadows outside the parlor door. She would tell her granddaughters that she knew already then, that she was to marry Hans Lemmich Juell.

The story would be unimportant, save for the fact that Minda treasured it so. Her fondness for it makes it a little mirror into Minda Blehr Juell; and in it we catch a glimpse of a girl who loved romance and the fantasy of the soul mate. Dagny would carry the fantasy to a fatal extreme. Minda believed her destiny had been fulfilled when she married Hans. She spoke of the happiness she had known with him as the gift of her life, and she "hung on to every shadow of life" in him, as Ragnhild said, until he died.[19]

Yet if Minda was a romantic, she was and remained above all a devoted mother. When her husband first wrote to Stach in 1894, inviting him to

Rolighed, he had said that she was suffering from melancholy with all the children gone. She seems to have welcomed the responsibility of her two small grandchildren when Dagny went traveling the world. In truth, she made it easy for Dagny to leave them with her. Sometime after the death of Hans, Minda took Otto Blehr's son, suffering from a nervous disorder, to live with her for a time. In her last letter to Dagny she expressed her loneliness in a house abandoned by its children:

> It is such a painful feeling not knowing where a letter can reach you. Here it is full summer with narcissus and lilacs and fruit trees in bloom, but without children it is empty and sad. Life in nature contrasts so sorrowfully with this desolately lonely home, so the future looms twice as large.

She reasoned that by selling Rolighed she would regain the freedom to live as she should, that is to say, for the sake of her children.

> . . . so I'm having Mr. Engelbretsen put "Rolighed" up for sale, if that will work, so I can be nearer my children and at their disposition if they need me. I still have, God be praised, my children and my grandchildren to live for and they are precious treasures over whom I sincerely ask God to hold his protecting hand. [June 2, 1901][20]

She admonished Dagny, so far away near the Black Sea, "Live well, then, dearest Dagny, and you too guard with tenderness the treasures that have been entrusted to you, your husband and your children."

Within an absolutely traditional framework, Minda Juell was able to reconcile the romantic ideal of love and the bourgeois ideal of family. Middle and upper-class nineteenth-century women grew up with the notion that marriage would ensure their fulfillment as spiritual partners, mothers, and legitimate citizens in the eyes of God and the world. Historically, the reality of marriage often proved disappointing for women, but the myth was maintained. In the case of Minda Juell, it may have been realized, almost to the point of cliché.

Dagny, on the edge of a new era, both rebelled against the idea of womanhood for which her mother unconsciously stood and fell victim to it. She wanted more than a husband, children, and a home, but she wanted them too; and she was simply incapable, as any woman would have been, of being all things to all people, including herself. Minda Juell, only twenty-two years older than Dagny, was shaped by such different experiences that it is unlikely that she could have even begun to understand her daughter's dilemma. In her last letter she was still trying to enlist Dagny's solidarity in the only conspiracy she knew, the family.

Minda's letter is at once a maternal plea and rebuke. She was concerned that Dagny had not yet settled down. "It seems to me that with your eternal traveling you use up a fortune that would go far to live on in a well-ordered home." She feared that Dagny had left Iwa behind. "You don't mention Iwi, perhaps you haven't managed to get her yet? If only I had her here in my loneliness, she is a dear little part of you, Dagny mine, which I would watch over with great tenderness." She suspected that things were not right with Stach and dared not really imagine why Dagny had left for Tiflis with Emeryk. "Is that man you mention rich? and are you to be his guests? or what?" Underlying Minda's long letter is the premonition that her daughter is in danger, and for all the tender feelings in the world, she cannot save her. "I'm always so worried about you. . . . Dear one, write immediately and send me your address."

Minda's maternalism must have engendered very conflicting feelings in Dagny, who lived a life that flew in the face of everything her mother held dear, yet who returned to her again and again. There were certainly tensions between the two women. In August of 1895, for example, when Dagny and Stach were at Rolighed while she was pregnant with Zenon, Ragnhild wrote to Helge in Stockholm: "Maya Vogt is here right now and it's not very much fun—they sit and play cards almost the whole day and Dagny assures Maya far and wide how she hates Mama etc., and now tonight she was very insulted because Mama didn't give Stach a toddy" (postmarked August 5, 1895).[21]

Yet even as Dagny lashed out at her mother, she sought and depended on her care. If she opposed her, she also tried to appease her. In her last surviving letter to her mother, written in the winter of 1901 after she and Zenon had been reunited with Stach, she went to extremes to paint a positive picture: Stach was overjoyed to have them back, he was more successful than ever, things were going well for them economically, they were on their way to a new life in Warsaw. She sounded more like a girl than a woman of thirty-three with painful years of experience behind her.

"Mama," she wrote, "now you can really be pleased with us . . ." (February 1901).[22]

Minda and Hans Lemmich Juell, independently and together as parents, were of both liberal and conservative bents. They raised their daughters with a progressive outlook and apparently a joyous spirit. All four sisters seemed confident of their own desirability. Their contagious charm and sense of fun were often remarked upon. Jens Thiis, art historian and good friend of Edvard Munch, remembered his initial encounter with the Juell sisters at Rolighed. It was the summer of 1894, when Dagny and Stach first came up from Berlin.

> Those few June days I spent, at Dagny Juell's invitation, in her home in Kongsvinger were an unforgettable experience for me. The district doctor was traveling, and the young people ruled over the house, the independent and captivating Dagny, the piquant Ragnhild who married the Swedish Dr. Bäckström, and the very young and beautiful Astrid . . . I mention it here because, in the first place, the Juell daughters were exceptional, sweet and fun girls.[23]

The Juells encouraged their daughters to be artists, and they welcomed their bohemian friends into their home. Yet they were parental in the extreme. No more poignant example could be found than Minda's handling of her daughter's death. She preferred to let Dagny's memory die rather than suffer the impressions of scandal. She commanded the silence that was to fall on Dagny, and in so doing she checked her daughter's history in a way that cannot be undone. Yet with her maternal blessing, she had also sent her out into the new, exciting, even dangerous world of art and music and culture in 1893.

THE "CHILDREN"

She was leaving, as always peaceful but sad.

Gave me the pictures of her family house and her sisters. Gave me too two old Swedish candlesticks made of copper. "They are from my home, please keep them for me."

Astrid, Hans, Minda, Dagny, Stach, Gudrun, Ragnhild, and Helge, Rolighed,
summer 1895. Dagny was then pregnant with Zenon.

I can see her right now, sitting in this armchair in front of me, her
silhouette so prettily sketched, slender, in a simple black dress. I am
looking at those candlesticks which she loved so much, because they
were a reminder of her home. [Lucyna Kotarbińska regarding Dagny's
departure from Kraków] [24]

The candlesticks did indeed play on Dagny's mind. She had few personal
possessions in Poland save for them. She incorporated them into the expressionistic womb sets of two of her plays. And in one of her last, placating
letters to Stach, she made a sad, fleeting reference to them. Perhaps they
were reminders of the home she psychologically really never left. Though
she became one of the most celebrated women of the *fin de siècle,* she also
remained so much the child. In this both Stach and, ironically, her parents
were her strong allies.

Though it may be difficult to imagine the bohemian Przybyszewskis in the context of the Juell's bourgois gentility, there is every reason to suspect that they mutually satisfied each others' needs. Minda and Hans Lemmich Juell were the ultimate parents. Dagny and Stach were the ultimate children. The Juells facilitated their coming home and seemed unwittingly to encourage their economic and psychological dependency. Dagny and Stach took every advantage. The picture that emerges of the Przybyszewskis' stays at Rolighed is one of fitfull children, their moods fluctuating between joy and boredom over being "home."

The Juells were remarkably accommodating, giving Dagny and Stach the run of the house and room and freedom to work. Stach was elated to be at Rolighed for the first time. He wrote to his mother during his visit in the summer of 1894 that his novel was going well and was soon finished.

> People here are extremely serious, taciturn. At first it was hard to get used to it, but now I feel completely at home. . . . I'd preferably like to stay here the rest of my life. I will probably stay here until Christmas, everyone is prepared to like me. Their friendliness is open and strong, since people here have great difficulty taking to anyone. [June 5, 1894] [25]

Ragnhild wrote to Helge from Rolighed a week later. She reported, too, that it was good to have the Przybyszewskis home and that both Dagny and Stach were working well, though the inevitable frustration for Stach, too little alcohol, was already taking its toll.

> Stachu is great—is already almost finished with a 300 page long novel and has a multitude of things going. He is magnificently elegant in a new suit, fine new spring coat and yellow boots. Naturally an advance on the novel. They're thinking a little about the hike, but of course they can't afford it. Have already borrowed 10 of my 20 to send to Stach's brother. He is, as a matter of fact, delightful at the moment and he was touchingly happy that I came. . . . To be sure, Stachu suffers greatly from a desire for alcohol, which he, of course, has difficulty satisfying. [June 13, 1894] [26]

The mood was tenuous. In a letter written two days later, Ragnhild reported that Dagny and Stach had been "less than good friends" since she had come. Stachu, she said, though he had finished the novel and was about to start on a play, was not very happy there (June 15, 1894). [27] In July,

Stach wrote to Richard Dehmel that they were bored to tears. The days were passing monotonously one after another, while all they did was wait for the mailman, eat, sleep, and play cards. By September the labile Stach wrote again to Dehmel: "An exceedingly sad country!—I haven't once seen dancing here—only in Christiania in the Cabaret, but there it was Germans dancing. You can imagine people who learn to dance from typical, beer-drenched Germans" (ca. September 10, 1894).[28]

During another long visit in the summer of 1895 when Dagny was pregnant with Zenon, Ragnhild wrote:

> Stachu and I speak a little German with each other during the day, for that matter I read or work and am with our boy, and the others play cards incessantly. Yesterday, however, we sat up in the big room and drank toddies and smoked until one o'clock and had a very good time. Maya Vogt is awfully sweet. Gudrun and Astrid are coming tomorrow and then things will get lively, I suspect. [Postmarked August 7, 1895][29]

Stach was soon frustrated, however. He wrote to Dehmel: "Here in Norway there are naturally no people to be found, at any rate none whom you've not had completely enough of after being with them twice" (August 15, 1895).[30] Dagny, too, was out of sorts, telling Maya Vogt how much she hated her mother.

Two years later, in the summer of 1897 when Dagny was pregnant with Iwa, there were again swings in mood. After Stach had joined Dagny at Rolighed, he wrote to his parents to assure them that "all was well." They had expressed fears that he was unhappy, and he was anxious to convince them to the contrary. He wrote that there was not another couple as happy or at peace as he and Dagny. He praised his parents-in-law for being as loving and proud as his own parents. Dr. Juell often talked to him of his artistic plans and literally beamed, he said, when he read something complimentary to his son-in-law. "My name is known here. Most of my books are translated and are much read." Stach took great pains to paint a picture of well-being at Rolighed (May 30, 1897).[31] But only weeks later Dagny wrote on the backside of a letter Stach had written to their friend, Hedwig Blix: "Dearest Hedwig, nothing much came of the trip to Christiania. . . . I hear from Fanny that you're living it up. God knows we're not."[32] Stach had left Rolighed already in July to return to Berlin.

The bohemian is in a certain sense synonymous with the child, immediate, self-indulgent, ignorant of any sense of future. Dagny and Stach worked and played at being all those things. As their friend Ida Auerbach Dehmel had written about them from their time in Berlin: "Both of them . . . entertained a bottomless contempt for all kinds of order. They found the thought of tomorrow ridiculous and unnecessary."[33]

Stach consciously cultivated a myth of the child in terms of himself, and Dagny, and the relationship they shared. In July 1895, he wrote to Franz Servaes from Rolighed that he and Dagny were like children, alone and at peace. Dagny was pregnant, he was happy. They went nowhere because they were completely self-sufficient. "Oh God, how we play together. In both of us there is so amazingly much of the child: now we've invented a new card game and spend hours playing together."[34]

In late June 1896, after Marta Foeder's suicide, Stach wrote to his parents, boasting of the good care Dagny was taking of him. She cooked for him, gave piano lessons, and was translating his works into Norwegian. But he lapsed into an infantile fantasy, telling his parents that he and Dagny had plans to move to Torun to be with them. They would live in the same building, and they would heed their advice, for they were both impractical and without experience.[35]

When Dagny was pregnant with Iwa, Stach again wrote to a friend that she was an absolute child. She dreamed big dreams, he said, she built castles in the air, but she never seemed to suffer if things did not turn out as she had planned (May 19, 1897).[36]

Children themselves in so many ways, Dagny and Stach seemed helpless to care for their own children. They left them with others for long periods of time. And they exposed them to decadent environments. Ewa Kossak wrote about their first months in Kraków. "The atmosphere of alcohol and drunkenness in the Przybyszewskis' home shocked some people who became attached to Dagny. 'She is queen-like—a little reserved, but a very natural and loveable girl—but you don't want to visit them too often, because their home resembles a tavern most of all.'"[37] The children were only too aware of the drinking. In one of Dagny's last letters to Stach, written from Warsaw in the spring of 1901, she wrote, "Zenon said, when he heard you were sick: Oh poor Papa! It must be that awful sickness you get from wine!"[38]

For his part, Stach often seemed jealous of his son and his daughter.

His letters from the time of both pregnancies reveal a growing obsession with his fantasy that he and Dagny were the world's children. In a letter to Dagny after Iwa's difficult birth, he asked only what his daughter was to be called. His primary concern was that he and Dagny should once again be playmates. "Now we have to earn a lot so that we can devote ourselves to the happiness of our love, without a care, like children, and proud as a royal couple."[39] Stach at first tried to borrow money to come to Rolighed, but within days he was exhorting Dagny to come to him, without their children.

> My God, how you must have suffered all this time, my golden queen, it is much better this way, that you'll come to me. It will be infinitely good for you here. People love you and adore you without reservation, but then, Good God, we don't need any people! More than anything else in the world, I'd like to be just with you alone. [November 4, 1897][40]

And to Hans, who had urged him to come and offered to pay his fare, he wrote on December 1, 1897:

> Dear Papa, I thank you from the bottom of my heart for the invitation, and I ask forgiveness because my telegrams caused such anxiety. I was very upset, but all is well now. I thought about coming, but decided not to. If I could have left the first of October that would have made some sense, but now it is too late, and in ten days Dagny can come here. And then everything will be all right. I am very nervous, of course, but that is because I have not seen Dusi for six months, and that's terrible for me, because I can't live without her and consequently I suffer so much. But when she is with me, then all is fine. Also my play will be performed on the fifteenth of December in Lipsk and I must definitely be there. . . . I am longing to see Iwi, but what can I do, I'll probably see her in May. I gratefully kiss the hands of Mama and Papa and remain your grateful son.[41]

Ever concerned with himself, Stach referred to his new daughter as if in passing.

Stach's negligence as a father eventually bordered on the criminal. He had, for example, little to do with his daughter by Aniela Pająkówna, Stanisława Przybyszewska, until she was a teenager. When he did pay her some attention, he also introduced her to heroine. She became an addict for life.[42]

Dagny was never so cruel, but she was improvident and at times puzzlingly irresponsible. The greater responsibility for the children fell to her, particularly during their years in Poland, where she was forced to move with them from place to place. From the summer of 1899 to 1900 she spent much of the time in Zakopane, where they lived in rooms in various pensions, changing residences as the money slipped through her fingers. When she left Stach in January, she took Zenon with her but entrusted Iwa to Stach's care. Within weeks she had sent her son to her family in Scandinavia and did not see him for several months.

In March Stach wrote to Aniela Pajākówna, who was then caring for Iwa, that Dagny had written him from Prague. She wanted to come back to Kraków and she desperately wanted to see Iwa. She was threatening suicide if Stach did not arrange it. Stach had Iwa brought to Kraków; but when he and Dagny did not reconcile, Dagny left again to be with Wincent Brzozowski, and she may have never seen Iwa again. When she returned to Poland in 1901, she wrote to her mother, just before she, Stach, and Zenon were about to leave Kraków for Warsaw: "Ivi is still with Mrs. Professor Morasjewska in Lemberg and I'm really happy about that. We have no maid here and naturally little room in a hotel."[43] Dagny never brought Iwa to live with her in Warsaw.

The Juell family lived according to a paradoxical set of norms. Minda and Hans encouraged independence and personal freedom in their children. Yet they were larger than life as parents, and they created an environment both psychologically nurturing and inhibiting from which their children would not, perhaps could not, free themselves. Dagny, who was intense and internally torn, swung ever more fatally between the emotional poles of woman and child, just as she traveled back and forth between Rolighed and foreign places increasingly far away.

8 : THE SISTERS

*Think how sweet all of you always were toward Dagny—yes, that sibling love you shared I
have otherwise never seen, completely unique.*
[Maya Vogt to Ragnhild after Dagny's death, December 3, 1901]

. . . dear Stacho, . . . none of us has a forgiving word for Dagny in this.
[Gudrun to Stach after Dagny left him, March 8, 1900]

*I am so happy that beloved Papa did not experience this, it would have upset him so
enormously and insurmountably.*
[Astrid to Stach after Dagny left him, May 7, 1900]

. . . you knew Dagny's and my relationship to each other and know how I am suffering now.
[Ragnhild to Munch after Dagny's death, July 3, 1901][1]

Dagny was the second of four sisters, all born within five years of each other. Her younger brother died at the age of one. As if a reflection of the contradictions inherent in their parents, the sisters split into two pairs, the one set drawn to convention, the other to the opposite extreme. They inevitably came into conflict, yet they were, and they remained, extremely close.

Dagny, Astrid, Gudrun, Ragnhild.

GUDRUN

Dagny grew up in the shadow of her imposing older sister, Gudrun. Born in 1866, one year before Dagny, Gudrun was musically very talented, exceptionally beautiful, temperamental, and vain. It was Gudrun who said to the Swedish king, when he asked if there were many beautiful girls in Kongsvinger, "There are four of us." She was also reputed to have said, when asked if there was anything of note in Lund, "Yes, the cathedral and myself."[2] Of the four sisters, she was the classic beauty. Dagny's daughter, Iwa, whom Gudrun raised, said that her aunt's magnificence simply took her breath away when, as a little girl, she would watch her dress for the evening.[3]

Dagny and Gudrun chose diametrically opposed ways to live their lives, the one so radically, the other so conservatively. Unlike Dagny, Gudrun pursued her academic studies, attending a private academy in Stockholm; and though she supposedly played the piano with greater virtuosity than

Dagny,[4] she never took it up professionally. At the age of twenty-two, Gudrun married Wilhelm Westrup, the son of wealthy landowners from Lund, and became part of Lund's high society. As Dagny sought herself in the cultural bohemias of the Continent, Gudrun sought herself in the upper-class worlds of Sweden. Ultimately, though, these two older sisters shared a common dissatisfaction, for neither woman seemed to find what she was looking for. "Gudrun is the same as always, nervous and frantic so that you can cry blood over her," Ragnhild wrote in 1905.[5]

"Fine people and clothes are their only real passion . . . ," she also wrote, at a time when she was exasperated with Gudrun and Astrid (September 16, 1897).[6] The judgment was no doubt partially true: In contrast to Dagny and their father, Gudrun was impressed by pomp and circumstance. When Otto Blehr was appointed prime minister, Gudrun wrote to him that she, her husband, and Astrid "screamed so the house rang, hurray for our dear uncle the prime minister" (April 11, 1891);[7] thereafter, she thoroughly enjoyed being a part of the social world of the ministerial Blehrs. Though Dagny was close to her aunt and uncle, having served as their governess for a year, she was not overly impressed with their status and what that might imply for her own.[8] The difference between the two sisters is amusingly illustrated by their responses to an invitation from their Aunt Randi to attend the ministerial ball of January 1893, just before Dagny was to leave for Berlin. Taking it upon herself to reply for the family, Dagny wrote from Rolighed:

> Thank you very much for your kind invitation. It was terribly nice that you would want us, and we, of course, would really like to come. But that is unfortunately impossible. I have been in Lund for a whole month. And then none of us has dresses. So we think that it would be a little too expensive a pleasure. . . . Gudrun and Wilhelm have already gone back to Lund, so as far as they're concerned, it is out of the question. [January 11, 1893]

Three days later Gudrun wrote from Lund:

> . . . your enormously friendly [letter] came today, dear Aunt, and that *we actually could not resist.* A thousand million thanks for your and uncle's great kindness!! At this very moment I have sent for my seamstress and together we shall do our best to ensure that your niece

is not an embarrassment at the ball. Can we really also come to the palace? I'm making a white [dress] too to be safe. It would be so lovely. [January 14, 1893][9]

Gudrun seemed to play a parental role in her relationship to Dagny. Her protective shadow is captured in the clothes she passed on to her younger sister, clothes from another world, richer, more traditionally stylish than those Dagny came to wear.[10]

From Poland, Lucyna Kotarbińska wrote that Dagny usually looked "sorry, barely covered, simple, plain, almost poor"; but "sometimes a better dress, a piece of velvet or other fabric. These were gifts from her sister, who sent a blessed package with gifts from time to time."[11] Another friend from Poland, Boy-Żeleński, wrote that "she wore with regal dignity the old clothes she inherited from her rich sister . . . , for Przybyszewski had no understanding whatsoever of a woman's need, and all the money that didn't go for strong drinks he thought wasted. It was easier to ask him for a bottle of champagne than for a pair of stockings."[12]

It was Gudrun who was sent out three times to bring her sister back home. The first time, in May of 1893, was prompted by Strindberg's letter to Birger Mörner about Dagny and Bengt Lidforss. The second time was again in May, seven years later, when Dagny had gone to Paris with Wincent Brzozowski. Discretely Gudrun wrote to Randi Blehr at the end of April, "May 4 we're going to Paris."[13] She did not say why. She apparently convinced Dagny to return to Rolighed.

The third time was in June 1901, after Dagny's death. She traveled with her mother to Poland to bring Dagny's children and her few possessions back to Norway. From Warsaw she wrote her uncle, Otto Blehr, asking for his help in facilitating Zenon's departure from Russia. She added, "You'll get to hear everything when we come home—though you should know that it was *not* a love drama, as the papers have wanted to make it" (June 21, 1901).[14]

In her letter Gudrun was extremely sympathetic to Stach. "You can't imagine what sums Stachu has had to employ and what *unbelievable* difficulties the Russian authorities have created to squeeze money out of that unhappy man. To have Dagny identified,—to have Zenon and her things brought out, he has spent unnecessary money ten times over, telegrams,— endless disappointments, anxiety." Obviously Gudrun did not know that

Dagny, Stockholm, 1894. According to Dagny's daughter, Iwa, Dagny was wearing Gudrun's dress.

it was primarily because Stach had failed to send Dagny's and Zenon's passports that difficulties then arose over identification of the body and the boy's passage home. But Gudrun was of no mind to blame Stach in any case. "Never have we been so necessary as here for Stachu in his desperate position, so we thank God that we could come."

Dagny's feelings for Gudrun have gone unrecorded. Stach's have not. He found her formidable, pompous, and disagreeable.[15] He was particularly enraged over her suggestion in the spring of 1900—after Dagny left him and sent Zenon to her family in Scandinavia—that Gudrun keep the boy. In a letter to Ragnhild he wrote, "Gudrun wanted to capitalize on my misfortune and wanted me to give Zenon to her. I find that shocking. I would dig gold out of the earth and fetch Zenon and take both children to my mother" (postmarked on arrival in Stockholm, April 11, 1900).[16]

Yet Gudrun had sympathized with Stach not only at the time of Dagny's death, but as well when Dagny left him a year and a half earlier. In March 1900, she wrote to him:

Dear Stacho! Yesterday I came from Stockholm, where I had visited Ragnhild and Helge for 14 days. I naturally told them about the great, incomprehensible misfortune that had befallen you and us, and Ragnhild was overwhelmed with sympathy for you, dear Stacho, and none of us has a forgiving word for Dagny in this. But when she says that she has never loved you, then she is lying,—if she has ever loved any person on earth, then it's you! I long very much for a letter from you—and cannot comprehend why you don't write. Maybe you now know Dagny's address? Then give it to me immediately. [March 8, 1900][17]

Gudrun asked if he had received her Christmas money and entreated him to send a picture of Iwa for her mother and herself. She ended with "a thousand heartfelt greetings from Astrid and your devoted sister-in-law."

Gudrun was not alone in her betrayal of Dagny. All the Juell women supported Stach when Dagny left him. Their betrayal was significant, and probably not an isolated moment. Yet typically they rallied around Dagny when she came home to Rolighed in the late spring of 1900. Ultimately their affections were much stronger than their antagonisms. One is, however, left with the uncomfortable feeling that in Dagny's case, in spite of the "unique" sisterly bonds of which Maya Vogt wrote, there was also a sisterly resentment.

Surely with mixed feelings on both sides, Gudrun had tried to protect and correct her younger sister during her lifetime. After Dagny's death her memory was in a profound sense entrusted to Gudrun in the lives of her children. According to Iwa, Gudrun refused to talk about Dagny because it caused her too much pain.[18]

ASTRID

Astrid was born in 1869, two years after Dagny, one year after their brother had died. As a young woman, Astrid was considered frail. Whether her health was truly poor, or whether she was instinctively responding to some uncommon worry her parents may have had about her in the wake of their only son's death, is difficult to judge. The fact that she, like her mother and her sister Gudrun, lived well into her eighties suggests that there was a psychosomatic dimension to her frailty.

Astrid's poor health became her signature. She took seriously ill and was feared to be close to death when Dagny was in Berlin. Dagny's letter home suggests her own and her family's immeasurable distress:

> Oh thank God, thank God! At this moment I got the telegram saying there is more hope. Oh God, how desperate I've been! I have cried continually since I got the first telegram. I've been as if in a fever, until I got the second telegram today. It is not possible, simply not possible, that Astrid should die and leave us. We simply can't do without her.
>
> Poor Papa and you! I see how extremely desperate you are. [Undated][19]

Astrid recovered, but she was forever seeking cures for chronic illness. She and Dagny could not have been more different in this regard. Dagny continually wrote of Stach's poor health, but she never portrayed herself as sickly, in spite of the fact that she suffered periodically from malnutrition and fatigue, and in spite of the fact that she almost died in childbirth.[20] It is poignant that when Dagny was in real danger, traveling toward her death in Tiflis, her sister Astrid, who would live a long life, was undergoing a water cure at a Swedish health spa. All the Juell women were attending her. Minda wrote in her last letter to Dagny:

Astrid has begun her water cure in Norrköping and Ragnhild is now with her, then Gudrun is going to relieve her, for she cannot be alone, she is too weak for that. God grant that this can help her get her health back, but it is a strenuous cure, so I'll be very anxious until I see her strength return. And then I have to be here during all this and take care of the farm, and cannot be with her. Meaningless. . . . [June 1901][21]

Ragnhild and Astrid were together when the news came of Dagny's death. Ragnhild wrote to Helge, "It was easier than I had thought to inform Astrid of the dreadful thing that has happened, but it was terrible, as you can imagine"; and shortly thereafter from the spa:

Astrid is *considerably* much better and has taken this with incredible strength, so it's almost worse for me. But I take care of myself conscientiously and then I will get better. . . . it is absolutely necessary that I still be here. It is painful to be alone among so many strange people in such a situation as ours, you see, and even worse then to be alone if you are as nervous as Astrid. [June 24, 1901][22]

Though Dagny was so unlike her delicate, protected younger sister, her feelings for her were strong. She had been in despair at the thought of her dying. She entrusted her children to her. And she had personally dedicated her lyric poem cycle to her. It was, in fact, Astrid who had kept the manuscripts of Dagny's poems and plays and eventually passed them on to Dagny's daughter, Iwa.

Yet of all the Juell women, Astrid seems to have been the most conflicted about Dagny. If she feared she had a rival in the family, it was probably her unorthodox older sister. Astrid and Gudrun shared the same conservative world view. They spent much time together, and they had the same concerns with status, fashion, and important people. There was a hint of Cinderella's wicked sisters in Ragnhild's description of them in a letter to Helge from 1897. "They're coming tomorrow at 11:30 and you know, I almost have stage fright at having to receive such spoiled and critical guests. . . . they somehow usher in an atmosphere that is strange to me" (September 16, 1897).[23]

Astrid took the news of Dagny's death remarkably well. In *her* consoling letter to Stach a year earlier, she had been uncomfortably willing to take emotional advantage of the situation, calling upon her dead father's disapproval of Dagny, while alluding to the greater intimacy that she now felt existed between her and Stach. In early May she wrote:

Dearest Stachu!

Mama and I both greatly appreciated hearing from you and getting little Ivi's picture, thank you very much for both. So sweet and beautiful she is, and she looks so much like Zenon, and since he is the most wonderful thing we know, then you can understand that we think it's fun.

Yes Stachu, we had also so much looked forward to having you all home this summer, it's been such a long time, and so terribly many and difficult things have happened since that time and now that bind us, I think, even closer together, so that we would have twice the benefit of being together. The terrible misfortune that has befallen you and the children—yes all of us, is such a big mystery to me that I'm struck dumb in the face of it—absolutely can't understand it! But dear Stachu, rest assured that Mama and I feel for you and perhaps are fonder of you now than before.

. . . I am so happy that beloved Papa did not experience this, it would have upset him so enormously and insurmountably. We don't doubt that you are a good and dear papa to Ivi, dear Stachu, and it is so good for you that you have her constantly with you, now that she must be without her mother, the poor little thing, kiss her from Gramma and Auntie!

Many heartfelt wishes, we think so much about you, wish so that we could do something for you. Your devoted *Astrid* [May 7, 1900][24]

Astrid watched over Dagny's children both during their early years at Rolighed and later when they came to live with Gudrun in Lund, and she lived with and cared for her mother until she died. Her nieces and nephews came to love her dearly as both a kind and very generous aunt. Certainly though, in ways subtle or not, she must have made Dagny feel her resentment.

We can only surmise what Dagny experienced growing up in between the imposing Gudrun and the frail Astrid. Dagny herself expressed only love and concern for her sisters in her surviving letters. Though her most publicized relationships were with Stach and with men in general, she liked women and was liked by them in return, which must in some way be a reflection of her relationships to her sisters.

Whether in a chastened or forgiving mood, she ended her long letter to her mother in February 1901, on her way back to Poland with Stach: "Sweetest Mama, I'm not going to get a chance to write to Gudrun or Astrid before we get to Warsaw, so please send them this letter so they will know where we are and how we are. . . . Stachu . . . is naturally overjoyed to have us back."[25]

RAGNHILD

Dagny found her truest friend in Ragnhild. They were both artistic and rebellious and their bond was unusually strong. Working to reconstruct Dagny's life, it becomes impossible to imagine her without Ragnhild, the one constantly loving and accepting figure in her world.

Ragnhild was the Juell's youngest daughter, born four years after Dagny in 1871. She was the last member of her family to whom Dagny wrote, sending her those poignant picture postcards from her journey toward Tiflis. After Dagny's death Ragnhild wrote to Helge from the health spa at Norrkjöping:

> Today is midsummer eve and the most beautiful weather—chamber music everywhere, May pole in Himmelstadlund Park and a lot of happy people in party clothes. But we are not in party clothes, I'm afraid—God how terrible it is about Dagny, I don't know how it is possible to ever get over such a blow, and even for a little while be able to forget that something like this has happened to one of our most dear. [June 24, 1901][26]

When she was back in Stockholm a little more than a week later she wrote to Munch to thank him for the interview he had given about Dagny in *Kristiania Dagsavis:*

> I just wanted to thank you for what you have done for Dagny's memory at this time, and you must absolutely believe that all of us closest to her are forever grateful to you.
>
> It is terrible that her life should have such an end, and that the

press now takes its pleasure in defiling her memory in any way it can. You are the only one who has said anything good about her, and I can never be grateful enough to you—you knew Dagny's and my relationship to each other and know how I am suffering now. [July 3, 1901][27]

Of all the Juell sisters, Ragnhild seemed to be the one with the greatest joy of life, both outwardly more determined and resilient and inwardly more at peace. She was the least beautiful of the girls but the most ebullient. She charmed many men as a young woman, most of them artists, including the Norwegian poets Vilhelm Krag and Nils Collette Vogt,[28] and the English pianist Frederick Delius, with whom she spent a great deal of time in Paris during the fall and winter of 1892.[29]

Ragnhild was also very close to the two men and the two artists so significant in Dagny's life, Stach and Munch. Munch painted Ragnhild twice, first in *Two Music-Making Sisters* and then alone as *Fru Bäckström* in 1894. Commissioned by her husband, Helge, this was the portrait her father asked Munch to take down. When Ragnhild died at age thirty-seven, Helge wrote him: "Dear Friend! Thank you for your flowers! Today they adorn her portrait" (August 12, 1908).[30]

Ragnhild and Stach were intimate friends. They exchanged letters and when at Rolighed often played and sang together. She thoroughly enjoyed his company and displayed a genuine affection for him. She also seemed to know him better than the others. When her mother and Gudrun had gone to Warsaw, she wrote to Helge: "It is wonderful to know that Mama and Gudrun are in Warsaw and will see both Stachu and Zenon, if only Stachu can be honest with them, so we can stop living with this terrible uncertainty about everything."[31]

Dagny and Stach met and fell in love in Berlin at approximately the same time as Ragnhild and Helge in Paris. In May both sisters returned to Norway, "secretly engaged." Dagny was almost twenty-six, Ragnhild twenty-two, and they were like best girlfriends involved in the adventure of their lives. Ragnhild wrote to Helge in the middle of June:

Dagny has, you see, gotten engaged in Berlin to a Polish writer and scientist, Stanisław Przybyszewski—I don't know if you've ever heard of him—and she's probably going back down again on the 7th of July to get married. In that regard there'll naturally be a great to-do among us, so there can't be talk of any relaxation up here until after that time. And if Mr. Przy.—meets her in Copenhagen and they get married there, then I'll probably go down there [with her] and then come right back home again when they go to Berlin. Dagny would so much like to meet you before she leaves—therefore I think you should come to Christiania on the 5th, then we'll meet there, and then we can at the same time decide where we'll put you this summer. It will be, you see, a very difficult matter, when I don't want Papa to suspect anything for anything in the world, and I don't want any small town gossip either. All this about Dagny is the *deepest secret*. [June 14, 1893][32]

Through Ragnhild we catch a glimpse of Dagny's mood when she came home from Berlin with her "secret." Their father was a major consideration. Ragnhild feared his reaction to both her and Dagny's engagements, but her fears seem to have been a bit puffed up for the occasion. She was shortly able to tell Helge that her father was pleased.

Ragnhild was excited by the very secrecy of her relationship. Once she had eliminated her father as an obstacle, she threw another in the path. She gave Helge, coming to Rolighed for the first time in July, instructions to come in disguise, i.e., as an old friend of Astrid and Gudrun from Lund. She had won a music scholarship which she felt could be jeopardized by any talk of an upcoming marriage. Helge was not at all amused. But furtiveness was one way Ragnhild had of thumbing her nose at the bourgeoisie.

Ragnhild's need to rebel is a mild reminder of what Dagny must have felt. Her youngest sister, emotionally more harmonious, was nevertheless at odds with the world of Rolighed, if only temporarily. Ragnhild and Helge had already enjoyed a sexual relationship in Paris, and the knowledge made her feel powerful. A week before their wedding she wrote:

As a matter of fact, it will be an awful day with priest and sextons, aunts and uncles and all the necessary accessories for such an act to take place in all decency. Only the veil and white gown are missing. But then when that purgatory is over with, we'll enjoy life to the fullest and thumb our noses and kick them all. Oh God how we'll laugh at those who are left with the comfortable belief that again they have participated in blessing a marriage—ah they don't know what kind of marriage this is going to be—have never in their lives been to something like this before. [November 20, 1893][33]

Dagny was Ragnhild's safe haven. In the same angry letter she wrote: "Dagny is fiercely looking forward to having us down in Berlin—I got a long letter from her yesterday—she asks me, and Stachu too, to give you their love. I can't deny that I am more looking forward to going there than to Lund, though they'll be lavish down there too."

Ragnhild, more so than Dagny, was caught in a conscious conflict between career and family. Whereas Dagny seemed to choose neither the one nor the other, Ragnhild painfully chose the latter. Once she had made the decision, her commitment was complete. She gave birth to six children, and they and her husband became the sum of her life. The path Ragnhild took suggests a path Dagny too might have taken, had she not been who she was. Ragnhild had been open to both the radical and conservative impulses in her family and was ultimately able to resolve the conflict in favor of tradition. Dagny could not do that.

Shortly after Dagny's death, Ragnhild wrote to Helge: "Oh, how hard and bitter life is, God grant that our children will never have to have a taste of what we have experienced lately, and you and I must *vow* to do *everything* so that our children's lives will be as bright as possible."[34] Seven years later Ragnhild died of breast cancer, only three years older than Dagny had been when she was shot in Tiflis.

It is fitting that Ragnhild, through her many letters, shed the most intimate light on Dagny and the Juell family; for Dagny felt the greatest love for her, this warmest, most ingenuous of her sisters. As if attempting to reenact the relationship in later years, Dagny tended to choose friends younger than herself, including Stach, Hjalmar Christiansen, Boy-Żeleński, Wincent Brzozowski, and Władysław Emeryk.

Though Ragnhild cared for Dagny like no other of her sisters, she, too, extended her sympathies to Stach in 1900. Her letter to him has not survived, but his reply has. It began: "My dear, beloved Trucha, I read your golden words with powerful feelings that shook me deeply. How thankful I am to you for your letter. You see, I am completely dead inside, but I feel that you would like to know everything and because of your love, must

Dagny and Ragnhild, Rolighed, summer 1895.

know. So on New Year's day she left me . . ." (postmarked on arrival in Stockholm, April 11, 1900).[35]

Stach went on to give his version of the events in great detail, portraying Dagny as the persecutor and himself as the martyred Christ. "This is my Golgatha," he wrote, "and God grant that it is not my undoing." To be sure, it was the beginning of Dagny's, not his own.

THE "SON"

The sisters' judgment of Dagny has both a familial and an historical dimension. They were encouraged to enter the man's cultural domain, but they were judged—and they judged themselves—by one standard and men by

Dagny and Zenon.

another. They were encouraged to be independent but to seek fulfillment in men. Men held the special place in the Juell family.

Stach wrote to his mother from Rolighed that Minda Juell adored Zenon "as if he were her own. Because she has only daughters and the boy, who would have been my age now, died" (May 30, 1897). Stach himself was a trickster, an inspired charmer and a liar. He won the hearts and, remarkably, the confidence of all the Juell women. He attributed his own acceptance, as he did Zenon's, to the fact that he became the son the Juells had lost.

How great a role the death of Minda's young son, whom they had named Hans Lemmich, played in her life, is difficult to ascertain. Still, it is apparent that for Minda Juell the man was sacrosanct. She idolized her husband. She idolized her grandson. And she welcomed the most unlikely son-in-law into her house. Her influence could not have failed to affect her daughters. When Ragnhild gave birth to her second child, Dagny wrote from Berlin: "Oh, my God, if I could come and see you just for a minute! And it's a little boy again. Just think: two sons! It's a proud feeling, isn't it? . . . Think, two sons, two sons! I must constantly think about it, all day long. Two sons! Little Truls with two sons!" (undated, but written around the New Year, 1896–97).[36]

Dagny's own son became her "prince." She kept him with her when she left her daughter behind. She clung to him those last months in Warsaw when Stach was spending more and more time with Jadwiga Kasprowicz. And she took him with her on the long journey to Tiflis. Emeryk, the man who shot her, wrote in his letter to Zenon: "You alone meant everything to her. She, the first and only queen, bowed humbly down to you. She believed that she came to earth simply so that you could be born."[37] Disturbed though Emeryk was, there may have been truth in his words.

The Juells fostered an ideal of the man as father, lover, and son that could only have resulted in a very ambivalent sense of self in their daughters. Again, it was Dagny who seemed to suffer the ambivalence most acutely. As a woman she literally reshaped existing female roles. She asserted her right, like men, to develop all sides of herself—intellectual, sexual and spiritual—and to make her choices as freely as they. Yet she was addictively attached to her husband and her son, as if only they could give her the identity she appeared so tragically to seek.

9 : WHEN THE SUN GOES DOWN

The Disintegration of the Woman and the Myth

. . . even a woman's truth is an unconscious lie.

The social liberality Dagny seemed to enjoy in the early years in Berlin was the exception, not the rule of her life in ways that would genuinely have made a difference. For if she fell victim to her family's —and her own—double standard, she also fell victim to Stach's. Though the bohemians appeared to give women greater freedom of movement both literally and figuratively, their progressivism was often either superficial or partial and made to serve highly egocentric ends. There was no greater offender than Stach. There is no better illustration than his attitudes toward sexual freedom and equality.

Both Dagny and Stach had other lovers in the course of their relationship, though their patterns were very different. Stach was promiscuous, before and during his eight-year marriage to Dagny. Marta Foerder, Maya Vogt, Aniela Pająkówna, and Jadwiga Kasprowicz were only the most visible of his many women. He seemed to consider affairs his right and had no qualms about disclosing them to his friends. One must wonder how concerned he was about concealing them from his wife.

Dagny was not so simply categorized as Stach. She formed relationships with several men during her first months in Berlin, though the knowledge

Edvard Munch's Stanisław Przybyszewski, *1895.*

of whether those relationships were sexual or not remains with her and the men she might have known. There is little to suggest that she had other relationships during the first four years of her marriage to Stach. When the Przybyszewskis moved to Poland, however, they grew increasingly estranged and betrayals apparently began on both sides. Ewa Kossak suggested that Dagny's failure to learn Polish was the critical if not the primary reason for their estrangement. Unlike in Berlin, Dagny was intellectually cut off from Stach, who was surrounded by his circle of passionate fans. A supportive, enamored circle also formed around her, made up of men who spoke German and French. These were men who also admired Stach and were themselves part of his *Paon* group. They included, among others, Alfred Wysocki, Tadeusz Boy-Żeleński, Wincent Brzozowski and his brother, Stanisław, and Władysław Emeryk. As in Berlin, there was talk of affairs. And again, Dagny's secrets died with her. Boy-Żeleński said that he had taught her to play billiards at *Paon* to amuse her during the long hours she and Stach spent there. But the fact alone that she played billiards, he claimed, scandalized people sufficiently to give rise to gossip.[1]

The details of the Przybyszewskis' love lives are, however, not the issue. The issue is the violent prejudice that Dagny, as a woman and as a sexual woman, suffered under Stach, if initially it was disguised as a mantle of ecstatic reverence.

Though Stach freely permitted himself multiple affairs, he seemed to exempt himself entirely from censure. As a form of radical new behavior for society in general, he rejected it. In Scandinavia the social notion of "free love" had been celebrated, in particular, by the Christiania bohemia of the 1880s, under the leadership of the Norwegian writer Hans Jæger and his countrymen Oda and Christian Krohg, who later were frequenters of the *Schwarze Ferkel*. By "free love" they had not meant promiscuity but the right of both men and women to choose their partners voluntarily and according to their own consciences. In an 1897 article on Edvard Munch, Stach seized the opportunity to lambast the Christiania bohemia's advocacy of both "free love" and "woman's sexual equality," which he rightly understood as being interdependent in the bohemia's terms.

> At that time Hans Jæger's famous novel, *Fra Kristiania-Bohêmen* (From the Christiania bohemia), was published. In it he completely openly proclaimed "free love," and that "free" love was elevated to a kind of sacred status. . . .
>
> But the breakdown soon followed. The Bohemia's moral about women's sexual equality and the sacredness of free love drove some people to suicide, some women from the Bohemia became prostitutes, for in this giving of themselves first to one and then another there was less of a love act than of a scandalous "proud" protest against the "decent" people. . . .
>
> Thus the Bohemia fell apart. The women were corrupted under the

influence of the moral of "free love," and the men fell away in drink or suicide, or they themselves became—"decent."[2]

Stach's underlying presumptions about the nature of women and men are clearly manifest. Women were of the body and always potentially corrupt. Men were of the mind and always potentially in the throes of despair. Women were physical, men existential. Thus, "free love" drove women to prostitution and men to suicide. There is a cruel irony in the fact that in Stach's own life, it was a woman who chose suicide as a solution.

One of the most radical and, in personal terms, the most successful of the Christiania bohemians was Oda Krohg. Unlike her countrywoman, Dagny, who was close-mouthed about her relationships, Oda revelled in her many affairs with, among others, Hans Jæger, Jappe Nilssen, Holger Drachmann, and Gunnar Heiberg. She flaunted her right to "free love." Carla Lathe, in her dissertation on the *Schwarze Ferkel* circle, told a story that arose in an interview she conducted with Oda's sister, Bokken Lasson, then ninety-seven years old. Lathe recounted that "Oda was unconcerned with the opinions of others, telling her younger sister Bokken, who was worried by people's insinuations about her liaison with Holger Drachmann, 'just let them talk—they don't know the half of it.'"[3]

In light of his own behavior, Stach's reaction to Oda would be humorous if it did not reveal such intense animosity toward the sexual woman. In April 1897, he wrote to his Czech publisher, Procházka, regarding Hans Jæger's *roman à clef, From the Christiania Bohemia*, in which Oda figured centrally:

> Fru Krohg plays a big role in Norwegian literature. She has ruined five married men and five married men have written novels and plays about her. Julia in Gunnar Heiberg's *The Balcony* is her. As you can see, this one fact illustrates the situation in Norway better than everything else put together. In the woman interpreted as the griffin Munch has, quite unceremoniously, portrayed her features in colossal exaggeration.[4]

Stach's remarks about Oda smack of Strindberg's diatribe against Dagny four years earlier. Stach's imagery speaks for itself. The sexual, equal woman was an abomination: a destroyer, a femme fatale, a monster.

There was certainly truth in Stach's assessment of the "free love" movement, which left many people, men and women, emotionally and spiritually bereft, because "free" often had come to mean "promiscuous" and "love" to mean "sex." But Stach's insight is not of significance here. At issue is his discriminatory view of women, in particular, sexual women, who seemed to transform themselves into off-color creatures before his very eyes.

The interpretation of "woman" which Stach imposed on Oda Krohg and the women of the Christiania bohemia corresponded to ideas he promulgated in his aesthetics. The genius of a work of art, he argued, was directly dependent on how deeply it originated in the instincts of the unconscious. Ole Michael Selberg wrote of Stach's aesthetic doctrine: "Only two ways stand open to the deepest levels of the psyche where the individual can communicate with the Absolute, with Genesis: madness, the pathological states of mind—and sex, sexual desire and pain."[5] Thus, madness and desire were the only legitimate sources for artistic inspiration. "Woman" was the vehicle through which to provoke both, and she was therefore quintessential to the creative process.

In classic nineteenth-century tradition, Stach determined man and woman to be opposites and always at war: ". . . the man and the woman are two completely differently organized creatures who feel differently, think differently, that *never* can understand each other, and where this seemingly happens, the one or the other must have been raped or overpowered."[6] The man, who is the sexually more powerful by virtue of his "incessant hunger," loses the upper hand to the woman because he "always must court and always must crawl, if he does not prefer to turn the woman into an apathetic and willing object for his passion," thus ending the struggle. And the struggle must be maintained, according to Stach, because the suffering soul is life's, consequently art's, only truth. "The joyful, rejoicing soul is a monstrosity, a square wheel. The soul is dark, because it is passion and the abyss, the endless pain of immersion and invention."[7]

Stach attributed great powers to the "woman," conceiving of her as an androgynous god who would reveal the over-intellectualized man to himself once again. She was "the black god," "the born whore, indifferent as to whether she prostitutes herself physically or morally." She was also "the good god," though "this god," he wrote, "is only an ideal, that perhaps someday will rise from man's kingdom of dreams and into reality." Stach saw her in Munch's *Madonna*.

Edvard Munch's hand-colored Madonna, *1893–94, dedicated to Przybyszewski.*

. . . there are moments when the woman ceases to be the vampire. In giving herself absolutely to a man the dirt is washed off and her lust to destroy and her shame disappear without a trace, her face shines in conception's terrifying beauty.

There is a moment in the woman's soul when she forgets herself and everything around her and transforms herself into a formless,

Gustav Vigeland's De nedbøyde, *1895.*

timeless and dimensionless creature, a moment when she conceives in virginity: "Madonna."[8]

But if his surrendering woman was a goddess, she was also a conquered victim. Speaking of Vigeland's sculpture entitled *De nedbøyde* (Bowed down), Stach wrote:

One of Vigeland's works especially seems to me to be unsurpassable in spiritual power: the woman kneels, with her head agonizingly bent toward the earth; her long hair flows down around her. Over her lies the man, also kneeling; with both hands he holds tight, painfully tight around her body and presses his face violently down into her neck.

It is the young girl's tragedy—the tragedy of the conquered, passive one. Pain is here intensified into something that is no longer pain: a passive tumbling down into the abyss, a passive giving-of-oneself unto the Satan of sin and destruction. She has fought until the last second, but his brutal will has constrained her. Yet now, when he has reached the goal of his desire, now he does not dare take her. He only presses her to him, he would really like to press her completely into himself in his desperate awareness of spiritual torture.[9]

Stach operated aesthetically with some of the most blatant, sexist clichés of the turn of the century. There were no women, only "woman," a sexual principle anchored at once in the unconscious and the cosmos. Her meaning derived only from her ability to quicken the artist's creativity, either through pain or purity. She was a tortuous mirror, a sexual/aesthetic vehicle. She was both the way to knowledge and eternal deception: ". . . even a woman's truth is an unconscious lie."[10]

Though Stach may have been revolutionary in his theories of the unconscious, he was typical rather than exceptional for his time in his view of "woman." It was not that he underestimated "her." The underlying impetus for his own as well as much of the misogynous iconography of the late nineteenth century was a defensive reaction to the power women were perceived to have won. Stach himself wrote about Munch that he painted the "inferior man's tragedy under the matriarchy's oppressive yoke, that never has been more powerful than perhaps precisely in our age."[11]

In *Woman and the Demon*, Nina Auerbach had attempted to recover the integrity of the various mythological projections of women in art and life. Where traditional feminist criticism had sought to expose the dehumanizing impetus in the iconography of the late nineteenth century, Auerbach sought to revive its underlying power. "It may be time," she wrote, "to circle back to those 'images' of angels and demons, nuns and whores, whom it seemed so easy and liberating to kill, in order to retrieve a less tangible, but also less restricting, facet of woman's history." Auerbach believed that those "images," by virtue of their different powers—metaphysical, spiritual, satanic, corrupting—were actually subversive, challenging and undermining the image of the woman in the home. In composite she saw them giving birth to the magic, mobile, transcending woman who, she believed, "functioned above all as a shaping principle, not only of fictions but of lives as well."[12] The composite image of woman, new and indivisible, was Auerbach's truly radical idea, for potentially it *was* empowering.

Dualistic thinking like Stach's and so many others of his time, while contributing to aspects of a new myth of womanhood, essentially divided and isolated the images and dehumanized the woman behind them.[13] The impetus may have been both awe and distrust, but the real consequences could be debilitating. Most certainly they were for Dagny.

One cannot, of course, assume correlations between artists' theories and the conduct of their lives. Yet Stach made the notion of "woman" so central to his aesthetics, that he could not have viewed individual women free of the prejudices which to him were absolute truths. Ultimately, inevitably, he had to turn them against Dagny.

The irony is that the very myth-making process which gave Dagny such a remarkable identity in the world in the end took it from her.

In the first years of their relationship, Stach worshiped Dagny—at least in print—in near reverential ecstasy, attributing to her a godlike fire that burned in his soul. In a letter to her a month after they were married, Stach wrote:

> A nature such as mine, it resides only in you, because you happen to be my most absolute, highest and intimate ideal; you are what I am, only finer, more aristocratic. . . . In you and through you I am; I owe everything to you, without you I am nothing. You are my beginning and my end, my heavy lightning bolt, my cosmic fire and everything —everything. . . . I want it to be known that you have created me, and I want to possess you as I have never possessed you: your naked, trembling Soul, your most naked, trembling thoughts. . . .[14]

She was purifying soul and creative fire all in one.

But where the cosmic madonna loomed in Stach's imagination, the whore lurked as well. In a letter to Adolf Paul earlier that spring, when Stach and Dagny were falling in love, he wrote that he could not concern himself with her past affairs.

> People have slandered her in the meanest ways. . . . Much of it is true, and I know about all her earlier relationships. But what does that concern me?
>
> What does it matter to me that a picture that I love earlier hung on a dirty tavern wall?
>
> I couldn't even be jealous—because that which I love in her—that

which through her I've learned to love in myself, no one can take that from me, no one can dirty it or stain it.[15]

The troubling notion is, of course, that Dagny's relationships prior to Stach had made her potentially unclean. She was now kept immaculate by virtue of the love, in particular, the self-love, she inspired in him. Though he claimed that no one could "dirty" or "stain" that love, Dagny's pure state was obviously a function of Stach's own caprice.

When privately and publicly he turned his pen against Dagny in 1900–1901, he chose metaphors of defilement and infection to describe her. To Ragnhild he wrote: "How she has dirtied things, she has desecrated the child. . . ."[16] While Dagny was at Rolighed in the fall of that year waiting for word of Stach's plans, he was finishing his *roman à clef* about a woman who betrays her artist husband. He entitled the first part of *Sons of the Soil* "Malaria," which began appearing in installments in the journal *Chimera* just weeks before Dagny returned to him.[17] The woman of the novel is portrayed as an exotic disease infecting the creative genius of her artist-husband.

Stach had also written privately to Dagny, speaking of the past with her as "the poison of the plague." She responded in a letter to him sent to Lemberg: "Oh Stasiu, you speak about thoughts and memories that effect you like the poison of the plague! And I! What shall I say!!"[18] Adopting his own metaphor of disease, she wrote in a letter from the same time, telling him that she had read "Malaria":

> Yes, Stasiu, Stasiu, God in heaven knows I'm desperate! In the end I didn't know if I was coming or going. Now in these past days I too have read your novel in Chimera—I can read that much Polish—yes, you can imagine how I looked inside! My God! When Zenon had gone to sleep last night I sat motionless at the table, hour after hour, just whimpered softly like a sick animal, and felt that I could not live, that it would be corrupt of me to live longer.[19]

A set of Stach's comments on women, real or aesthetic, cannot possibly tell the story of the Przybyszewskis' complex relationship. But it can suggest an attitude toward women that, unchecked, would finally destroy the marriage and seriously wound the woman. As free as Dagny was, or as free as she felt when she came to Berlin, she would inevitably have been crippled by the sexual prejudice, if not the sexual hatred, that informed Stach's thinking.

There are persistent suggestions in memoirs from the time of the extreme forms his thinking took. Stories exist from both Berlin and Poland of his use of women as *objets d'art*. It was told, for example, that he offered Strindberg the key to his apartment on New Year's Eve, 1892, so that the master could enjoy Marta, the disciple's "finest possession." (Strindberg was said to have declined the gift.) Kossak included the account of an acquaintance of Stach from Kraków, who accompanied him home one very warm summer night. Dagny was asleep, he said, with only a sheet over her. Literally using her as his metaphor, Stach uncovered her to demonstrate that we must not fear lifting the veil that separates us from the truth. Kossak would have assumed that the story was concocted but for the fact that similar anecdotes occurred in several contemporary memoirs. She also included one concerning Stach's second wife, Jadwiga. Supposedly Stach told her to undress for someone, because she was a "work of art, and art does not know anything of shame."[20] If there are hints of passive violence against women in Stach's history, there are also hints of active violence. Boy-Żeleński believed that Stach eventually began to abuse Dagny physically and Wincent Brzozowski that Stach actually sold her to Władysław Emeryk.

There may be no truth to any of these tales. Like so much of the lore surrounding Dagny, they may be the result of prurient fantasy. But there is no doubt that they are the *possible* consequences of thinking like Stach's. If only symbolically, they are reminders of the emotional abuse which Dagny, as a woman, suffered in her relationship with Stach.

Disturbing questions arise. How long did Dagny live with Stach's hostility? If we are to believe her, a long time. In her letter about "Malaria," she wrote: "I know, of course, that you love me only from a distance, that when you see me and hear my voice, your heart will slowly be filled with the old hatred, that has found such brutal expression in your novel."[21]

Why did she remain with him? Partial answers suggest themselves. Dagny and Stach shared powerful bonds. They were passionately in love and committed to each other in the early years of their marriage. Together they enjoyed celebrity status as the renegade royalty of Europe's most avant-garde circles. Together they endured the tragedy of Marta Foerder, the ensuing isolation, and perennial poverty. Dagny's family embraced Stach as a son and sided with him when she tried to leave.

But there were even more powerful bonds. Dagny had a strong, charismatic personality and an intense longing to be free. Yet she had a correspondingly weakened sense of self, divided and vulnerable. The fragmented inner image—the crux of her writing—is as naked a self-portrait as she could have painted. Masked as it may often have been by her commanding presence, it revealed itself in her ambivalent attitude toward herself as a writer; in her relationships to her parents and her children, whom she repeatedly left and to whom she repeatedly returned; and in her love for Stach, which was at once so assertive and so self-annihilating.

In a unique sense Dagny could not have made a more perfect match than Stach. When she met him she was nearly twenty-six, looking for her calling and most likely herself. Stach wooed her with the fantasy that she was his creator. His adoration could only have inspired her with the feelings of wholeness so painfully absent from her poetry. His rebellious behavior must have promised exhilarating possibilities. At the same time, his erratic personality corresponded to her own inner extremes. Ecstatic and depressed, loving and indifferent, gregarious and solitary in turn, he could unconsciously serve as her internal mirror, a seductive, psychic twin. Her identity so tied to his, she would have found it very difficult to leave him.

Though she did try. Whether in the first instance she left for Wincent Brzozowski or because of Stach is ambiguous; certainly, however, she was attempting to extract herself from a desperate situation. Before she went to Paris in May and then home to Rolighed, she and Stach had apparently discussed divorce. He even initially rushed to Berlin in the belief that she had gone there to begin proceedings, supposedly to preempt her.[22] Divorce was not an unheard of course of action to take in 1900, particularly in Scandinavia. It would have been more of a scandal in Catholic Poland but, nevertheless, a possibility in the progressive circles in which the Przybyszewskis circulated.

What Dagny's family might have thought of divorce, even whether she discussed it with them, is not known; though we must suppose that they encouraged her to return to Stach. And Dagny's own desire to begin again with him must not be underestimated. She wrote to her mother in 1901: "I am endlessly happy to be back with Stachu again."[23]

In every aspect of the Przybyszewskis' relationship there were disturbing signs of Dagny's subservience to Stach. Yet the difficulty of interpreting any of her actions is crystallized in an anecdote from the Berlin years told by Meier-Graefe.

> She was intelligent and witty and ready for everything, but not for this circle's most beloved preoccupation. I would not wonder if the eternal sexual problem was not the reason why the marriage with Stachu came apart.
>
> Once we walked through Friedrichstrasse by night. It was cold, and the street was so slippery that we had to slide. As usual, Stachu expounded on his Physiology; spoke to me, but meant his wife. That was familiar to me. At that moment a train passed over the bridge. "The locomotive engineer," said Ducha, "is more interesting than all of you put together." She spoke to me but meant Stachu. Stachu attempted to employ the locomotive engineer for an erotic purpose. Ducha declared herself ready to stop there. He then, of course, really got going. She stood standing. "If you do not stop, then I will lie down on the street before you!" We laughed. Yet she lay already in the middle of the sidewalk.
>
> This was one of the occasions. Imagine the situation as crass as possible: the street, the people; and when you have all that, then let me tell you that at this very moment she lost nothing. She lay there as if poured. That is how her forbears lie in the church on the stone sarcophagus.
>
> Munch said reluctantly: "The Lady."[24]

Was Dagny's lying down in the street a signal of protest or provocation, defiance or surrender? Was she playing the rebel or the victim? In the same way we are left to wonder if her devotion to Stach—whether it took the form of caring for him after Marta's suicide, or leaving her children to travel with him through Europe, or going back to him in Poland—was an assertion of freedom or submission. The inevitable, if paradoxical conclusion is that each action was potentially both, for both impelled Dagny forward.

Finally, though, she was robbed of her freedom, deprived of her roles and even a stage on which to play. The extreme consequence of Stach's philosophy was to deny to women an identity of their own. This was the fate Dagny suffered, physically, emotionally, and socially, when she returned to him in 1901. Stach, her family, the times, and Dagny herself may have shared the blame that such a thing should come to pass. But Dagny was the sufferer. And as much as she was the archetypal modern woman of the myth, she was the archetypal victim of reality. Whether bourgeois or bohemian, the notion that a woman was an extension of a man was equally insidious, and it simply brought Dagny down.

This is not to say that she did not fight. She fought even as she acquiesced; and she fought with the grace and dignity so characteristic of her. Meier-Graefe had called her a "spiritual aristocrat." And truly, it is this image of her that rises from the ashes of her final tragedy.

Dagny herself is able to tell at least parts of the story. Her few surviving letters from that last winter-spring reveal a woman in great emotional pain, trying to hold her self and her world together by clinging to Stach and the roles she had always played vis-à-vis him. In the end Dagny was clinging to a void.

DAGNY

—yes, you can imagine how I looked inside!

The weather was extremely cold. Dagny, Stach, and Zenon moved into a room on Marszalkowska Street in the center of Warsaw. Stach soon left and was away for much of the spring, lecturing and preparing one of his plays for production in Lemberg. He was also seeing Jadwiga Kasprowicz and Aniela Pająkówna, both of whom lived in Lemberg. He did not communicate with Dagny for long periods of time and gave her no indication of when he would return. She was depressed, ill, and confused. There were once again rumors of the presence of admirers, including Wincent Brzozowski's brother, Stanisław. Dagny's letters suggest, however, that her world centered on Stach, particularly in his absence.[25] All her energies were devoted to appeasing him.

She entreated him to return:

And then Stachu come back to Warsaw soon! You are absolutely needed here!

It is infinitely sad and gloomy here! And it is snowing and terribly cold! Sad, too sad! And why do you never write when you will return?

Write often: it comforts me! And come back soon. . . .

And Stasiutulek, come soon! I long for you!

She felt imprisoned in her one room,[26] longing for space in which she could work and find peace of mind.

What shall I do about a place to live? How many rooms do you want? . . . I am so terribly tired of not having a permanent place. Don't you understand that? Dearest, dearest write a little about all of this, I would be so grateful to you!

And the gods only know when you'll finally come back here someday. You have no idea how I long to put things in order, to settle down! To be able to play, read, write! It's completely impossible here! The whole pension is now full and we have to stay in our room. Oh God, if you'd only come back soon, Stachu! I long for you.

She was separated from Iwa and both she and Zenon were in poor health.

I am terribly nervous and neither Zenon nor I am really well yet. Zenon always has something new, earaches, stomachaches, tooth-aches, never really first class, and he wonders why you don't write, he thinks you're in Warsaw.

Stach had written that he was ill himself. She wanted to believe him, but she had suspicions. She was cautious and indirect.

Stasiu, dearest! how frightful about your illness! And that you should just at that time be in Lemberg among strangers! [She added a postscript:] Where have you seen Ivi since you have been so sick the whole time?

In another letter, she wrote:

. . . I'm so happy you're well again and that your illness was the reason for your not writing. . . . !

But she feared that there were other reasons.

I opened the enclosed letter out of curiosity, I recognized the hand-writing and knew that it wasn't dangerous.

She treaded gingerly, but she knew Stach was lying to her.

> The theater director . . . says that he never visited you, so that the stories you have told me are again rather incomprehensible.[27]

Dagny was on treacherous ground. Everything depended on Stach, and he provided her with nothing, not a place to live and work, not a relationship, not the truth. He was sending her messages, both privately and publicly, that she had become his infectious demon; but he alternated with words of affection, it would seem indiscriminately. In the same letter about being sick at heart over "Malaria," Dagny wrote to him:

> And today, when I got your letter, your very warm letter, full of tenderness and sounding so honest, I thought again that life might be possible, that life could bring good days and maybe even a little happiness, but I'm afraid of my incurable optimism . . .

Dagny was kept as if on quicksand, off-guard and vulnerable. She did not seem to know whether to fear her naiveté or her wisdom.

Dagny showed no anger toward Stach, only deep hurt which she turned against herself. She even attempted to demonstrate to him, in the meekest possible ways, that she was innocent and still worth loving, if only by another.

> The little Swedish violinist is so sweet and so delighted with me. She is completely a child, open and natural, truly a fine, wise, naive and loving little lass. . . . Believe me, she is a very sympathetic little artist-child—23 years old.[28]

And that she was true to him:

> I see no one besides *Władysława* and *Krzyżanowski* . . .

Władysława Tomaszewska was an older friend who, after Dagny's death, would travel to Tiflis to bring Zenon out of Russia.[29] Konrad Krzyżanowski was an artist who painted Dagny's portrait that last spring. He seemed to capture, in horrific fashion, her own dark mood.[30]

The deference Dagny had always shown to Stach as the artist surfaced now as pathological self-denial. Strength came into her voice only when she was discussing his career. She wrote the long, resolute letter trying

Konrad Krzyżanowski's portrait of Dagny, Warsaw, spring 1901.

to convince him to change publishers, because she believed he was being swindled by his present one. She was grateful for any news of Stach's works, still as involved as she had always been in their fates. "Your play still at the censors! but good Lord! When is it going to be performed then? Thank you for sending me the German review! It was so fun to read!"

Dagny was also actively involved in promoting Munch's works that spring. She revealed vitality in making her plans for Munch, as for Stach, but kept near total silence about her deprived circumstances. She showed more sympathy for Munch's problems than for her own. "Live well! I'll write soon again. I am so sorry that you are so sick, good Lord, illness is worse than having no money."

She stressed Stach's success, as if it were a sign that their world was not collapsing and that things were as before. In retrospect it is apparent that Stach's career was actually on the wane. Dagny did not seem to know. "Stachu has written several new, strong things, but in Polish, dramas, I think they are magnificent. In a while I'll send you the last book by him in German verse."

Dagny was a woman literally without a room of her own. She no longer had the physical space, much less a productive environment, in which to work at the things that she loved and which gave her personal definition. She could not play the piano. She could not write. She could not read. She did not even have the silence she so cherished.

But if Dagny's ability to think and create was diminished, so too were her powers vis-à-vis her children and, crucially for her, her husband. None of the roles she had played in her relationship to Stach, and through which she might now begin to assert herself once again, any longer existed, for Stach had drawn away. She was not really his wife or his companion. From his muse he had made her his evil spirit. She was trying still to function as his advisor and agent, but he seemed either to be lying to her or ignoring her.

Kossak noted that that spring she had begun to take courses in Scandinavian literature at the University of Warsaw.[31] This may have been the one way she had of keeping intellectually and emotionally connected to something she knew.

Paradoxically, the only company she had in her pain was Stach. In her letters she vacillated quite helplessly between her hurt and her longing for him to return. In nearly the same breath she sighed over how sick his words had made her feel and how comforting his letters were to her. She juxtaposed trivialities and despair. As if a physical manifestation of her uncertainty, she in one letter switched back and forth between Norwegian and German, as she would in her very last letter to him from Tiflis. Though Stach was destructive to her, he must have seemed to be her only organizing principle, both in an external and an internal sense. Holding on to him, or an image of him, was a way of holding herself together.

For she could not rely on her own image—"You can imagine how I looked inside!" She felt it would be literally "swinish" of her to go on living, interpreting Stach's acrimony as her sin. Yet if she herself felt corrupt, she spoke with a voice verging on innocence in these letters.

Meier-Graefe had written that Stach's verbal ironies were powerless over her, "because she did not defend herself."[32] Her defenselessness may very well have been the invisible seat of her power, giving to her actions, as to these letters, a kind of extraordinary, very personal moral independence, like a pacifist's in the face of violence.

Who is to say whether that invisible spirit might have saved her, had Emeryk not shot her? For if Dagny was weak, she was also strong.

Leaving for Tiflis may have been her boldest or her most helpless course of action. She had written to her mother on the way to Russian Georgia, promising that all was well. Her mother was unconvinced: "Your welfare in all ways is so eternally dear to my heart, I am also so worried about you, how you are, you and your precious children and husband. Your letter from the trip did not set my mind at ease at all, that you're leaving Warsaw now, even before Stachu can be with you, but I'll learn later why you now have decided to leave."[33]

No one, however, would learn of the exact circumstances. According to Ragnhild in a letter to Helge written in late June 1901: "Stachu says that she left him against his will, but that judging from everything she was coming back to Warsaw." Kossak wrote that "all the witnesses from the time agree that Stach as well as Dagny intended to travel to the Caucuses."[34]

Dagny's and Stach's friend, Lucyna Kotarbińska, believed it, too. She wrote that "there was no choice. Przybyszewski was going to go to Lemberg probably in order to resolve commitments unnecessarily imposed upon him, because in my mind he loved only Dagny. Thus she was going to leave before him with Emeryk and her son, Zenon. Przybyszewski was going to follow shortly thereafter."[35] The imposed commitments to which Kotarbińska was referring were to Jadwiga Kasprowicz. Kossak quoted Stach as saying long afterward to a friend that the trip to the Caucuses was seen as "a way out for both parties. Dagny would be saved from Brzozowski and Przybyszewski himself from Jadwiga."[36] None of these statements is trustworthy, whether Stach's or Kotarbińska's. Kossak herself cast some doubt on Stach's intentions ever to follow and warily allowed for the possibility that he facilitated Dagny's departure to have her out of the way.

Macabre rumors were rampant: Stach sold Dagny to Emeryk and sent him on a death mission; several of Dagny's friends and admirers, including Emeryk, made a pact to put her out of her misery. The ever-present desire to sensationalize Dagny's life was certainly at play and has been ever since. Even Kossak could not avoid it. She wrote, for example, that Stanisław Brzozowski poisoned himself on April 29, 1901, one in a chain of suicides linked to Przybyszewski's decadent circle: "One mentions Dagny's name."

Some of the residents of the pension in Warsaw informed Dagny of Brzozowski's death.

"Ja, er hat das getan," she said resignedly. (Yes, he has done it.) It seemed that she had already earlier suspected his intentions. . . .

The debts the dead man left after him were paid by Władysław Emeryk. It is difficult to say if it was because he was the only one in the circle of friends who had the means or if some kind of earlier agreement had been made between them. Brzozowski had left his revolver to Emeryk. In light of what later happened, this came to be interpreted as a sign or a signal from the other side of the grave, particularly since Stanisław Brzozowski was known for his attraction to spiritism.

The burial took place one of the last days Dagny was still to be seen in Warsaw. The recent happenings had left deep physical and psychological traces. She was seen a few more times at restaurants and lectures. Her fading beauty was admired by those listening to Przybyszewski's lecture on the poet Kasprowicz [Jadwiga's husband] on May 2. Dagny seemed then completely in control, though she was surely bothered by the sensation-seekers, as well as occasional hostile glances. . . .

Two days after Przybyszewski's lecture Dagny said a sorrowful good-by. It was May 4. For those who followed Dagny to the train, it seemed like attending yet another funeral.[37]

Such is the insidious stuff of rumor that plagued Dagny throughout the years of her public life. The fact is that she had left Warsaw days before any of these events took place. On the day of her departure, April 26, 1901, she wrote Ragnhild, "Beloved! Next station Tiflis!"; and on April 28 from Kiev, "Will write a letter from Rostoff on the Asiatic Sea!"

In leaving was Dagny heeding or defying Stach's wishes? Was she surrendering even more of herself or was she asserting herself? Was she trying to save her marriage or end it? To have remained in a deteriorating relationship and such disabling circumstances would seem to have been the more suicidal choice. But then why did she not go home one last time? There was something undeniably and troublingly careless in the way she left. Emeryk was young, in his early twenties, and unstable. Iwa was being cared for by another woman. And Dagny and Zenon were without passports through thousands of miles of foreign country. In both a metaphorical and a real sense she left her identity in the hands of Stach, and the fact simply was that he was willing to put her at risk. Stach's failure to send her passport confirmed what had begun to happen to her on all levels of her life, i.e., a loss of identity to a man who wished her ill. One can read the shock of recognition in her last letter to him written shortly before she died. She wrote in German, save for the last few lines in Norwegian:

> I'm about to lose my mind. Not a word since a month ago. I have telegraphed to Kraków, to Lemberg, to Warsaw. No answer. Fine.
>
> Tomorrow we're leaving Tiflis and going to Emeryk's partner in the country near the Black Sea.
>
> I can't decide anything as long as I've not gotten an answer from you. My address is still the same, *Grand Hotel, Tiflis.*
>
> *Very important!*
>
> You must absolutely send my and Zenon's passport right away. Otherwise I can have a lot of difficulty.
>
> You promised me to send a passport already the following day!
>
> I beg you: send it right away.

Emeryk embraces you many, many times! I am dumbfounded, completely dumbfounded.

Zenon kisses you.

Dagny[38]

Stach had led Dagny's family to believe that she was desperate for her passport because she had grown frightened of Emeryk. Ragnhild wrote to Helge: "The same day it happened Dagny telegraphed Stachu, 'Send passport immediately,' so she had probably become afraid of [Emeryk] and wanted to leave rather than be alone with him."[39] Dagny's letter suggests, however, that the person she had actually grown frightened of was Stach. She had obviously written to him about the future, and he had failed to respond. She had been wiring for her and Zenon's passports for at least a month and again he failed to respond. For the first time Dagny seemed to get angry. For the first time she seemed to realize that Stach might really mean her harm. Though she still acted as the conduit for others' love to Stach, she did not send her own. She could not believe what was happening. "I am dumbfounded," she wrote, "completely dumbfounded." Possibly this could have been a beginning.

According to Ragnhild, "she was found fully dressed on a chaise longue at 1:00 after just having eaten lunch, when he, in all likelihood, had given her some sleeping potion in her wine, for he had planned the murder for a long time."[40]

Emeryk wrote six letters concerning his plan to take Dagny's life. He sealed them and left them for the police to find, asking them to deliver the other five unopened to the addressees. Already on May 29 he had composed one to a friend in Tiflis, Antoni Keller, asking him to make the funeral arrangements.

No one, absolutely no one must see her. Don't let any curiosity-seekers in. Mme Przybyszewska must have the best burial, in a word, a fine casket, a faultless catafalque, a good place in the cemetery. In time she should have some kind of monument. See to it that the grave lies in a place where it will be easy to put up a gravestone (Mme Przybyszewska is Christian, her first name is Dagny). My remains anyone can have. Bury me where you want and how you want. If it is possible, I ask you to see that no autopsy is performed on Mme Przybyszewska. There will not be any doubt that I killed her, an autopsy is therefore unnecessary. Cover Mme Przybyszewska and her entire casket with fresh flowers, preferably roses.[41]

Emeryk seems to have suffered a mental breakdown in the wake of impending bankruptcy. Shortly after Dagny's and his arrival in Tiflis he had written to a friend for financial help.

> My future prospects are not bad, I will soon be independent and rich. . . . Oh, it would be terrible if I didn't manage, terrible if I had to go under because I didn't reach the goal I've been working toward for a whole year. I therefore turn to you with my prayer. I'm ready to fall on my knees to you. Save me. [May 20][42]

Dagny became the victim of Emeryk's personal crisis. It is unlikely that she knew how dangerous he had become. His letters about the impending murder suggest he maintained a very controlled, concerned presence. Kossak commented, "There is an enormous contrast between the horror of the planned crime and the impression of touching goodness, sensitivity, even humility in Emeryk's letters."[43] He gave his thoughtful instructions for Dagny's burial, as well as for Zenon's care, even to details about his health and diet. He informed the police that he himself was in his right mind, and he made his sincere apologies to Stach and Zenon. But he maintained that he was doing it for Dagny's own good.

It is when he spoke of Dagny that the insanity of his obsession revealed itself. To Zenon he wrote:

> She was not of this world, she was far too ethereal for anyone to understand her true nature. . . . That she was an incarnation of the absolute, that she was God, you will learn from others. I only want to tell you that she, to put it in an earthly way, was a saint. She was goodness itself, the kind of goodness that is called regal, and that arises from contempt. You alone meant anything to her. She, the first and only queen, bowed humbly down to you. She believed that she had come to the world only so that you might be born.[44]

And to Stach:

> What can I say? Not much. I have done what you should have done. She knew everything. First she wanted it, then the mother in her got the upper hand. She loves Zenon far too much. I'll have to postpone

the whole thing and kill her at a moment when she least expects it. She wanted to write to you, that she knows I am going to kill her; that she sees it as the only way out, that it had to happen. She wanted to write that she loves you and always will love you. Because her whole life she has never loved anyone but you.

You must know that I look up to you, I adore you, love you. Still I know that you curse me, and that is my great desperation.

Stach. I'm killing her for her own sake.

Oh, if you could refrain from damning me.[45]

Whether Emeryk ever really spoke to Dagny of death by his hand is another of the unknowns of her life. Ragnhild wrote to Helge: "[Stachu] is in despair, but says that for her death was the greatest happiness, and then we must try to see it that way too."[46] This would have meant that Dagny had completely resigned herself. Why then would she wire for her passport? Why would she vent her anger at Stach?

Dagny was not killed by a jealous lover. She was killed by an obsession about "woman" that was the logical tragic consequence of a philosophy such as Stach's. This is not to lay the immediate blame at his feet. His role remains ambiguous. But his ideas did dominate the particular bohemian circles in which Dagny lived; and his ideas were representative, if in the extreme, of attitudes in the times.

Dagny was killed because she was seen to be a goddess, or a demon, a metaphysical absolute, not a woman, not a human being. In the name of her life being worth so much, a crime was committed demonstrating that her life was worth nothing at all. "I have done what you should have done," Emeryk wrote to Stach. One surmises that he believed that Stach in essence already had delivered her her death blow by abandoning her. She was seen as the world's queen, the son's vehicle, the man's tragic victim. She was denied identity, individuality, indeed life, killed "for her own sake" by a world view whose real obsession was still "the man." "You must know that I look up to you, I adore you, love you," Emeryk wrote to Stach. "Oh, if you could refrain from damning me."

Dagny Juel Przybyszewska's life bears out and refutes at one and the same time the powerful myth of the magic, mobile, transcending woman, who functioned "as a shaping principle, not only of fictions but of lives."[47]

Unique woman that she was, Dagny made people think for a moment that they were looking into the future. She *was* the "shaping principle" of her own grand myth, and she became a "shaping principle" for others, symbolizing a myriad of unimaginable possibilities. The myth itself was made up of many faces, projections of the people who wished it into being. Like Stach, some saw madonnas and vampires, others saw wood nymphs, biblical apparitions, creatures of the wild, and transcending dancers. But no one face ever stood for the whole, for no one face could ever describe Dagny. Because of her the myth was more than the sum of its many, often contrasting parts. Because of her the clichés *were* transformed into something radical, new, and indivisible.

Dagny was at the heart of the myth. She brought to it her intelligence, her dignity, her yen for freedom, and her grace. She brought her many contradictions: her quiescence and her vitality, her despair and her optimism, her spirituality and her physicality, her independence and her will to submit, her inner fragmentation and her outer presence. Within herself she contained every possibility. Defenseless and silent, she could suggest them all, depending on what others yearned to see.

But her story was in the end one of possibilities tragically unfulfilled. The myth failed to translate into real life. Dagny herself became a victim of the very process of this myth-making that made of her everything but human and individual.

CHRONOLOGY

1867 Dagny was born on June 8 in Kongsvinger, Norway.

1888 From the fall through the spring she served as governess to the children of Randi and Otto Blehr, her aunt and uncle, in the small, west coast Norwegian town of Førde.

1892 In February-March she went to Berlin for a short stay, probably to study music.

1893 In early February she went again to Berlin, to study music at Holländers Conservatory. Shortly thereafter she went to *Zum schwarzen Ferkel* and made her historical impact. She met Stanisław Przybyszewski, to whom she was engaged when she returned to Norway that summer. They were married in Berlin on August 18. Dagny wrote her first known work of fiction, "Rediviva," in December.

1894 That spring she went to Rolighed,

her parents' home in Norway. Stach followed and they lived at Rolighed—with trips to Christiania and the environs—through the summer. In the fall they returned to Berlin, living in an apartment in Louisenstrasse 6.

1895 Dagny became pregnant and returned to Rolighed in April. Stach followed in May. They stayed for over half a year. Dagny's Norwegian translation of Stach's *Unterwegs/Underveis* was published in Christiania and Copenhagen and her German translation of Sigbjørn Obstfelder's "Liv" in the third issue of *Pan*. Zenon was born on September 28. In late December Dagny and Stach went to Stockholm and then on to Copenhagen.

1896 In January Dagny submitted her play *The Stronger* to the Christiania Theater. In February, for lack of money, she returned to Rolighed and Stach went on to Berlin. In May Dagny and Stach were reunited in Copenhagen. On June 6, Marta Foerder committed suicide, and the Przybyszewskis went immediately to Berlin. Stach was held in jail for two weeks. Their friends abandoned them. Dagny held their lives together through the summer and fall. *The Stronger* was published in *Samtiden*. In December they moved to a cheaper apartment in Nieder Schönhausen on the outskirts of Berlin. They were impoverished and Dagny suffered from fatigue and malnutrition. She was also probably writing the lyric cycle, *Poems*, throughout the fall and winter of 1896–97.

1897   Dagny became pregnant with Iwa and returned to Rolighed in March. Stach followed in May. Dagny was probably working on her plays *Ravenwood*, *The Sin*, and *When the Sun Goes Down*. In July Stach returned to Berlin. Dagny went through an extended pregnancy of ten months, giving birth to Iwa on October 5. Dagny almost died. In December Stach wrote to his Czech publisher, Arnošt Procházka, about publishing Dagny's plays. Dagny joined Stach in Berlin, leaving her children at Rolighed.

1898   In January Dagny and Stach traveled first to Paris and then on to Spain, to the small town of Playa del Mera. Dagny may have been writing her prose poems, *Sing mir das Lied vom Leben und vom Tode*, at this time. In April they returned to Paris. In May Dagny learned that *The Sin* was to be performed in Prague. (It finally received only a reading at Intimní Volné Jeviště.) In June, first Dagny and then Stach returned to Rolighed where her father had grown seriously ill and was operated on that summer. In September Stach left Kongsvinger for Kraków to take over the editorship of *Życie*, the journal of the Young Poland movement. Dagny and the children followed later in the fall. The Przybyszewskis moved into a house on Karmelicka Street. They became the central figures of the *Paon* bohemia. Dagny's *The Sin* was published in Czech translation in *Moderní Revue*.

1899   Dagny's father died in January. In June Stach began affairs with two women in Lemberg. Dagny spent most of the summer with the children in the mountain resort town of Zakopane. Dagny's *The Sin*, *When the Sun Goes Down*, and *Sing mir das Lied vom Leben und vom Tode* were published in *Życie* in Stach's translations.

1900   In January Dagny left Stach, initially with Wincent Brzozowski, and traveled to Lemberg, Kraków, Prague, back to Kraków and then to Paris. In May Dagny went home to Rolighed, where Zenon was staying with her mother. Iwa was in Poland. *Sing mir das Lied vom Leben und vom Tode* was published in *Samtiden*. Dagny waited for word from Stach.

1901 In February Dagny, Zenon, and Stach were reunited in Berlin and then went on to Kraków and finally Warsaw, where they moved into one room in a pension on Marszalkowska Street. Stach was away for much of the spring. In late April Dagny, Zenon, and Władysław Emeryk left for Tiflis in Russian Georgia. They arrived at the Grand Hotel in mid-May. On June 5 Emeryk shot Dagny and then himself. Dagny was buried in Tiflis on June 8, her thirty-fourth birthday.

Notes

INTRODUCTION

1. Lucyna Kotarbińska, *Wokoło teatru* (Around the theater) (Warsaw: F. Hoesick, 1930), pp. 348–49. Lucyna Kotarbińska was married to the director of the Kraków Theater, where a number of Stach Przybyszewski's plays were performed. She and her husband were friends of the Przybyszewskis. They asked her to be their daughter's godmother when Iwa was baptized in 1899. *Wokoło teatru* includes a chapter on Dagny and Stach. Polish translations by Roma King, unless otherwise indicated.

2. Gina Krog, "Hos Gina Krog. Frøkenen udtaler sig om Situationen," *Kristiania Dagsavis*, 27 June 1901, p. 1.

3. Nina Auerbach, *Woman and the Demon* (Cambridge and London: Harvard University Press, 1982), p. 1.

4. Maya Vogt, sister of the Norwegian poet Nils Collett Vogt, was a friend of Dagny both early in Christiania and later in Berlin. The letter, undated, is in Ragnhild Juell Bäckström's correspondence, now in the possession of Dr. Lennart Hellström in Stockholm; hereafter cited as Bäckström correspondence.

5. This was told to me by various members of the Juell family in personal interviews in the summer, 1985.

6. Personal interview with Jadwiga P. Westrup, summer, 1985.

7. Kotarbińska, pp. 344, 345.

8. Erik Vendelfelt, *Den unge Bengt Lidforss: En biografisk studie med särskild hänsyn til hans litterära utveckling* (Lund: Gleerup, 1962); Sonja Hagemann, "Dagny Juel Przybyszewska: Genienes inspiratrise," *Samtiden* 72 (1963), pp. 655–68.

9. Professor Ole Michael Selberg discovered three of Dagny's plays in the possession of her daughter, Iwa Dahlin. He received permission to publish them in *Synden*

og to andre skuespill av Dagny Juell in 1978. Martin Nag had earlier found a cycle of lyric poems, *Digte*, also in Iwa Dahlin's possession, and published them in 1975. He discovered a short story, "Rediviva," in the Munch Museum in Oslo, and published it in 1977. Nag has written numerous articles about Dagny and become something of a champion on her behalf. His enthusiasm has been a double-edged sword, however, for he has idealized her in ways she could not survive.

10. Ewa K. Kossak, *Dagny Przybyszewska: Zbłąkana gwiazda* (Warsaw: Państwowy Instytut Wydawniczy, 1973; enlarged edition, 1975); Swedish translation, *Irrande stjärna: Berättelsen om den legendariska Dagny Juel*, trans. Christina Wollin (Stockholm: Bonniers, 1978). I have worked primarily with the Swedish translation, but I have had my Polish translator compare the two and consult the original on significant points. References here are to the Swedish translation.

11. When I visited the Jan Kasprowicz Museum in Inowrocław, Poland, I was surprised to find two portraits of Dagny and a small sculpture of Dagny and Stach which I had not seen before. The director told me that they were all done in a 1977 competition for the best artistic reproduction of Dagny and Stach on the fiftieth anniversary of his death. The museum, located in eastern Poland (in the vicinity of Poznań) where Przybyszewski was born, is devoted to memorabilia relating to him and to his fellow poet Jan Kasprowicz. It is both apt and ironic that they should share the museum. Kasprowicz's wife, Jadwiga, left her husband for Stach even while Dagny was alive. Jadwiga and Stach married soon after Dagny's death.

12. Kossak, for example, often relied on contemporary literature, such as the plays of Ibsen, to explain or justify Dagny's behavior, when there was no connection at all. However, in the course of my research, when I have been able to document a particular event more fully, I have often been delighted by the accuracy of Kossak's intuition.

On the other hand, though Kossak does not read Norwegian and was not aware of the existence of all of Dagny's works, she did know the plays and the prose poems in Polish translation. Yet she did not deem them intrinsically valuable.

13. Elisabeth Aasen, *Kvinners spor i skrift* (Oslo: Det Norske Samlaget, 1986); *Norsk kvinnelitteraturhistorie: Bind 1, 1600–1900*, ed. Irene Engelstad, Jorunn Hareide, Irene Iversen, Torill Steinfeld, Janneken Øverland (Oslo: Pax Forlag, 1988). I was invited to write the last chapter, "Eros og ære" (Eros and honor), about the drama at the turn of the century. Dagny is central to my discussion.

14. The Kongsvinger Museum in Kongsvinger, Norway, Dagny's birthplace, has recently begun to collect material on Dagny. Under the direction of Kari Jacobsen, the museum held a week-long reassessment seminar on Dagny in August 1987. The Juell home, Rolighed, has also been saved from demolition by Jacobsen and others and may be designated as a women's museum.

15. At the time I began my research I knew of a small collection of letters in Universitetsbiblioteket in Oslo and several letters quoted by Kossak, which I found to be in private hands in Poland. Though Dagny's mother had insisted that all correspondence relating to her daughter be destroyed, I discovered that some had been saved. In Riksarkivet in Oslo I found letters from Dagny, as well as other members of her family, to

Randi and Otto Blehr, her maternal uncle and Norwegian prime minister to the king of Sweden-Norway from 1891 to 1905. Dagny's daughter, Iwa Dahlin, gave me access to letters Dagny had written to her mother and her youngest sister, Ragnhild Juell Bäckström. In turn, Ragnhild's grandson, Dr. Lennart Hellström, allowed me to read a large collection of Ragnhild's correspondence that her husband, Helge Bäckström, had saved. Ewa Kossak said that Dagny left her own correspondence in Poland to a friend from Kraków, Ludwik Janikowski (p. 171). It has disappeared. Kossak believes that it was destroyed during WWII. I have also used Stach Przybyszewski's letters as they appear in *Stanisław Przybyszewski: Listy*, vol. 1, ed. Stanisław Helstyński (Warsaw: "Parnas Polski," 1937). The letters in volume 1 cover the period up to 1906. The difficulty with the Przybyszewski letters is that Stach was a pathological liar and thus never to be relied upon.

16. A collection of books which Dagny had with her in Poland is located in the Jan Kasprowicz Museum in Inowrocław. The director of the museum, Janina Sikorska, found the books at an auction in Warsaw. Dagny wrote her name in any number of them. Up until 1889 she signed them Dagny Juell. In 1890 she wrote both Juell and Juel, and by 1891 only Juel. She did, however, sign her marriage certificate "Juell." The feminine ending in Polish is "a": Przybyszewska.

17. I made a similar decision to refer to her husband and the members of her immediate family by their first names, since they were closest to her. Przybyszewski was normally called Stachu, the nickname used by his family and friends. I refer to him as Stach, which is the shortened form used in the literature about him in Poland.

18. The first part of the quote is from an undated letter, the second part from a following letter dated 3 December [1901] in the Bäckström correspondence. I have not been able to locate the photograph.

CHAPTER 1

1. Julius Meier-Graefe, "Geschicten neben der Kunst: Ducha," *Berliner Tageblatt*, 7 March 1930. Translated by Thomas Haeussler.

2. The most extensive discussion of *Zum schwarzen Ferkel* bohemia is an unpublished dissertation by Carla Lathe, "The Group Zum schwarzen Ferkel: A Study in Early Modernism," The University of East Anglia, 1972. It is a fascinating study. Lathe's bibliography alone is invaluable to anyone interested in the period.

3. Arne Eggum, *Edvard Munch* (Oslo: Stenersens, 1983), p. 93.

4. Julius Hart, "Aus Przybyszewskis Sturm- und Drangjahren," *Pologne Littéraire*, no. 2 (1928), p. 2. Carla Lathe gives the full quote: "Wie ein Meteor leuchtete Stanisław Przybyszewski—unser Stachu!—einige Zeit lang auch über den Himmel unserer deutschen Literatur dahin" (p. 41).

5. Adolf Paul, *Min Strindbergsbok* (Stockholm: Norstedt, 1930), p. 54.

6. Dehmel's entire poem, entitled "En evig" ("An eternal"), is quoted—in Swedish—by Adolf Paul in *Min Strindbergsbok*, pp. 78–79. Edvard Munch also recorded the event

in an unpublished literary fragment dedicated to Strindberg, in Munch's unpublished papers, OKK N 25, in the Munch Museum, Oslo.

7. The other women mentioned in connection with the *Ferkel* circle were, in particular, the Norwegian painter Oda Krohg, the Finnish actress Gabrielle Tavastjerna, and the Norwegian Sigrid Lund.

8. Meier-Graefe, "Geschicten neben der Kunst," 7 March 1930.

9. Paul, a Finnish writer, was considered a lacky of Strindberg by the members of the circle. His book is entertaining but unreliable; Frida Strindberg, *Strindberg och hans andra Hustru* (Stockholm: Bonniers, 1933); Polo Gauguin, *Edvard Munch* (Oslo: Aschehoug, 1933); Olof Lagercrantz, *August Strindberg* (Stockholm: Wahlström & Widstrand, 1979); Reidar Dittman, *Eros and Psyche: Strindberg and Munch in the 1890s* (Ann Arbor: UMI Research Press, 1982); Per Olof Enquist, *Strindberg: Ett liv* (Stockholm: Norstedt, 1984); *Northern Light: Nordic Art at the Turn of the Century*, ed. and with an intro. by Kirk Varnedoe (New Haven: Yale University Press, 1988).

10. Arne Brenna, "Edvard Munch og Dagny Juell," *Samtiden* 87 (1978), pp. 51–64, in response to Knut Heber, "Kunst og Kultur," no. 1 (1977), pp. 1–18.

11. The story that Dagny and Munch were childhood friends seems to have gained validity in people's minds from the belief that Dagny's and Munch's fathers were doctors in the Hedmark area at the same time. Brenna showed, however, that Dr. Juell began his practice in Kongsvinger in 1863 and that the Munchs left Hamar for Christiania in 1864 (when Munch was one year old and Dagny not yet born). Brenna also pointed to the fact that Dr. Juell wrote Munch a letter in 1895 from which it is clear that the two men had never met. Dr. Juell referred to himself as, "a man who is a perfect stranger to you. . . ."

12. Munch kept notebooks throughout his life, some of them literary, some of them not. He wrote profusely about his various relationships, often using pseudonyms. He referred to his primary love interest of the early 1890s, Milly Thaulow, as Fru Heiberg. Munch's notebooks are voluminous and still not fully catalogued. They are in the archives of the Munch Museum.

13. Brenna, p. 55. Also in 1978, Ragna Stang published her book, *Edvard Munch: Mennesket og kunstneren* (Oslo: Aschehoug). In a long footnote, she exposed some of the same erroneous assumptions as did Brenna (p. 296), but she clung to certain others.

14. Sigrid Lund appears in a number of accounts from the time, including Adolf Paul's and the Pole, Alfred Wysocki's, as Sigrid L. Carla Lathe learned from Torsten Eklund, editor of Strindberg's letters, that the L. stood for Lund (Lathe, p. 47). Sigrid lived in the same pension as Strindberg and Paul, who described her as "a young and beautiful Norwegian, dark-eyed and with locks black as the night" (Paul, p. 57). According to *Ferkel* lore, Sigrid was enamored with Munch and Strindberg with Sigrid. Accounts of the jealousies Sigrid was to have aroused (see Paul, pp. 57–58) have also been attributed to Dagny (for example, in Swedish Television's *Strindberg* from 1985). What is known is that both Dagny and Sigrid studied piano in Berlin, and Dagny considered Sigrid a close friend. In his memoirs, Wysocki mentions that Dagny said to him in Kraków in December 1898: "It is so difficult for me to get used to my new

surroundings. In Berlin I had Sigrid, Maya [Vogt]—Here I have no one I am close to" (quoted from Kossak, p. 175).

15. Dagny's original letters to Munch are in Universitetsbiblioteket in Oslo. They were first published in *Edvard Munchs brev: Familien,* ed. Inger Munch (Oslo: Johan Grundt Tanum, 1949). They were incorrectly dated by Inger Munch.

16. *Klostret* takes its primary inspiration not from the *Schwarze Ferkel* but from Strindberg's engagement and marriage to Frida Uhl. Strindberg wrote *Klostret* in 1898, but it was never published in its original form in his lifetime. He intended to write a second part but never did.

In 1901 Strindberg revised *Klostret* and published it under the title *Karantänmästarns andra berättelse* in a volume of poems and stories entitled *Fagervik och Skamsund/Fair Haven and Foul Strand.* In 1965 C. G. Bjürström published a French translation of the original manuscript, and in 1966 Bonniers published the original Swedish manuscript. An English translation was published in 1969 as *The Cloister,* trans. Mary Sandbach (New York: Hill and Wang). It is to Mary Sandbach's commentary that I owe the above information. She said that Bjürström thought that the reason the original novel had not been translated in Strindberg's lifetime "may have been due to its 'blatantly auto-biographical character, involving as it did not only Strindberg and his second wife, Frida Uhl, but also the whole of the group from *Zum schwarzen Ferkel* '" (p. 147). Sandbach herself considered its greatest merit to lie in its historical authenticity! In the first place, only the few first pages concern themselves with the *Ferkel* circle. More importantly, however, Strindberg's most recent biographer, Olof Lagercrantz, in his book *August Strindberg* (1979), has demonstrated that Strindberg's so-called autobiographical fiction is a myth. I use Lagercrantz's argument in my ensuing discussion of Dagny's relationship to Strindberg.

17. I have read painstakingly through Munch's notebooks and found only one clear reference to Dagny. It is contained in "Litterære opptegnelser," registered "T.nr.2759," a black notebook kept by Munch probably in 1902–3 at the time he was recovering from a breakdown triggered by his troubled relationship with Tulla Larson. His notes at times appear to be literary ravings. He wrote, using Fru D. for Dagny, Fru L. for Tulla:

"He lay for three days then he could not lie [any longer]—he stood on his head in bed. Then he said—I do not understand this—then death.

Then he shot up—Fru D. dead—Shot in Tiflis by a lover. —Fru D. whom he had accompanied to the ship when he met Fru L. —Whom he had envied with her children. . . ."

Shortly thereafter he imagines a woman coming to him. He is startled. He thought it was Fru L., but it was Fru D. She was acting as an intermediary, trying to get him to return to Fru L. "I come from her—Come to her . . . She loves you so." He says it has been hell, he can no longer endure it, and Fru D. leaves.

The passage seems to be a rendering of a hallucination having to do with fears of death and whatever anxieties Munch's relationship to Tulla Larson brought on. The Fru D. character appears to be an emissary of both death and reconciliation, but without a context in which to interpret this, little more can be made of it. I do think it is extremely significant that Munch does not in these notebooks use Dagny as a character onto whom he projects his internal demons, as he obviously does with, among others, Milly Thaulow and Tulla Larson. It is further proof, I think, of the friendship and trust that existed between Dagny and Munch. His first reference to Dagny as a woman whom he envied, a woman with her children, suggests a longing for something that does not have anything to do with passion.

18. "Edvard Munch fortæller om Fru Przybyzewski (sic)," *Kristiania Dagsavis*, 25 June 1901.

19. Munch often kept drafts, or fragments of drafts, of his own letters. This one, to an unknown addressee and written in his sister's hand, is in archive N– in the Munch Museum.

20. In her dissertation Carla Lathe showed the intense, inspirational interaction that existed between Munch and Przybyszewski. Stach had published the first treatise on Munch's works in 1894, *Das Werk des Edvard Munch* (Berlin: S. Fischer), and used Munch's paintings in his own works at least eleven times (Lathe, p. 294). The dependence was mutual, Lathe suggested. "Where the Jugendstil sought to escape horror in a mask of beauty and distance, Munch tried to express the existential situation by the archetypal symbols Przybyszewski recommended" (p. 296). Dagny's real role may have been as a kind of symbolic vision shared by both artists.

21. "Edvard Munch fortæller om Fru Przybyzewski."

22. Lagercrantz's *August Strindberg* was translated into English by Anselm Hollo (New York: Farrar, Straus & Giroux, 1984). I have not always found Hollo's translation accurate. I quote in the main from his edition, but I have taken the liberty of correcting his English when I found it necessary. I will give page references to both the original Swedish and the English translation. These quotes are from Lagercrantz, pp. 284–86, and from Hollo, pp. 238–39.

23. *August Strindbergs brev*, vol. 9, ed. Torsten Eklund (Stockholm: Bonniers, 1965), p. 188. In a letter to Birger Mörner, dated 9 May 1893.

24. August Strindberg, *Inferno, Alone and Other Writings*, trans., ed., and with an introduction by Evert Sprinchorn (Garden City, New York: Anchor Books, Doubleday & Company, Inc., 1968); Nils Beyer, *Bengt Lidforss* (Stockholm: Norstedt, 1968).

25. It is also the version told by the Juell family.

26. Strindberg, *Brev*, vol. 9, pp. 187–88.

27. Strindberg, *Brev*, vol. 9, p. 214.

28. Lagercrantz, p. 283; Hollo, p. 237.

29. Early on in his relationship to Frida Uhl, Strindberg was also supposedly involved with Gabrielle Tavastjerna and Sigrid Lund. He wrote a series of letters maligning Dagny in 1893 and 1894 to Mörner, Adolf Paul, and in particular Bengt Lidforss. They are all to be found in volume 9 of *Brev*.

30. Lagercrantz, p. 282; Hollo, p. 237.

31. See note 16.

32. Lagercrantz, p. 290; Hollo, p. 243.

33. Ola Hansson wrote his name in the top, left-hand corner. The book is among those in the Jan Kasprowicz Museum in Inowrocław. Rumor in Poland has it that Dagny's mother destroyed other Strindberg editions in Dagny's possession when she came to Warsaw to take her grandchildren home after her daughter's death. I have no reason to believe that is true, except for the fact that Minda Juell did order all family correspondence having to do with Dagny destroyed.

34. Alfred Wysocki was a young Pole who knew the Przybyszewskis in Berlin. He befriended them during a very difficult time in 1896–97, and came together with them again in the *Paon* circle in Kraków. In 1956 he published his memoirs, *Sprzed pół wieku* (A half century ago), parts of which were translated into Swedish—"För ett halvsekel sedan"—by Martin von Zweibergk for Swedish Radio in 1986. Mr. von Zweibergk has been kind enough to give me access to his translations. Wysocki's memoirs are a valuable source, specifically with regard to the state of affairs in which the Przybyszewskis lived in 1896–97. Quoted from von Zweibergk's translation, pp. 10–11.

35. The English film maker, Peter Watkins, portrayed Dagny as the seductive/destructive muse in *Edvard Munch* from 1976, produced by Norsk Rikskringkastingen and Sveriges Radio. The Norwegian director, Håkon Sandøy, directed *Dagny*, produced by Norsk Film and Polish Film, in 1976. Though based on Kossak's book, it did little to uncover the myth or the woman. It was simply a passionate love story, not so passionately portrayed. Even Lise Fjeldstad, the Norwegian actress who played Dagny, later said that she thought it was rather remarkable that she had played a woman who wrote plays and poetry, and yet she had never had a pen in her hand.

Swedes Johan Bergenstråle (director) and P.O. Enquist (screen writer) collaborated on Swedish Television's sensationalist series *Strindberg: Ett liv* in 1985. Based on Enquist's book script (1984), Dagny was portrayed as a hard-talking, foul-mouthed seductress who would stop at no lengths to seduce Strindberg. At one point she attempted to keep him at the *Schwarze Ferkel* by inviting him to a black mass as she masturbated in front of him on the table. Enquist completely violated the historical integrity of the woman and the myth, almost as if he were intent on turning white into black. For example, he had Dagny and Frida Uhl meet in the tavern, Dagny screaming hysterically at Frida that she would get revenge. Since we do have Uhl's account of their only, very reserved meeting in a pension, during which not a word was spoken, we must wonder what Enquist's intentions were. The only thing that can be said for his portrayal of Dagny is that he understood that Strindberg was afraid of her and perceived her to be powerful beyond his imagination.

CHAPTER 2

1. In 1956, twelve years after Munch's death, Christian Gierløff published an article entitled "En kvinne i Munchs malerier" in *Arbeiderbladet*, 10 March, p. 10. Gierløff,

who had been a friend of Munch, called the article an interview he had had with Munch prior to his death. Munch seems to have repeated many of the same things to Gierløff that he had said in the interview he gave in 1901 to *Kristiania Dagsavis*. It must be assumed that Gierløff remembered Munch's words somewhat creatively. He may also have refreshed his memory with Munch's earlier interview.

2. "Livet i 'Den sorte Gris,'" *Dagbladet*, 20 June 1901. The article had previously appeared in a German newspaper. Though this particular quote does not demonstrate it, the article is vicious in intent. It has been attributed by many to Bengt Lidforss. Dagny's sister, Ragnhild, however, believed that it had been written by Strindberg. In a letter to her husband, postmarked 6 July 1901, she wrote: "The article, 'Svarte Grisen,' is the most revolting, loathsome, dirt-slinging attack on a dead person that you can imagine, probably Strindberg's last attempt to hurt her and us" (Bäckström correspondence). Munch's article, "Edvard Munch fortæller om Fru Przybyszewski," was in many respects a response to the "Sorte Gris" article. He debunked its veracity and denied that it could have been written by anyone who really knew Dagny or was a part of the circle. Ragnhild wrote Munch to thank him: "I just want to thank you for what you have done during this time for Dagny's memory, and you must absolutely believe that all of us closest to her are eternally grateful to you." (The letter, postmarked 3 July, is in the Munch Museum.) Privately Ragnhild had written to Maya Vogt complaining that Munch had not gone far enough in his article. Maya wrote back: "Thank you for M[unch]'s article. I think like you do that if Munch was first going to speak out, he should have done so with greater force" (undated, Bäckström correspondence). Olof Lagercrantz noted that Strindberg had pasted Przybyszewski's announcement of Dagny's death, which appeared in the Scandinavian press, into his journal without comment. This obviously struck Lagercrantz as odd, given Strindberg's tendency to delight verbally when he learned that his "enemies" had been "punished" (Lagercrantz, p. 364; Hollo, p. 305).

3. *Min Strindbergsbok*, p. 91.

4. Paul included parts of Stach's letter in his book on Strindberg. Stach wrote the letter in April of 1893, having known Dagny only since February or March. He was in an extremely productive period, and he told not only Paul but many others that he felt he owed his newfound creativity to Dagny. Quoted from *Min Strindbergsbok*, p. 117.

5. The name Aspasia was used primarily by Strindberg and his friends, Lidforss, Paul, and Uhl, in correspondence and memoirs. Munch, in his "interview" with Gierløff, remarked: "One evening, very high, [Strindberg gave] a speech for Dagny and said that she reminded him of Pericles's blond Aspasia. From this, one or two base natures who just happened to be there hatched the hetaera legend, and imputed her to be vile."

6. Quoted from Kossak, p. 103.

7. "Przybyszewski wie ich ihn sah," *Pologne Littéraire*, no. 96, 15 September 1934. Ida Auerbach knew both Dagny and Stach during the Berlin years. She eventually married the poet Richard Dehmel, who was an intimate member of the *Ferkel* circle and a good friend of the Przybyszewskis in the early Berlin years. Ida Dehmel had money and

was a patron of the arts and artists. She helped Dagny and Stach on several occasions. She remembered Dagny with great sympathy, both in this article and in an interview she gave Stanisław Helstyński, Przybyszewski's Polish biographer.

8. One of Stach's admirers from Kraków, speaking about the *Paon* group's initial reaction to Dagny. Quoted from Kossak, p. 165.

9. Quoting a Kraków source, Kossak noted: "It was Dagny's presence that lured the elegant clientele because 'the young ladies longed to see what the beautiful Mme Przybyszewska looked like—since this was the place where it was easiest to meet Mme Przybyszewska, people decided to go there after the theater.'" p. 169.

10. *Sprzed pól wieku*, quoted from von Zweibergk's translation, p. 3.

11. From the anonymous "Livet i 'Den sorte Gris'" article. It is a highly charged and very questionable description of the real woman. No other portrait "paints" the hair brown and bristly, the mouth big and bright purple-red. Nevertheless, it is a rather magnificent description of a woman. And indeed, Dagny's hair does often appear in photographs to be darker than the "golden" it is consistently "colored" in the verbal portraits. The word Pre-Raphaelite is not used in this description. It was, however, the most common art word used to describe Dagny's beauty.

In view of the fact that Dagny's sister, Ragnhild, believed that the article was written by Strindberg, it is interesting to compare this description of Dagny to Strindberg's description of Henriette, supposedly modelled on Dagny, in *Crimes and Crimes*. Maurice says of her: ". . . she left her impression on the air behind her. I can still see her standing there." "She seemed to suck herself out through the door, and in her wake rose a little whirlwind that dragged me along. . . ." "Yes, her clothes rustle as when the clerk tears off a piece of linen for you." Trans. by E. Björkman and N. Erichsen in *August Strindberg: Eight Famous Plays* (New York: Charles Scribner's Sons, 1949).

12. Johannes Schlaf was a German writer who frequented the *Schwarze Ferkel*. Quoted from Kossak, p. 105.

13. The reference is to Dagny during her first year in Kraków, i.e., the fall, winter, and spring of 1898–99. Quoted from Kossak, p. 171.

14. "En kvinne i Munchs malerier."

15. "Fra livet i 'Den sorte Gris.'"

16. *Wokoło teatru*, p. 345.

17. Hagemann, "Genienes inspiratrise," p. 659.

18. *Strindberg och hans andra hustru*, p. 317. Uhl devoted considerable attention to Strindberg's reaction to "Aspasia," retelling much of the story as he saw it and as he supposedly told it to her. There is a curious similarity to Adolf Paul's remembrances. Frida Uhl and Dagny met only this one time, according to Uhl. It is interesting to note that she found Dagny neither "malicious" nor "hateful," only "curious" and "matter of fact." She remarked at the end of her account of their meeting, "I can't help but wonder about the underside of the woman who in reality is so different from the way the man [Strindberg] sees her" (p. 318).

19. *Strindberg och hans andra hustru*, p. 318.

20. "En kvinne i Munchs malerier." In both this and his earlier interview from 1901, Munch referred to the fact that Dagny had done so much to further Scandinavian art and literature abroad, including Gustav Vigeland's and his own.

21. Servaes was referring to Dagny's earliest months in Berlin. Quoted from Kossak, p. 36.

22. Auerbach, *Woman and the Demon*, p. 10.

23. Auerbach, pp. 138–39.

24. Quoted from Kossak, p. 103.

25. Quoted from Kossak, p. 105.

26. Quoted from Kossak, pp. 104–5.

27. This man had met Dagny in Zakopane when he was thirteen or fourteen years old. It would have been sometime in 1899. Quoted from Kossak, p. 180.

28. "En kvinne i Munchs malerier."

29. Quoted from Kossak, p. 79.

30. *Strindberg och hans andra hustru*, p. 316.

31. "Livet i 'Den sorte Gris.'"

32. Dagny and Stach were in Paris in the spring of 1898, on their way to Spain. Quoted from Kossak, p. 160.

33. Tadeusz Boy-Żeleński was a Polish writer, critic and translator, and a central figure in the *Paon* bohemia. He was a metropolitan figure, a man of great knowledge and wit. It was he who essentially wrote the history of the *Paon* bohemia (*Kennst Du das Land* and *O Krakówie* (Kraków: Wydawnictwo Literackie, 1923), devoting considerable attention to Dagny and, of course, Stach. This particular quote is taken from Kossak, p. 168.

34. Nina Auerbach discussed the magic hands, simultaneously mobile and drooping, that appear in so much of Pre-Raphaelite art, in particular Rosetti's. "This mystic movement of hands reminds us of the totemistic aura parts of a woman's body acquire in disjunction from the woman herself. . . . In Dante Gabriel Rosetti's paintings of explicitly mythic subjects these twining female hands move to the center of the composition, often giving the still paintings their only movement. . . . The hands of Rosetti's women are so vital that in one curious chalk drawing, 'La Donna della Fiamma' (1870), a flame leaps from the palm of an otherwise inert woman . . . , an experiment in the mythmaking that crystallizes the metamorphic vitality of female hands as it was perceived by Rosetti and his circle" (pp. 49–51).

35. *Strindberg och hans andra hustru*, pp. 180–81. Supposedly Uhl asked Strindberg what Dagny looked like. He responded that he had not yet met her, but that he knew how Munch saw her. The entire passage reads: "—What does the beauty look like? I asked gayly.

—I don't know, answers Strindberg. I haven't seen her. But I know how Munch sees her. What she is to others doesn't concern him. That man asks nothing of a woman other than the ability to awaken an illusion in him and at the same time destroy it. Woman is and remains the clay out of which each and every one creates an ideal according to his own needs.

—And how does Munch see and paint her?

—Most modern type, slender and fine, a spiritual seductress more than a physical one. A vampire of the soul with a longing for the higher world and full of the finest nuances. No Fryne, but instead an Aspasia. —The face is singular, aristocratic, winningly full of life. There is something searching in it, something testing the air; there's a trembling around the nostrils, she holds her eyelids lowered, but the eyes still stare out audaciously. The neck is narrow, but the shoulders are in feminine fashion spread out challengingly." If you pay close attention to this description, you begin to suspect that it is a very subjective interpretation of Munch's painting of Dagny Juel Przybyszewska (see the end of this chapter). Whether Strindberg actually formulated this description, having seen Dagny, or having talked to Munch, or having seen a sketch Munch was doing, or whether Uhl, in retrospect, used the painting to refresh her memory, is impossible to know.

When Uhl had completed her book, she wrote to Munch, inquiring about his portrait of Dagny, asking if she might use it. (The letter is in the Munch Museum.) I do not know what Munch replied, or even if he did. Uhl did not, however, use Munch's image, but rather a photograph of Dagny, in side profile, from before her marriage.

36. Jappe Nilssen was a Norwegian writer and journalist and art critic for Dagbladet. Also part of the Ferkel circle, he was for a time desperately in love with Oda Krohg, then married to Christian Krohg. Munch used Nilssen as the model for the man on the beach in Melankoli. Quoted from Kossak, p. 33.

37. Quoted from Kossak, pp. 179–80.

38. In the Polish newspaper, Głos Narodu. Quoted from Kossak, p. 234.

39. "En kvinne i Munchs malerier."

40. Quoted from Kossak, p. 160.

41. Quoted from Kossak, p. 159.

42. Quoted from Kossak, p. 103.

43. "En kvinne i Munchs malerier."

44. Min Strindbergsbok, p. 91.

45. Strindberg och hans andra hustru, p. 220. As Uhl remembered it, Strindberg claimed that he had at this point only seen her in passing.

46. Gabriella Zapolska was a Polish writer and critic, who knew the Przybyszewskis in Kraków. Zapolska reviewed the production of Dagny's play, Ravnegård, performed in Kraków in 1902. Quoted from Kossak, p. 172.

47. Meier-Graefe's account is quoted by Hagemann in "Genienes inspiratrise," p. 659. (This version is slightly different from the one that appeared in Berliner Tageblatt.) Hagemann speculated that the fourth man was Bengt Lidforss. That could be correct. The time Meier-Graefe described was the fall-winter of 1893–94, after Dagny and Stach were married and living in their apartment in Louisenstrasse 6. Lidforss was supposedly a frequent visitor to the Przybyszewskis.

48. "Przybyszewski wie ich ihn sah."

49. Quoted from Tone Vikborg's Gustav Vigeland: Mennesket og kunstneren (Oslo: 1983), p. 51. There are two versions of this sculpture, Vals I and Vals II. According

to Vikborg, Vigeland did the first one in 1893, and, therefore, Dagny and Stach could not have been the initial models, since Vigeland did not meet them until a year later. Vigeland did this second sculpture in 1896. He did a bust of Przybyszewski in 1895, which is in the Vigeland Museum in Oslo. He also apparently did one of Dagny, but he destroyed it as he did many of his works from that time in Berlin.

50. Hagemann, "Genienes inspiratrise," p. 657.

51. Quoted from Kossak, p. 172.

52. Quoted from Kossak, p. 79.

53. Quoted from Kossak, p. 125. She said that the woman was a childhood friend who saw Dagny in Berlin sometime in 1894–95.

54. Quoted from Kossak, p. 167. She referred to Helena Pawlikowska as "a known and respected woman in Kraków." This story of Dagny sleeping on the coats is also told by someone from the time in Berlin.

55. Schlaf remembered Dagny this way from the first time he saw her, standing in the yard of Richard Dehmel on a sunny afternoon in Berlin. Quoted from Kossak, p. 106.

56. Quoted from Kossak, p. 155.

57. Quoted from Kossak, p. 171.

58. Amelie Posse, *Kring kunskapens träd* (Stockholm: Natur och Kultur, 1946), p. 418. Posse was a young friend of Dagny's sister, Gudrun Westrup. In 1900, Posse met Dagny when she and her son, Zenon, were visiting Gudrun. Her remembrance of Dagny is from that time.

59. Quoted from Kossak, pp. 179–80.

60. *Strindberg och hans andra hustru*, p. 220.

61. Stanisław Wyspiański was one of the best writers and artists of the Young Poland circle that gathered at *Paon* around the Przybyszewskis. He was also a frequent visitor to the Przybyszewski home. According to Kossak, he was very kind to Dagny. After having been involved in the life of the bohemia for several months, he retreated into his own more peaceful and more productive isolation. No one has portrayed the Kraków of the 1890s, particularly its trees, as beautifully as Wyspiański. This drawing of Dagny was used as the frontispiece for Stach's poem, "Am Meer," published in Poland in the late 1890s.

The cartoon drawing, a well-kept secret for many years, is on the lower edge of a famous tapestry that covered an entire wall in *Paon*, and on which the artists "doodled." The tapestry, I learned after much searching, is located in the National Museum in Kraków. When I visited the museum in May 1985, and asked to see the canvas, unaware of what I would find, I was told that it was in the workshop, about to undergo restoration. The museum officials were extraordinarily gracious and helpful and actually had the huge canvas unrolled for me in the workshop. It is a marvelous collage of the artists of *Paon*, done by themselves. In the middle there is a picture of Stach. The museum staff could not say who painted it. The drawing of Dagny is to the lower right on the canvas. It is only about eight inches high, with Wyspiański's well-known initials underneath. The museum director was kind enough to let me take pictures of the drawing.

The canvas was treated like a living work of art by the artists, who freely painted over what was already there. Kossak wrote that the canvas contained portraits of both Stach and Dagny by the painter Josef Mehoffer. The museum staff did not know if that had been true at one time.

62. The painting is housed in the Munch Museum.

63. Quoted from Kossak, p. 225.

CHAPTER 3

1. According to another family version, Gudrun said, "There are two of us," meaning Dagny and herself.

2. Her father mentioned the scarlet fever in a letter to Otto Blehr, dated 25 May 1878. The letter is in the Blehr archive in Riksarkivet in Oslo, hereafter cited as Blehr archive. In a letter to Dagny dated 3 October 1882, her cousin, Rolf Lunderbye, congratulated her on her confirmation and told her to write him when she got to Germany. He said that he had asked the painter, Lærum, to be her traveling companion and to watch out for her. This letter is in the Kongsvinger Museum.

3. Posse, *Kring kunskapens träd*, p. 417.

4. In a letter from Birgit Blehr to Randi Blehr, dated in Sigurd Blehr's hand, November 1888, Blehr archive. Birgit Blehr was married to Dagny's mother's brother, Theodor.

5. Mr. Bull may have been a relative of Dagny. Her paternal grandmother was a Bull, i.e., Mathea Isabella Bull (1810–88).

6. Undated letter to Randi Blehr, written around 12 February (Randi Blehr's birthday) 1889, Blehr archive. Reminiscence of Iwa Dahlin in the summer of 1985.

7. Undated, but written in the fall of 1889, Blehr archive.

8. Undated; Sigurd Blehr wrote in "November," Blehr archive.

9. Undated, but written at Christmastime, 1888, Blehr archive.

10. Blehr archive.

11. Undated, but written sometime in early 1889, Blehr archive. Hjalmar Jonsson is not mentioned anywhere else.

12. Dated Bergen, 30 December [1888], Blehr archive.

13. Dated Bergen, 10 January 1893, Adam Mickiewicz Museum of Literature, Warsaw.

14. Meier-Graefe, "Geschicten neben der Kunst: Ducha."

15. Dated only "Saturday," but written in the fall of 1889, Blehr archive.

16. Before 1892 Maria (Maja) Blehr had a "Husholdningskole" and a pension in Victoria Terrasse 42. In 1898 she became the owner of the Hotel Westend on Karl Johansgate 45. Dagny and her sister Ragnhild stayed there when they were in Christiania again in 1900.

17. Undated, Blehr archive.

18. From a letter Ragnhild Juell wrote to Randi Blehr from Paris in December 1892, it is apparent, however, that she had previously met the painter Fritz Thaulow, and his wife, who was Oda Krohg's sister. The Thaulows were in Paris that winter, and Ragn-

hild said she spent quite a lot of time at their house. That Ragnhild knew the Thaulows suggests that she and Dagny could have met, for example, the Krohgs as well, and that they could also have met Munch at this time.

19. Vilhelm Krag seemed to have been quite taken with Ragnhild. In a letter to a friend in Paris from 22 October 1892, he wrote, "If you should meet a Norwegian singer, Miss Ragnhild Juell, then greet her too from me and ask her to stay in Paris until March when I'm coming." (Universitetsbiblioteket, Oslo.)

20. They are both in the Jan Kasprowicz Museum in Inowrocław.

21. Dated only "26," but written sometime in the fall of 1901, Bäckström correspondence.

22. Dated "3/2–92." Gudrun must have exchanged the numbers by mistake, for she says later in the letter that it is already March. In a letter dated 7 February 1892, also to Otto Blehr, Gudrun ended by saying simply, "Dagny is now in Berlin." Both letters are in the Blehr archive.

23. Quoted from Kossak, p. 29.

24. Lidforss's two major biographers, Erik Vendelfelt, *Den unge Bengt Lidforss* (1962), and Nils Beyer, *Bengt Lidforss* (1968), both came to this conclusion.

25. The Juells and the Lidforsses had known each other previously. Dagny's oldest sister, Gudrun Westrup, knew them, of course, from Lund, and her youngest sister, Ragnhild, had earlier been romantically involved with Bengt's younger brother, Erik, though she was not engaged to him, as sources have suggested.

Bengt Lidforss, as much as Strindberg, spread libelous stories about Dagny, if he did seem to alternate between befriending her and betraying her. In the wake of Strindberg's meddling efforts to "save Lidforss from Juel" in the spring of 1893, Strindberg and Lidforss had a falling out, apparently in part because Lidforss reacted negatively to having been brought back to Lund by his friends. He did not interpret it as Strindberg's efforts to "save" him but rather as interference in his life. He had also written to Strindberg, insisting that he retract statements he had made about Dagny in his letter of 9 May to Birger Mörner. Strindberg wrote to Mörner in a letter dated 8 June: "Whereupon I now answer: the facts I related were based on Lidforss's verbal reports to me, especially concerning Aspasia's setting herself up on Karlstrasse, which Lidforss alternately found proper and abominable" (*Brev*, vol. 9, p. 202). Strindberg may have been telling the truth when he said that his stories about Dagny originally came from Lidforss. Ragnhild Juell seemed to think that not only Bengt, but also the other Lidforsses, had acted reprehensibly with regard to Dagny that spring. She wrote to her fiancé Helge Bäckström in June, just before Dagny returned to Norway: "Apropos Dagny I've lately had my eyes cruelly opened to all the Lidforsses, Bengt, Gärda and to a certain extent Erik, and I'm writing to him to get my letters back" (Bäckström correspondence). Lidforss seems to have played a malicious game with Dagny, accepting her friendship, but maligning her behind her back. One must speculate that his ambivalence arose from his own situation, not hers.

26. Posse, *Kring kunskapens träd*, p. 415.

27. Dated 10 January 1893, Adam Mickiewicz Museum of Literature.

28. Fru Nilsen replied to Dagny's letter (which does not exist) on 10 January 1893, saying, "Yes, it is your life's dream to go to that world famous city." The letter is the same as in note 27.

29. Dated Rolighed, 26 January, Blehr archive. Dagny reminded her uncle that he had secured this passport (called "ministerpass") for Ragnhild when she went to Paris earlier that fall, and said she would appreciate it if he would do the same for her.

30. Maya Vogt had written to Ragnhild after Dagny's death that she had been with Oda Krohg, ". . . and we also talked about Dagny; she thought her death had been beautiful, absolutely enviable" (Bäckström correspondence).

31. Auerbach, *Woman and the Demon*, p. 1.

32. Kossak goes into specific times and events in Dagny's life in considerable detail.

33. The date of their marriage has often been given as September 18, 1893. Ewa Kossak published a copy of their marriage certificate, however, which was dated August 18. Illustrations numbered 19 and 20 in *Dagny Przybyszewska: Zbłąkana gwiazda* (1975).

34. Dehmel, "Przybyszewski wie ich ihn sah."

35. Meier-Graefe, "Geschicten neben der Kunst."

36. In "Edvard Munch fortæller om Fru Przybyzewski," Munch said that Dagny had named the journal one night at the *Schwarze Ferkel* "in an inspired moment." The name "was accepted with enthusiasm by the whole circle."

In her dissertation on the *Schwarze Ferkel*, Carla Lathe wrote regarding Strindberg's fantasy that the group did not survive Dagny and, perhaps more importantly, his own absence: "The proof that Strindberg's group could continue and expand without him lay in the fact that its greatest corporate achievement came after his departure. This achievement was the founding of the journal *Pan*, which was the culmination of the circle's efforts to extend the cultural scene in Berlin in spite of inauspicious circumstances. *Pan* was to be finer, more international and more modern than any other art journal circulating at the time. By common consent of art historians today, it largely fulfilled its aims. According to Philippe Jullian [*Dreamers of Decadence*, 1969] *Pan* was the most splendid and interesting review of the period" (p. 48).

37. Stach to Adolf Paul, April 1893, quoted by Paul in *Min Strindbergsbok*, p. 117. Stach's biographers, the Pole, Stanisław Helstyński (*Przybyszewski* [Kraków: Wydawnictwo Literackie, 1958, rpt. 1966]) and the Frenchman, Maxime Herman (*Un sataniste polonais: Stanislas Przybyszewski (de 1868 à 1900)* [Paris: Société d'Edition "Les Belles Lettres," 1939]), and Ewa Kossak all say the same.

38. Undated, but written in May 1896, Universitetsbiblioteket, Oslo.

39. Holger Drachmann wrote this in his "Berliner-Breve," which appeared in *Verdens Gang* on 29 May 1894. It is also told by others, including surviving members of Dagny's family. The truth is, however, that when Dagny came home from Berlin in June 1898, she said that she was engaged. Obviously she intended to marry.

40. Dehmel, "Przybyszewski wie ich ihn sah."

41. Dated Rolighed, 8 November, Blehr archive.

42. Stanisław Helstyński did not believe that Dagny and Marta ever met. Kossak, based on a scene between two women which Stach wrote for *Homo sapiens*, believed

they did. She suggested that Dagny, at some point in the early years of their marriage, "decided to insist that Przybyszewski should break all ties with his illegitimate children and their mother, yes, strike them from his life" (p. 117). Kossak believed that Dagny would have acted not only out of jealousy but also out of fear that their economic resources could not support two families.

Maxime Herman asserted that Dagny's correspondence from the time revealed that she had not played "the seemly role" ("*le beau role*") in Stach's break with Marta. Herman accused Dagny of literally stealing "the inconstant and feeble Przybyszewski" from Marta (*Un sataniste polonais*, p. 193). Herman based his assumptions partly on Adolf Paul's *Min Strindbergsbok*, which does not lend credibility to them. Ewa Kossak was unable to find the correspondence to which Herman referred. Neither have I found it. It is, though, a curious, if French, reversal to accuse the wife of stealing the husband from the mistress.

43. Much of this information is based on a letter Stach wrote to his parents in late June 1896, praising Dagny for the good care she was taking of him (in *Przybyszewski: Listy*, vol. 1, p. 124; in Kossak, p. 141).

44. Undated, "Berlin, Halldorferstrasse 39" written in the top left-hand corner, Universitetsbiblioteket, Oslo.

45. Meier-Graefe added, "Your lithographs have given them much joy." According to Stach's letters from the time, he sent them to his Czech publisher, Arnošt Procházka, telling him he could choose the ones he wished to use in his journal, *Moderní Revue*. Meier-Graefe's letter, dated 15 August 1896, is in the Munch Museum.

46. Undated, in the possession of Iwa Dahlin.

47. Quoted from Kossak, pp. 145–46.

48. Quoted from Kossak, p. 146.

49. According to Kossak, Maya had met Stach through Dagny in Berlin. She "had corresponded with Stach for a long time. Their contacts went far beyond the context of a normal acquaintance. Their friendship dated from 1894 when Przybyszewski dedicated his 'Notturno' to Maya. When he returned to Berlin from Kongsvinger [in the summer of 1897] he met her again" (p. 150). Stach had written to Alfred Wysocki from Rolighed, 19 May 1897, that he should not mention anything about "M," because Dagny liked to read his letters (in *Przybyszewski: Listy*, vol. 1, p. 154). The editor of Stach's letters, Helstyński, said in a note that "M" could refer to either Marta or Maya. Since Marta had been dead a year, it is likely that the reference is to Maya. Kossak said "M" was Maya. She quoted a letter from Stach to Wysocki after Stach had returned to Berlin that summer. Referring to Maya, he wrote: "What shall I say about her? The same nice girl as always, but for me she's a stranger. I like her and I wish her well with all my heart, but there is nothing between us. Sic transit etc. Ducha, Ducha, for ever Ducha, only Ducha, the queen of Heaven and Earth" (*Przybyszewski: Listy*, vol. 1, p. 161; Kossak, p. 150).

If Stach and Maya had earlier had an affair, then everyone acted as if they had not. Maya came to Rolighed in the summer of 1895 when Dagny and Stach were home.

Ragnhild, who was also there, wrote very warmly about her. Dagny and Maya seemed to remain good friends, if they did not have a great deal of contact in the later years. They saw each other in Christiania in the fall of 1900 when Dagny was in Norway. Ragnhild definitely considered Maya a good friend of Dagny, sending her a photograph of Dagny after her death, a photograph for which Maya was very grateful.

50. Stach Przybyszewski wrote to Iwa many years after her mother's death to explain her name. "Dagny and I were in Copenhagen (very poor, but very happy). There we got to know a wild, but exceptionally beautiful dancer from the Samoa Islands. Dagny, who found her absolutely enchanting, suddenly said to her: 'If I have a daughter, I'm going to call her the same as you.' When you came into the world a year later, we had already called you Ivi for a long time" (*Przybyszewski: Listy*, vol. 3, p. 321). Iwa Dahlin told me that when she came to be baptized in Kraków, the Polish priest would not allow the name Ivi, because it was pagan. He baptized her Ewa, which her family subsequently pronounced Iwa. In letters in the early years, the family wrote Ivi.

51. This letter, written to Margarete Ansorge on 17 November 1898, is quoted by Kossak, p. 170.

52. Astrid's letter is in the Blehr archive; the letter to Dagny from her mother is in the Adam Mickiewicz Museum of Literature.

53. The house in Kraków still stands, though a second story has been added to it.

54. *Przybyszewski: Listy*, vol. 1, p. 208. The source of this information is Boy-Żeleński. Helstyński included it in a footnote.

55. She was Stanisława Przybyszewska, the author of *Danton* and other plays.

56. Stach wrote to many people during this time, bemoaning his situation. In April he wrote a letter to Ragnhild, in which he told of Dagny's actions and of his own pain. It is a very self-serving, self-indulgent letter, blaming Dagny for the tragedy that had befallen them, concealing his own affairs with Kasprowicz and Pająkówna. It cannot be trusted as accurate, for Stach was so anxious to gain sympathy for himself and lay the blame for everything on Dagny. (In the following years he would go to great lengths to paint his early years with Dagny as black as possible.) The letter, postmarked on arrival in Stockholm 11 April 1900, is in the Bäckström correspondence.

57. Postmarked Kongsvinger, 10 October 1900, Bäckström correspondence.

58. Postmarked 14 October 1900, Bäckström correspondence.

59. Dated Monday, 3 December, Universitetsbiblioteket, Oslo.

60. Undated, Universitetsbiblioteket, Oslo.

61. In a letter postmarked 5 October, 1900, from Ragnhild to Helge, Bäckström correspondence.

62. Undated, in the possession of Iwa Dahlin.

63. Quoted from Kossak, p. 209.

64. Ewa Kossak referred to a portrait of Dagny done in the spring of 1901 by Konrad Krzyżanowski (see page 162). Kossak described what she thought Krzyżanowski saw: "Dagny already bore the stamp of death on her face. The black dress buttoned high around her neck, made her look older than she was. She bit her lips together, as if

she wanted to keep them from quivering" (p. 205). Comparing Krzyżanowski's vision with that of the Warsaw journalist, Kossak asked, "Which of the two women is the real Dagny?" (p. 209).

65. Postmarked Kongsvinger, 4 August 1901, Bäckström correspondence. Ragnhild's information came from her mother and her sister Gudrun, who had gone to Warsaw to bring back Dagny's children and her belongings. Their source was undoubtedly Stach.

66. These postcards are in the possession of Iwa Dahlin.

67. Kossak dated the letter 4 May (p. 226). She quoted an earlier letter that began in the same way as 22 May (p. 219).

68. Undated, in the possession of Iwa Dahlin.

69. Emeryk left six letters in all. Kossak quotes them in part on pages 221–28.

70. In researching her book, Ewa Kossak went to the cemetery where Dagny is buried. After a day's hunt, she and her husband found a rose-colored, marble tombstone with the epitaph in Polish and Norwegian: "Here lies Dagny Przybyszewska, died 5 June 1901 at the age of 33." The Norwegian inscription has added, "born Juel" (p. 30). Kossak guessed that Maya Vogt, who had married the Russian count Avalof and moved to Tiflis after Dagny's death, had arranged for the stone. She was right. Maya sent a postcard to her brother, Nils Collett Vogt, on 5 November 1905, in which she said, "Am going to put a stone on Dagny's grave. Have asked the sister to send me 1000 crowns." (In Universitetsbiblioteket, Oslo.)

CHAPTER 4

1. Wysocki, *Sprzed pół wieku*, 1956, quoted from von Zweigbergk's translation, p. 4.

2. Munch, "Min venn Przybyszewski," *Oslo Aftensavis*, 30 January 1929.

3. *Glåmdølen*, 11 December 1895.

4. Dated 15 June 1894, Bäckström correspondence.

5. Kungliga Biblioteket, Stockholm. This quote has been used by a number of scholars to date Dagny's writing. The first sentence has generally been omitted, apparently so as not to offend people's sensibilities. Yet to omit it is to prejudice the truth.

6. Paul, *Min Strindbergsbok*, p. 92.

7. Sandra M. Gilbert and Susan Gubar, *The Madwoman in the Attic: The Woman Writer and the Nineteenth-Century Literary Imagination* (New Haven and London: Yale University Press, 1979), p. 4.

8. Gilbert and Gubar, p. 8.

9. *Przybyszewski: Listy*, vol. 1, p. 175.

10. Dagny Przybyszewska, *Kiedy słońce zachodzi . . .*, trans. Stanisław Przybyszewski (Warsaw: Jan Fiszer, 1902), pp. 3–4.

11. Quoted from Paul's *Min Strindbergsbok*, p. 117.

12. Undated, in the possession of Iwa Dahlin. Aunt Birgit was Birgit Blehr from Bergen, and Gerhard Gran was the editor of *Samtiden*. Dagny had actually written "misunderstanding" (*misforståelse*), then crossed it out and written "surprise" (*overraskelse*).

13. Dagny's note accompanying the manuscript, dated "Copenhagen, 2 January 96," is in the Munch Museum. It was given to the museum by Sonja Hagemann.

14. The letter, dated 12 June 1899, is found in Helstyński's biography, *Przybyszewski*, in the 1966 edition, p. 227.

15. The letter, dated Kraków, 23 May 1899, is in Prague; a copy is in the Jan Kasprowicz Museum. Letters from the museum translated by Thomas Haeussler.

16. Stanisław Przybyszewski, *Underveis*, trans. Dagny Juel Przybyszewska (Christiania and Copenhagen: Alb. Cammermeyer, 1895).

17. Bäckström correspondence.

18. Universitetsbiblioteket, Oslo; the last part of this undated letter is missing.

19. The original of this letter is in Prague; a copy is in the Jan Kasprowicz Museum.

20. Undated, Universitetsbiblioteket, Oslo.

21. Postmarked 20 August 1895, Bäckström correspondence. Aunt Henrikka was Dagny's maternal aunt, Henrikka Lunderbye.

22. Kossak, p. 146.

23. Kossak, p. 326.

24. Boy-Żeleński, *O Krakówie*, p. 329.

25. Kossak, p. 149.

26. Ragnhild wrote a series of letters to Helge while on tour, discussing with him her fears of giving up her career. The letters are in the Bäckström correspondence.

27. In an interview with Iwa Dahlin in the summer of 1985 she told me that she too believed Ragnhild had been the model.

28. Whether her works suffered the same fate as her correspondence, of which much was destroyed or lost, is an unanswered question. I have discovered one unpublished poem, "På et fjernt og solbeskinnet sted."

29. Truman Capote, *Music for Chameleons* (1975; rpt. New York: Signet, 1980), pp. 7–8, from the short story called "Music for Chameleons."

CHAPTER 5

1. "Rediviva," *Dagbladet*, 22 January 1977, p. 22. The manuscript was discovered by Martin Nag in the Munch Museum and published by him. He republished it in *Kongsvinger-kvinne og verdensborger: Dagny Juel som dikter og kulturarbeider*, which he put together for the Kongsvinger Museum's week-long seminar on Dagny in August 1987. Bengt Lidforss, in his letter to Strindberg about Dagny's literary endeavors, said she was writing short stories as well as her memoirs. The memoirs have not survived, but "Rediviva" is, in fact, a short story in the guise of a personal reminiscence.

2. Both Ewa Kossak and Ole Michael Selberg, in his introduction to Dagny's plays, mention the fact that Stach Przybyszewski foreshadowed Foerder's suicide in his play. Kossak could not have known about "Rediviva," which was not discovered by Nag until 1977. But Selberg does not mention it either, in his introduction written a year later.

3. *Przybyszewski: Listy*, vol. 1, p. 175.

4. The letter from Hedvig Aubert, dated 18 June 1908, is in the Bäckström correspondence.

5. The publication history of Dagny's plays:

Den sterkere, Samtiden 7 (1896), 449–59.

Hrich (Synden), trans. Hugo Kosterka, Moderní Revue 9 (1898), 129–38. Kosterka's translation was also performed as a recitation at Prague's Intimní Volné Jeviste.

Kiedy słońce zachodzi (Når solen går ned) and Grzech (Synden), trans. Stanisław Przybyszewski (1898), Życie.

Kiedy słońce zachodzi (Når solen går ned), a collection containing Przybyszewski's dedication to their children and his translations of Synden, Når solen går ned, and the four poems of Sing mir das Lied vom Leben und vom Tode (Warsaw: Jan Fiszer, 1902).

Osoby (Ravnegård), trans. Stanisław Przybyszewski (Warsaw, 1902). In December of 1902 the play was performed in Kraków.

6. Synden og to andre skuespill av Dagny Juell, ed. and intro. Ole Michael Selberg (Oslo: Solum Forlag, 1978). Selberg found the original manuscripts in the possession of Iwa Dahlin.

7. Synden og to andre skuespill, pp. 10–11.

8. For a more extensive discussion of the women dramatists at the turn of the century, see my chapter "Eros og ære," in Norsk kvinnelitteraturhistorie, vol. 1, pp. 235–43.

9. In the 1870s, the Danish critic, Georg Brandes, had called on writers "to debate problems." Ibsen's Pillars of Society and A Doll House became classics of the tendens genre.

10. For further discussion see Åse Hiorth Lervik's Evig din (Oslo: Universitetsforlaget, 1985).

11. For example, Amalie Skram portrayed a woman who lied, drank, stole, and was divorced in Agnete (1893) and Hulda Garborg a woman capable of murder in Mødre (1895).

12. Lervik pointed out that in the literature of the 1870s and early 1880s, one of the lovers often died before the earthly union could take place. Death was a sign of the true nature of the union (pp. 18–26). The conclusion to be drawn is that innocence was insured at the same time as the woman was made whole through spiritual love.

13. Dagny had a copy of Heiberg's Balkonen with her in Warsaw. It is among her books in the Jan Kasprowicz Museum.

14. It is an interesting footnote that Munch, in his copy of Når vi døde vågner—Samlede Værker, 1908—had marked the scene between Rubek and Irene, in which Rubek attempts to defend what he has done to the art work for which she was the original model. Munch had written at the bottom of the page, "Ducha and Stachu." He had put an "X" by Irene's condemnation of Rubek: "Poet!" she calls him. "Why poet?" he asks. "Because you're soft and lazy and full of self-forgiveness for every sin of your life, the acts you've done and the thoughts you've had. You killed my soul—and then you model yourself in remorse and penance and contrition—(Smiles.)—and you think that settles the score." Trans. by Rolf Fjelde in Ibsen: The Complete Major Prose Plays (New

York: Ferrar, Straus, and Giroux, 1978). Martin Nag, who noticed Munch's markings in his book, wrote a short article in *Verdens Gang*, 16 July 1978, entitled "Er Dagny Juel Irenes modell?" He speculated that Ibsen sensed the "complications in the relationship between 'Ducha' and 'Stachu'."

15. Sigbjørn Obstfelder, *Samlede skrifter*, vol. 1, ed. Solveig Tunold (Oslo: Gyldendal, 1950), pp. 184–85.

16. Kossak, p. 204.

17. *Synden og to andre skuespill*, p. 18.

18. Alice Miller, *The Drama of the Gifted Child*, trans. Ruth Ward (New York: Basic Books, 1981), p. 10.

19. Miller, *For Your Own Good*, trans. Hildegarde and Hunter Hannum (New York: Farrar, Straus & Giroux, 1984; orig. prt. 1980), p. 85.

CHAPTER 6

1. For a study of Obstfelder in English, see my book, *Sigbjørn Obstfelder* (Boston: Twayne Publishers, 1982).

2. *Oeuvres complètes de Baudelaire* (Paris: La Pléiade, 1934), p. 4.

3. *Singt mir das Lied vom Leben und vom Tode*, trans. Stanisław Przybyszewski, *Życie* 2 (1899); *Sing mir das Lied vom Leben und vom Tode*, *Samtiden* 11 (1900), 289–97. Przybyszewski used the second person plural form, "Singt," while Dagny used the second person singular "Sing," when she published the poems in Norwegian.

4. An account of this time is given by Kossak, pp. 156–58. Dagny's letter is quoted on p. 157.

5. Recounted by Kossak, p. 158. The edition is now the property of Professor Roman Taborski of Warsaw.

6. *Digte*. In "Dagny Juel: Norsk lyrikks Camilla Collett?" by Martin Nag, *Samtiden* 84 (1975), 512–24. Nag subsequently published them in *Kongsvinger-kvinne og verdensborger* (1987) for the Kongsvinger Museum. The poems are untitled and are referred to by their first lines.

7. Both letters undated, in the possession of Iwa Dahlin.

8. The letter to Arnošt Procházka is in *Przybyszewski: Listy*, vol. 1, p. 140.

9. Undated, in the possession of Iwa Dahlin.

10. *Kiedy słońce zachondzi*, pp. 3–4.

CHAPTER 7

1. He took over the practice of a certain Dr. Schjøtz.

2. Blehr archive.

3. Dr. Juell's letter is in Munch's correspondence in the Munch Museum.

4. Arne Eggum, the director of the Munch Museum, told me he believed Dr. Juell feared that Ragnhild's portrait, hanging in the midst of the "love" portraits, suggested she was the "loving" woman (summer, 1985).

5. In Munch's notes, file N, in the Museum. Munch mistakenly remembered the year to be 1894. The missing word is not legible. It begins with a "b" in Norwegian. Possibly it was *bønfallende,* i.e., "pleadingly."

6. Blehr archive. In a series of letters to his brother-in-law that fall, Hans aired his plans for change. The Aker position was by appointment, and he was, therefore, seeking Otto's advice both in his capacity as "His Excellency Mr. Prime Minister" and "Dear brother-in-law." Hans could not free himself from the thought that he was currying favor. The sheer possibility made him feel pained and insecure.

7. After 10 December 1892, Hans did not mention the Aker position again in his letters to Otto Blehr. In his New Year's letter of 31 December 1892, he asked his brother-in-law to use his influence to help save the middle school in Kongsvinger, which was being threatened with closure. He said he did not mind asking for Otto's assistance, since it was not for himself but for the good of Kongsvinger. One senses that Hans was in some sense trying to "right himself" after the Aker affair. (Blehr archive.)

8. *Przybyszewski: Listy,* vol. 1, p. 159.

9. Bäckström correspondence.

10. The following announcement appeared in the newspaper, *Solungen,* in 1901. "The farm, Rolighed, very beautifully and well-situated right near Kongsvinger, with approximately 100 'mål' of cultivated land, some forest, good garden, large fruit garden, good buildings with fire insurance of 29,740 crowns, is for sale cheap. If not sold, the farm can be rented immediately either in its entirety or the main building with garden alone and the rest of the farm by itself. The main building has 12 rooms and kitchen, etc." On 15 July 1901, Ragnhild wrote that as of 30 September her mother had rented Rolighed to Candidate Stang, who would then buy it if he liked it. On 28 July she wrote that they were going to hold an auction on 20 September and had to be out of the house on 25 September.

11. March 1894, Adam Mickiewicz Museum of Literature.

12. Bäckström correspondence.

13. Bäckström correspondence.

14. Both letters in the Bäckström correspondence.

15. Both letters in the Blehr archive.

16. Kossak, p. 132.

17. After his operation, Hans stayed at Maja Blehr's hotel, Westend, in Karl Johansgate 45.

18. The story was told to me by Astrid Holmqvist, Ragnhild's niece, in an interview in Stockholm in the summer of 1985.

19. Undated, Bäckström correspondence.

20. In the possession of Iwa Dahlin.

21. Bäckström correspondence.

22. In the possession of Iwa Dahlin.

23. Jens Thiis, *Edvard Munch og hans samtid* (Oslo: Gyldendal, 1933), p. 211. Thiis's accounts in this book must always be taken with a grain of salt, because they can contain so many unwitting falsehoods. He remembered that he was at Rolighed in the summer of 1893, when it had to be 1894. He said that Astrid married a Swede, when Astrid never married. Thiis, like so many, believed that the Juell sisters and Munch had known each other as children. In spite of his mistakes, however, Thiis did capture an atmosphere.

24. Kotarbińska, *Wokoło teatru*, p. 348.

25. *Przybyszewski: Listy*, vol. 1, p. 92. In the following section I used a good number of Stach's quotes from his letters from the time. Ole Michael Selberg was kind enough to give me copies of his Norwegian translations of letters which he eventually used in part in his article, "Stanisław Przybyszewski og 1890-årenes norske kunst og litteratur," *Samtiden* (1977), pp. 103–18.

26. Bäckström correspondence.

27. Bäckström correspondence.

28. Both letters in *Przybyszewski: Listy*, vol. 1, p. 94 and p. 97.

29. Bäckström correspondence.

30. *Przybyszewski: Listy*, vol. 1, p. 107.

31. *Przybyszewski: Listy*, vol. 1, pp. 158–59.

32. Kongsvinger Museum.

33. Dehmel, "Przybyszewski wie ich ihn sah."

34. *Przybyszewski: Listy*, vol. 1, p. 104.

35. *Przybyszewski: Listy*, vol. 1, pp. 124–25.

36. The letter, to Maciej Szukiewicz, is in *Przybyszewski: Listy*, vol. 1, p. 157.

37. Kossak, p. 172.

38. This letter, undated, is in the possession of Professor Roman Taborski, Warsaw.

39. Dated 13 October, *Przybyszewski: Listy*, vol. 1, p. 168.

40. *Przybyszewski: Listy*, vol. 1, pp. 168–69.

41. *Przybyszewski: Listy*, vol. 1, p. 172.

42. Stanisława became a dramatist. She wrote *Danton*, among other plays. Iwa Dahlin befriended Stanisława and gave her money from time to time.

43. In the possession of Iwa Dahlin.

CHAPTER 8

1. The letter from Maya Vogt is in the Bäckström correspondence. The letters from Gudrun and Astrid are in the Adam Mickiewicz Museum of Literature, and the letter from Ragnhild in the Munch Museum.

2. This is told by members of Dagny's family.

3. From an interview with Iwa Dahlin in the summer of 1985.

4. Many of the Juell relatives tell of Gudrun's magnificent piano playing; but it was, in fact, Dagny's daughter, Iwa, who told me that she believed that her aunt was a greater artist than her mother.

5. Dated 10 February, Bäckström correspondence.

6. Bäckström correspondence.

7. Blehr archive.

8. Though Dagny seemed to have a good relationship with her aunt and uncle, always being invited to their residences when she was in Christiania or Stockholm, there seemed, too, to be distance between them. Ragnhild wrote to Helge on 6 July 1901, one month after Dagny's death, "I was at Blehrs yesterday for dinner, but it was just trying, because they are so untouched by what is filling all my thoughts for the moment and talk only of clothes and royalty and memories of their silver anniversary" (Bäckström correspondence).

9. Both letters in the Blehr archive. On 15 January 1893, Minda wrote, apparently to correct any wrong impression Dagny might have given. She assured Randi of their gratitude and particularly of Dagny's desire to attend the ball—dresses they could always arrange—but to explain that Dagny needed to prepare herself for her trip abroad to study music. "You understand, of course, that this reason must be respected" (15 January 1893).

10. In an interview from the summer of 1985.

11. Kotarbińska, *Wokoło teatru*, p. 341.

12. Quoted from Kossak, p. 168. Boy-Żeleński actually said the things came from Dagny's rich sister in Stockholm. That would, of course, have been Ragnhild. I assume that both Ragnhild and Gudrun sent packages to Dagny in Poland. But as for clothes, Ragnhild was a much smaller woman, and therefore dresses and such must have come from Gudrun.

13. Dated 22 April, Blehr archive.

14. Blehr archive.

15. This is made clear in letters he wrote from his times at Rolighed.

16. Bäckström correspondence.

17. Adam Mickiewicz Museum of Literature.

18. From an interview in the summer of 1985.

19. In the possession of Iwa Dahlin.

20. Kossak maintained that Dagny was proud of her "iron constitution." That may very well have been, though I have not found anything that Dagny herself has said in that regard. Kossak recounted that Stach had told his second wife Jadwiga that toward the end of their marriage, Dagny suffered from a skin disease and had sores on her mouth (Kossak, p. 187). Jadwiga Kasprowicz was, however, always anxious to hear terrible things about Dagny, and Stach often catered to her.

21. In the possession of Iwa Dahlin.

22. Both letters are part of the Bäckström correspondence; the first is undated.

23. Bäckström correspondence.

24. Adam Mickiewicz Museum of Literature.

25. In the possession of Iwa Dahlin.

26. Bäckström correspondence.

27. Bäckström correspondence.

28. Ragnhild's correspondence contains two poems written to her by Norwegian poets, the one from Nils Collett Vogt, entitled "Mairegn" ("May rain") with a postscript, "In memory of the rainy afternoon 12th June 92"; and the other from Carl Gjerud, entitled "Ekko" ("Echo") and dated "22/Sept.93."

29. During her first months in Paris in the fall of 1892, Ragnhild had met Delius, apparently through Randi Blehr. She wrote to her aunt: "I spend much time with Mr. Delius down here, and I like him very much. He is a fine, intelligent fellow, and very musical he is too. Through him I've gotten into a little Wagner society, which is terribly interesting—there are four men, Delius among them, who play eight-handed Wagner operas and then I and a splendid baritone sing. It's terribly interesting and instructive for me—all those men are, you see, splendid musicians, a couple of them pianists of absolutely the first order. —Christmas Eve I was at Mr. Delius's uncle, who also lives down here, and we had an awfully pleasant time. —In general, Delius has been terribly kind to me down here" (Blehr archive).

30. Munch Museum.

31. Undated, Bäckström correspondence.

32. Bäckström correspondence.

33. Bäckström correspondence.

34. Undated, Bäckström correspondence.

35. Bäckström correspondence.

36. In the possession of Iwa Dahlin.

37. Kossak, p. 225.

CHAPTER 9

1. Quoted from Kossak, p. 180.

2. Przybyszewski, "Edvard Munch," *Moderní Revue* 5 (1897). From a Norwegian translation (in the Munch Museum) of the Czech original, pp. 17–18.

3. Lathe, "The Group Zum schwarzen Ferkel," p. 47.

4. Berlin, April 1897, *Przybyszewski: Listy*, vol. 1, p. 147.

5. Selberg, "Stanisław Przybyszewski og 1890-årenes norske kunst og litteratur," *Samtiden* (1977), p. 112. In the following discussion, I will quote Stach, using his interpretations of Munch's and Vigeland's works. But as Selberg wrote: "When Przybyszewski contemplates a work of art that moves him and makes an impression on him, it invokes in him an image of a specific psychic situation or conflict that both is individual and universal and that can serve as an illustration of his own philosophy of life and art" (p. 113).

6. Przybyszewski, "Edvard Munch," p. 12.

7. Przybyszewski, "En Ubekendt," *Tilskueren* 13 (1896), p. 809. Originally published in the German journal *Die Kritik*, in May 1896.

8. Przybyszewski, "Edvard Munch," pp. 13, 14. Munch portrayed the Madonna in many forms. (Stang, *Edvard Munch*, p. 136.)

9. Przybyszewski, "En Ubekendt," pp. 801–2. Carla Lathe included a picture of the sculpture in her dissertation, with the following notation: "Vigeland made a sketch for it in his notebook in Berlin, 13.2.1895. Jens Thiis called it 'Berlinergruppe'/'Berlin Group.' When Munch saw it, he was so enthusiastic, he said he would like to use it for his Frieze of Life series. As a sculpture, it is a poignant contrast to Vigeland's *Vals* II. (See p. 29.)

10. Przybyszewski, "Edvard Munch," p. 13. Stach also wrote this on the *Paon* tapestry, under his own portrait and next to Wyspiański's drawing of Dagny.

11. Przybyszewski, "Edvard Munch," p. 13.

12. Auerbach, p. 3.

13. Bram Dijkstra's *Idols of Perversity: Fantasies of Feminine Evil in Fin-de-Siecle Culture* (New York and Oxford: Oxford University Press, 1986) is a virtual kaleidoscope of all the possible fantasies male artists could dream up in order to marginalize women and lay them completely to rest in the form of household nuns, clining vines, draculas, beasts, serpents, virgins, whores, etc. While concentrating on the thrust in late nineteenth-century iconography to render women powerless, Dijkstra actually operates with the same notion as Auerbach in *Woman and the Demon*. Women were perceived to be powerful. Thus, turning them into everything but human beings was a defensive reaction, limiting their power in the very ways that men perceived themselves to be weak or undefended. Auerbach wrote: "The self-transforming power surging beneath apparent victimization lies at the heart of this study; the subjection of women is a defensive response to this vision" (p. 34). Auerbach's and Dijkstra's books are well read in tandem, the one a corrective of the extremes of the other.

14. A copy of this letter, written in German and supposedly written on 18 September 1893, is in the Jan Kasprowicz Museum in Inowrocław.

15. Quoted from Paul's *Min Strindbergsbok*, p. 119.

16. Postmarked on arrival in Stockholm, 11 April 1900, Bäckström correspondence.

17. Kossak said that Stach had begun writing the book already in 1899 (p. 205).

18. Undated, but from the spring of 1901, in the possession of Ewa Kossak.

19. Undated, but from the spring of 1901, in the possession of Professor Roman Taborski of Warsaw.

20. Kossak, p. 174.

21. In the possession of Roman Taborski.

22. According to Kossak, Stach claimed Dagny was spying on him, "in order to saddle him with a suit" (p. 198). In Berlin Stach met Maya Vogt and Tulla Larson, the major woman in Munch's life at the time. Together they sent Munch a greeting. Tulla Larson also wrote to Munch, apparently on 23 January, "Przy—— has left a long time ago, he is still looking for his wife—He told me his whole life story—not to her advantage." (The card and letter are in the Munch Museum.)

23. In the possession of Iwa Dahlin.

24. Meier-Graefe, "Geschicten neben der Kunst."

25. I quote from Dagny's last letters as if they were one final document. They have all been cited earlier, and I will therefore not give specific references to individual letters.

26. Dagny lived in a pension on Marszalkowska 84. Her landlady was a woman by the name of Madame Waruka, with whom Dagny seemed to get along. Either for her or for her daughter—which one is unclear—Dagny wrote to Stach, even in her anxiety that last spring: "Miss Waruka has asked me to do her a favor: to send two postcards to her with your full name, as an autograph. It's for a good cause. Please do it!" Minda Blehr and Gudrun stayed in the same pension when they went to Warsaw following Dagny's death. Ragnhild wrote to Helge: "Mama and Gudrun say that worse conditions than in Poland they cannot imagine." (Postmarked 4 August 1901, Bäckström correspondence.)

27. Scasjewski was an acquaintance of Dagny and Stach, who convinced Dagny that Stach should change publishers, and who was willing to help bring it about.

28. The violinist was a certain Miss Lindberg, who later visited Ragnhild in Stockholm.

29. Gudrun wrote to Otto Blehr from Warsaw, "Stachu has sent an older cousin for Zenon about 8 days ago, —she has still not arrived in Tiflis!" (Dated 21 June 1901, Blehr archive.)

30. According to Kossak, "Before 1939 the painting hung in the Polish embassy in Berlin, where Alfred Wysocki was minister. It disappeared during the Second World War and has never been found" (p. 207).

31. The original source of this information was Lucyna Kotarbińska in Wokoło teatru.

32. Meier-Graefe, "Geschicten neben der Kunst."

33. Dated 2 June 1901, in the possession of Iwa Dahlin.

34. Postmarked 24 June 1901, Bäckström correspondence; Kossak, p. 213.

35. Kotarbińska, Wokoło teatru, p. 350.

36. Kossak, p. 215.

37. Kossak, pp. 217–18.

38. Kossak dated this letter 4 May 1901.

39. Postmarked 4 August 1901, Bäckström correspondence.

40. Postmarked 4 August 1901, Bäckström correspondence. Dagny was shot in the back of the head. The actual time of the murder given in the papers from Tiflis was 1:20 P.M. Some reports said she was lying on the bed, others that she was sitting in a chair. (Władysława Tomaszewska returned from Tiflis with the latter account.) Emeryk was supposedly lying at the foot of the bed (Kossak, p. 228).

41. Quoted from Kossak, pp. 222–23.

42. Quoted from Kossak, p. 221.

43. Kossak, p. 224.

44. Quoted from Kossak, p. 225.

45. Quoted from Kossak, p. 226.

46. Postmarked 24 June 1901, Bäckström correspondence.

47. Auerbach, p. 3.

BIBLIOGRAPHY

WORKS BY DAGNY JUEL PRZYBYSZEWSKA

Den sterkere. Samtiden 7 (1896), 449–59.

Digte. In "Dagny Juel: Norsk lyrikks Camilla Collett?" by Martin Nag. *Samtiden* 84 (1975), 512–24. Reprinted in *Kongsvinger-kvinne og verdensborger: Dagny Juel som dikter og kulturarbeider*, Martin Nag. Kongsvinger: Solør-Odal og Kongsvinger Museum, 1987.

Grzech (Synden). Trans. Stanisław Przybyszewski. *Życie* (1899).

Hrich (Synden). Trans. Hugo Kosterka. *Moderní Revue* 9 (1898), 129–38.

Kiedy słońce zachodzi (Når solen går ned). Trans. Stanisław Przybyszewski. *Życie* (1899).

Kiedy słońce zachodzi. Trans. and with a dedication by Stanisław Przybyszewski. Warsaw: Jan Fiszer, 1902. (A collection containing translations of *Når solen går ned, Sing mir das Lied vom Leben und vom Tode,* and *Synden.*)

Osoby (Ravnegård). Trans. Stanisław Przybyszewski. Warsaw, 1902.

"Rediviva." *Dagbladet,* 22 Jan. 1977, p. 2. Reprinted in *Kongsvinger-kvinne og verdensborger.*

Sing mir das Lied vom Leben und vom Tode. Samtiden 11 (1900), 289–97.

Singt mir das Lied vom Leben und vom Tode. Trans. Stanisław Przybyszewski. *Życie* 2 (1899).

Synden og to andre skuespill av Dagny Juell. Ed. and intro. by Ole Michael Selberg. Oslo: Solum Forlag A/S, 1978. (A collection containing *Når solen går ned, Ravnegård,* and *Synden.*)

Translation of "Liv" by Sigbjørn Obstfelder. *Pan* (Sept., Oct., Nov. 1895).

Translation of *Underveis* by Stanisław Przybyszewski. Christiania and Copenhagen: Alb. Cammermeyer, 1895.

LETTERS

Håndskriftssamling, Universitetsbiblioteket, Oslo. Contains letters from Dagny Juel Przybyszewska and Stanisław Przybyszewski to Arne Garborg, Edvard Munch, Jappe Nilssen, and Lars M. Swanström.

Iwa Dahlin has a small collection of correspondence between Dagny and her mother, Minda Juell, and her sister, Ragnhild Bäckström.

Kungliga Biblioteket, Stockholm. Contains letters to August Strindberg from Bengt Lidforss and Edvard Munch.

Munch-Museet, Oslo. Contains letters to Munch from his contemporaries, including Hans Lemmich Juell and Ragnhild and Helge Bäckström.

Muzeum im. Jana Kasprowicza, Inowrocław. Contains copies of letters from Dagny to Arnošt Procházka and Stach Przybyszewski, as well as a letter to Dagny from Stach.

Muzeum Literatury Adama Mickiewicza, Warsaw. Contains letters to Dagny from her mother, Minda Juell, and Fru Nilsen, as well as letters to Stach Przybyszewski from Arne Garborg, Laura Marholm Hansson, Hans Lemmich Juell, Astrid Juell, Karl and Gabrielle Tavastjerna, Gudrun Juell Westrup, and Gustav Wied.

Riksarkivet, Otto og Randi Blehr Arkiv, Oslo. Contains letters from Dagny, her family, and her relatives to Otto and Randi Blehr.

Ragnhild Bäckström correspondence. The private correspondence of Ragnhild Juell Bäckström. In the possession of her grandson, Dr. Lennart Hellström.

Solør-Odal og Kongsvinger Museum, Kongsvinger. Contains various Juell family papers.

SECONDARY SOURCES

Aasen, Elisabeth. *Kvinners spor i skrift*. Oslo: Det Norske Samlaget, 1986.

Auerbach, Nina. *Woman and the Demon*. Cambridge and London: Harvard University Press, 1982.

Bab, Julius. "Die neuromantische Bohème," *Die Berliner Bohème*. Berlin, 1904.

Bakke, Oddveig Karin. "En feminist i bohem-miljø." Thesis, University of Oslo, 1979.

Baudelaire, Charles. *Oeuvres complètes de Baudelaire*. Paris: La Pléiade, 1934.

Beck, Inger Merete, and Frans Grandjean. "Hvad Satan er det I nøler efter? En analyse av den norske bohémlitteratur i perioden 1880–1900." Dissertation, Aarhus University, 1982. Contains a chapter on Dagny Przybyszewska's plays.

Berg, Mie. "Mytene om Dagny Juell," *Dagbladet*, 10 April 1979, p. 11.

Beyer, Nils. *Bengt Lidforss: En levnadsteckning*. Stockholm: Norstedt, 1968.

————. "Strindberg och Bengt Lidforss," *BLM* 31 (1962), 796–805.

Boy-Żeleński, Tadeusz. *O Krakówie*. Ed. Henryk Markiewicz. Kraków: Wydawnictwo Literackie, 1923.

————. *O Wyspiańskim*. Ed. Stanisław Witold Balicki. Kraków: Wydawnictwo Literackie, 1973.

Brandes, Georg. *Indtryk fra Polen*. Copenhagen: Gyldendal, 1888.

Brenna, Arne. "Edvard Munch og Dagny Juell," *Samtiden* 87 (1978), 51–64.

Dahl, Willy. *Norges litteratur II: Tid og tekst 1884–1935*. Oslo: Aschehoug, 1984.

Dahlerup, Pil. *Det moderne gjennembruds kvinner*. Copenhagen: Gyldendals Paperbacks, 1983.

Dauthendey, Max. *Maja: Skandinavische Bohême-Komödie in drei Akten*. Leipzig: Ernst Rowohlt, 1911.

Dehmel, Ida Auerbach. "Przybyszewski wie ich ihn sah," *Pologne Littéraire*, 15 Sept. 1934.

Dehmel, Richard. *Mein Leben*. Leipzig, 1922.

———. *Richard Dehmels Tagebuch*. Leipzig, 1921.

Dijkstra, Bram. *Idols of Perversity: Fantasies of Feminine Evil in Fin-de-Siècle Culture*. New York and Oxford: Oxford University Press, 1986.

Dittman, Reidar. *Eros and Psyche: Strindberg and Munch in the 1890s*. Ann Arbor: UMI Research Press, 1982.

Drachmann, Holger. "Berliner-Breve," *Verdens Gang*, 29 May 1894.

Eggum, Arne. *Edvard Munch: Malerier—skisser og studier*. Oslo: Stenersens, 1983.

———. "Det gröna rummet," in *Edvard Munch: 1863–1944*. Stockholm: Liljevalchs og Kulturhuset, 1977.

Enquist, Per Olov. *Strindberg: Ett liv*. Stockholm: Norstedt, 1984.

Gauguin, Pola. *Edvard Munch*. Oslo: Aschehoug, 1933.

Gilbert, Sandra M., and Susan Gubar. *The Madwoman in the Attic: The Woman Writer and the Nineteenth-Century Literary Imagination*. New Haven and London: Yale University Press, 1979.

Gierløff, Christian. "Dagny Juel: En kvinne i Munchs malerier," *Arbeiderbladet*, 10 March 1956, p. 10.

Gunnestad, Astrid. "Lise Fjeldstad som og om Dagny Juel," *Norsk ukeblad*, 14 Sept. 1976.

Hagemann, Sonja. "Brev som sannhets bevis," *Dagbladet*, 5 Feb. 1963, p. 5.

———. "Dagny Juel Przybyszewska: Genienes inspiratrise," *Samtiden* 72 (1963), 655–68.

———. "Femme-fatale," *Dagbladet*, 31 Dec. 1962, p. 3.

Heber, Knut. "Dagny Juel: Utløseren av Edvard Munchs kunst i kampårene 1890–1908," *Kunst og Kultur* 60 (1977), 1–18.

Helstyński, Stanisław. "Aspazja i Mefistofeles," *Stolica*, 19–26 Dec. 1971, p. 18.

———. *Przybyszewski*. Kraków: Wydawnictwo Literackie, 1958; 2d ed. 1966.

———. "Stanisław Przybyszewski and Scandinavia," *Baltic and Scandinavian Countries*, vol. 3, no. 1 (1937), 121–25.

Herman, Maxime. *Un sataniste polonais: Stanislas Przybyszewski (de 1868 à 1900)*. Paris: Société d'Edition "Les Belles Lettres," 1939.

Ibsen, Henrik. *Samlede Værker: Mindeudgave*. Christiania and Copenhagen: Gyldendal, 1908. Oslo Kommunes Kunstsamlinger, Munch-Museet.

Jaworska, Władysława. "Edvard Munch and Stanisław Przybyszewski," *Apollo*, 1974–75, pp. 312–17.

———. "Munch and Przybyszewski," *Polish Perspectives*, vol. 15, no. 12 (1972), 61–72.

Kolinska, Krystyna. *Stachu: Jego kobiety i jego dzieci.* Kraków: Wydawnictwo Literackie, 1978.

Kongsvinger kino- og teaternemden. "Dagny Juell," Kongsvinger, 1977.

Kossak, Ewa K. *Dagny Przybyszewska: Zbłąkana gwiazda.* Warsaw: Państwowy Instytut Wydawniczy, 1973; enlarged ed. 1975.

———. *Irrande stjärna: Berättelsen om den legendariska Dagny Juel.* Trans. Christina Wollin. Stockholm: Bonniers, 1978.

Kotarbińska, Lucyna. *Wokoło teatru: Moje wspomnienia.* Warsaw: F. Hoesick, 1930.

Krog, Gina. "Hos Gina Krog: Frøkenen udtaler sig om Situationen," *Kristiania Dagsavis*, 27 June 1901, p. 1.

Kuncewiczowa, Maria. *Fantasia alla Polacca.* Warsaw, 1979.

Lagercrantz, Olof. *August Strindberg.* Stockholm: Wahlström & Widstrand, 1979.

———. *August Strindberg.* Trans. Anselm Hollo. New York: Farrar, Straus & Giroux, 1984.

Langaard, Ingrid. *Edvard Munch: Modningsår.* Oslo: Gyldendal, 1960.

Larsen, Bjørg. "Dagny Juel var ikke bare et kjønnsobjekt," *Arbeiderbladet*, 6 Dec. 1974, p. 21.

Lathe, Carla. "Edvard Munch and the Concept of Psychic Naturalism," *Gazette des Beaux Arts* 93 (1979), 135–46.

———. *Edvard Munch and His Literary Associates.* Norwich: The University of East Anglia, 1979–80.

———. "Edvard Munch's Dramatic Images," *Journal of the Warburg and Courtauld Institutes* 46 (1983), 191–206.

———. "The Group Zum schwarzen Ferkel: A Study in Early Modernism." Dissertation, The University of East Anglia, 1972.

Lervik, Åse Hiorth. *Evig din: Om kjærlighet hos kvinnelige forfattere ca. 1870–1907.* Tromsø, Oslo: Universitetsforlaget AS, 1985.

Lysthuse. Ed. Liv Palmvig. Charlottenlund: Rosiante, 1985.

Meier-Graefe, Julius. "Edvard Munch: Zur Austellung im Kronprinsenpalais," *Frankfurter Zeitung*, 2 April 1927.

———. "Edvard Munch i tysk kunstkritikk," *Kunst og Kultur* 14 (1927), 111–16.

———. "Geschicten neben der Kunst: Ducha," *Berliner Tageblatt*, 7 March 1930.

———. "Geschicten neben der Kunst II: Ducha," *Mannheimer Tageblatt*, 22 Oct. 1931.

———. "Munch," *Grundstoff der Bilder: Ausegewählte Schuften.* Ed. Carl Linfert. Munich, 1959, 176–83.

Miller, Alice. *The Drama of the Gifted Child.* Trans. Ruth Ward. New York: Basic Books, Inc., 1981.

———. *For Your Own Good*. Trans. Hildegarde and Hunter Hannum. New York: Farrar, Straus & Giroux, 1984.

Moen, Erik. "Dagny Juell Przybyszewska," *Solör-Odal*, vol. 4, 183–89. Solör-Odal Historielag, 1975–76.

Munch, Edvard. "Edvard Munch fortæller om Fru Przybyzewski" (sic.), *Kristiania Dagsavis*, 25 June 1901.

———. *Edvard Munchs brev: Familien*. Ed. Inger Munch. Oslo: Johan Grundt Tanum, 1949.

———. "Mein Freund Przybyszewski," *Pologne Littéraire*. 15 Dec. 1926. Trans. "Min venn Przybyszewski," *Oslo Aftenavis*, 30 Jan. 1929.

———. *Notebooks*. Oslo Kommunes Kunstsamlinger, Munch-Museet, Oslo.

Möller, Lotte. "En ängel med cigarrett i munnen," *Vi*, Sept. 1989, pp. 8–12.

Nag, Martin. "Dagny Juel: Dramatiker 50 år forut for sin tid," *Verdens Gang*, 4 Jan. 1966, p. 10.

———. "Dagny Juel: En kommentar," *Aftenposten*, 29 June 1976, p. 7.

———. "Dagny Juel: En norsk tragedie," *Dagbladet*, 4 Aug. 1975, p. 3.

———. "Dagny Juel: En norsk Tsjekhov?" *Samtiden* 85 (1976), 57–64.

———. "Dagny Juel: Norsk lyrikks Camilla Collett?" *Samtiden* 84 (1975), 512–24.

———. "Dagny Juel: Portrett av en pionér," *Arbeiderbladet*, 12 Feb. 1975, p. 5.

———. "Dagny Juell: En pionér," *Arbeiderbladet*, 11 July 1972, p. 6.

———. "Dagny Juell og Håkon Sandøy," *Morgenbladet*, 2 July 1976, p. 6.

———. "Dagny Juell Przybyszewska: En ny-feminist?" *Sirene* 6 (1974), 28–31.

———. "Dagny Juel og Gina Krog," *Morgenbladet*, 2 Sept. 1975, p. 7.

———. "Dagny Juels dramaer," *Arbeiderbladet*, 3 April 1975, p. 5.

———. "Dagny Juels skuespill," *Friheten*, 28 Nov. 1978, p. 8.

———. "Er Dagny Juel Irenes modell?" *Verdens Gang*, 16 July 1970.

———. *Kongsvinger-kvinne og verdensborger: Dagny Juel som dikter og kulturarbeider*. Kongsvinger: Solør-Odal og Kongsvinger Museum, 1987.

———. "Om Dagny Juel og Edvard Munch," *Arbeiderbladet*, 12 July 1976, p. 16.

———. "Przybyszewski: Den nakne sjel," *Verdens Gang*, 7 Aug. 1967, p. 10.

New French Feminisms. Ed. and intro. Elaine Marks and Isabelle de Courtivron. New York: Schocken Books, 1981.

Norges litteraturhistorie. Vol. 4. Oslo: J. W. Cappelen, 1975.

Norseng, Mary Kay. "Eros og ære: Problemdiktning og sjeledrama rundt århundreskiftet," in *Norsk kvinnelitteraturhistorie*, pp. 235–43.

———. "Killing the Angel in the Plays of Dagny Juel Przybyszewska," in *The Modern Breakthrough in Scandinavian Literature 1870–1905*. Proceedings of the 16th Study Conference of the International Association of Scandinavian Studies, 4–8 Aug. 1986. Göteborg: Litteraturvetenskapliga institutionen vid Göteborgs universitet, 1988.

———. *Sigbjørn Obstfelder*. Boston: Twayne Publishers, 1982.

Norsk kvinnelitteraturhistorie: Bind 1. 1600–1900. Ed. Irene Engelstad, Jorunn Hareide, Irene Iversen, Torill Steinfeld, Janneken Øverland. Oslo: Pax Forlag, 1988.

Northern Light: Nordic Art at the Turn of the Century. Ed. Kirk Varnedoe. New Haven: Yale University Press, 1988.

Obstfelder, Sigbjørn. *Samlede skrifter.* Ed. Solveig Tunold. Oslo: Gyldendal, 1950.

Pan. Ed. Otto Julius Bierbaum and Julius Meier-Graefe. Berlin: Kritik-Verlag, 1895.

Paul, Adolf. *Min Strindbergsbok.* Stockholm: Norstedt, 1930.

Posse, Amelie. *Kring kunskapens träd.* Stockholm: Natur och Kultur, 1946.

Przybyszewski, Stanisław. *Androgyne.* Kraków, 1905.

──────. *Auf den Wegen der Seele.* Berlin: Kritik-Verlag 1897.

──────. "Dagny, Strindberg und ich," *Die Aktion* 15 (1913).

──────. *De profundis.* Berlin, 1895.

──────. "Edvard Munch," *Moderní Revue* 5, 1897. Norwegian trans. in Munch-Museet.

──────. *Erinnerungen an das literarische Berlin: Mit einem Geleitwort von Willy Haas.* Munich: Winkler-Verlag, 1965.

──────. *Homo Sapiens.* Trilogy: *Ueber Bord,* 1896. *Unterwegs,* 1895. *Im Malstrom,* 1896. Berlin: F. Fontane and Co.

──────. *Homo Sapiens.* Trans. Thomas Seltzer. New York: Alfred A. Knopf, 1915.

──────. Introduction to *Stanisław Wyspianski: Dzielz malarski.* Inst. Wyd. "Bibljoteka Polska," 1925.

──────. "Malarya," *Synowie ziemi. Chimera,* 1900.

──────. *Moi wspolczeani.* Warsaw, 1926–30.

──────. *Nad morzem.* Kraków, 1899.

──────. *Over Bord.* Translated in Copenhagen, 1896.

──────. "Psychischer Naturalismus," *Die neue deutsche Rundschau,* 1894, 865–89. Reprinted in *Das Werk des Edvard Munch.*

──────. *Satans Kinder.* Paris, Leipzig, Munich, 1897.

──────. *Snow: A Play in Four Acts.* Trans. O. F. Theis. New York: Nicholas L. Brown, 1920.

──────. *Stanisław Przybyszewski: Listy.* Ed. Stanisław Helstyński. Warsaw. Vol. 1, 1937; vol. 2, 1938; vol. 3, 1957. (Vol. 1 contains letters from 1879 to 1906.)

──────. *Totenmesse.* Berlin: F. Fontane & Co., 1893.

──────. "Ein Unbekanter," *Die Kritik* (1896), 836–42, 943–47, 983–89, 1035–42.

──────. "En Ubekendt," *Tilskueren* 13 (1896), 789–809.

──────. Translation and dedication of *Kiedy słońce zachodizi (Når solen går ned),* Dagny Przybyszewska. Warsaw: Jan Fiszer, 1902.

──────. *Underveis.* Trans. Dagny Przybyszewska. Christiania and Copenhagen: Alb. Cammermeyer, 1895.

──────. *Vigilien.* Berlin, 1895.

──────. "Das Werk des Edvard Munch." Berlin: S. Fischer, 1894.

──────. *Zur Psychologie des Individuums: I. Chopin und Nietzsche; II. Ola Hansson.* Berlin, 1892.

Rychter, Josef. "Przybyszewscy." Kraków, 1901.

Sandøy, Håkon, dir. *Dagny.* With Lise Fjelstad. Norsk Film/Polish Film, 1976.

Sawicki, Stanisław. "Listy Skandynawow do Przybyszewskiego," *Przeglad Wspolczesny*, no. 5 (1939), 28–40.

Schleich, Carl Ludwig. *Besonnte Vergangenheit*. Berlin: Ernst Rowohlt, 1921.

———. *Those Were Good Days*. Trans. Bernard Miall. London: George Allen & Unwin Ltd., 1935.

Schulerud, Mentz. *Norsk kunstnerliv*. Oslo: J. W. Cappelen, 1960.

Selberg, Ole Michael. "En kvinne i Munchs liv," *Arbeiderbladet*, 5 March 1974, p. 8.

———. "Munch-filmen og Dagny Juel," *Arbeiderbladet*, 21 Nov. 1974, p. 12.

———. "Stanisław Przybyszewski og 1890-årenes norske kunst og litteratur." *Samtiden* (1977), 103–18.

———. Ed. and intro. *Synden og to andre skuespill av Dagny Juell*. Oslo: Solum, 1978.

Stang, Ragna. *Edvard Munch: Mennesket og kunstneren*. Oslo: Aschehoug, 1978.

Stanisław Wyspiański. Intro. Napisala Helena Blum. Warsaw: Auriga, 1969.

Stenersen, Rolf. *Edvard Munch: Nærbilde av et geni*. Oslo: Gyldendal, 1945.

Strindberg: Ett liv. P. O. Enquist. Directed by Johan Bergenstraale. Sveriges Radio, Kanal 2, 1985.

Strindberg, August. *August Strindbergs brev*. Ed. Torsten Eklund. Stockholm: Bonniers, 1948–.

———. *The Cloister*. Trans. Mary Sandbach. New York: Hill and Wang, 1969.

———. *Inferno, Alone and Other Writings*. Ed. and intro. Evert Sprinchorn. Garden City, New York: Doubleday & Co., Inc., 1968.

———. *Klostret*. Ed. C. G. Bjurström. Stockholm: Bonniers, 1966.

———. *Skrifter*. Stockholm: Bonniers, 1983.

Strindberg, Frida. *Strindberg och hans andra hustru*. Stockholm: Bonniers, 1933.

Stubberud, Juel. "Kvinne i feil århundre," *Østlendingen*. 2 April 1977.

Thiis, Jens. *Edvard Munch og hans samtid*. Oslo: Gyldendal, 1933.

Vendelfelt, Erik. *Den unge Bengt Lidforss: En biografisk studie med särskild hänsyn til hans litterära utvekling*. Lund: Gleerup, 1962.

Vikborg, Tone. *Gustav Vigeland: Mennesket og kunstneren*. Oslo, 1983.

Watkins, Peter, dir. *Edvard Munch*. With Geir Westby and Gro Fraas. Norsk Rikskringkastingen and Sveriges Radio, 1974.

Westrup, Jadwiga P. "Dagny Juel: Femme fatale eller en kvinna före sin tid," *Røster i Radio TV*, July 1978.

Westrup, Zenon P. *Jag har varit i Arkadien*. Stockholm: Natur och Kultur, 1975.

Wysocki, Alfred. *Sprzed pól wieku*. Kraków: 1956. Translated in part by Martin vom Zweibergk for Sveriges Radio, "För ett halvsekel sedan," 1986.

Årsmelding fra Kongsvinger Museum. *Pionerkvinner i Kongsvinger*. Kongsvinger, 1986.

INDEX

PHOTO CREDITS

Special thanks are extended to Iwa Dahlin for permission to reproduce photographs belonging to Dagny's family: pp. xii, 38, 39, 50, 108, 111, 119, 120, 124

Also gratefully acknowledged are the photographs and paintings courtesy of the following:

Aschehoug Publishers, Oslo, Norway: p. 46

Ewa K. Kossak, from her book *Dagny Przybyszewska: Zblakana qwiazda* (Warsaw: Państwowy Instytut Wydawniczy; enlarged ed. 1975): pp. 33, 144

Kongsvinger Museum, Kongsvinger, Norway: p. 131

Munch Museum, Oslo, Norway: cover illustration and pp. 35, 43, 57, 58, 75, 113, 143, 147, 151

National Library, Warsaw, Poland: pp. 134, 162

National Museum, Krakow, Poland: p. 34

Vigeland Museum, Oslo, Norway: pp. 29, 152

ABOUT THE AUTHOR

Mary Kay Norseng is professor of Scandinavian literature and languages at the University of California, Los Angeles.